POLITICS AND NATIONALITY IN CONTEMPORARY SOVIET-JEWISH EMIGRATION, 1968–89

Politics and Nationality in Contemporary Soviet-Jewish Emigration, 1968–89

Laurie P. Salitan

Assistant Professor
Department of Political Science
The Johns Hopkins University

St. Martin's Press   New York

First published in the United States of America in 1992

Printed in Hong Kong

ISBN 0–312–06108–0

Library of Congress Cataloging-in-Publication Data
Salitan, Laurie P.
   Politics and nationality in contemporary Soviet-Jewish emigration,
1968–89 / Laurie P. Salitan.
      p. cm.
   Includes bibliographical references and index.
   ISBN 0–312–06108–0
   1. Jews—Soviet Union—History—1917– 2. Jews—Soviet Union–
–Migrations.   3. Soviet Union—Emigration and immigration.
4. Germans—Soviet Union—History—20th century.   5. Soviet Union–
–Ethnic relations.   I. Title.
DS135.R92S244   1992
947'.004924—dc20   91–8633
                                                                          CIP

To Marc

Contents

List of Tables and Figures

Acknowledgements

Many people were helpful to me during the various stages of writing this book. I am grateful to my dissertation supervisor, Harry Shukman, for his encouragement and assistance while I was in Oxford, to Howard Spier for his ongoing support and editorial advice, and to Lukasz Hirszowicz for his comments on an early version of this manuscript. I also thank Seweryn Bialer, Evelyn Brodkin, William Connolly, Germaine Hoston, Jerry Hough, Woody Howard, Robert Kaiser, Norma Kriger, Robert Lewis, Beth Mitchnek, Alexander Motyl and Sara Shudofsky for their suggestions here and in articles that formed the foundation for this book. The American Jewish Committee (New York), the Institute of Jewish Affairs (London) and Radio Liberty (Munich) kindly made their archives available to me. Elizabeth Karsk typed manuscript revisions. Patrick Lee and Diana Ohlbaum, who provided invaluable assistance editing, proofreading and verifying citation references, deserve many thanks for their sustained efforts. The Johns Hopkins University gave me a liberal leave of absence and the Duke University Center on East–West Trade, Investment, and Communications provided generous financial support through a grant from the Carnegie Corporation.

My family's encouragement since the very beginning of my graduate school days and their eager anticipation of this finished project has been enormously gratifying and is warmly appreciated. I owe my profoundest thanks to Marc Kushner, whose involvement in the long journey this study has taken from dissertation to its present form, and whose unfailing support throughout the process cannot be measured but will always be remembered.

October 1990

Introduction

Jews have always occupied an uneasy place in Soviet society. On the one hand, their high educational level, professional standing and achievements have often placed them in positions of prestige, respect and authority. But at the same time, those very characteristics have aroused anti-Semitic feelings long present in Soviet (and Russian) society. This mistrust of Jews, also stemming from their family ties abroad and connection with the State of Israel, hindered their full acceptance into Soviet society. One of the clearest manifestations of ambivalence toward Jews in the contemporary period is Soviet policy on Jewish emigration.

The emigration of Soviet Jews during the 1970s and 1980s is a much discussed but little understood subject. Despite several major policy reversals, emigration from the Soviet Union has remained an anomaly. With only a few exceptions – the most notable being the Jews, Germans and Armenians – voluntary emigration from the USSR has not been possible.[1] The reasons the emigration of Soviet Jews has been permitted to take place, notwithstanding the Soviet Union's restrictions on the free movement of its citizens, are the major subject of this study.

In part, misperceptions about contemporary Soviet emigration policy result from a tendency by Western scholars and analysts to view the issue from the perspective of US–Soviet relations, paying little or no heed to the domestic constraints on Soviet policy-making.[2]

Most explanations of contemporary Soviet emigration view the annual fluctuations that have characterized emigration trends from 1968 to the present in terms of US–Soviet relations. This consensus has led to what I term the 'barometer thesis'. Adherents of the thesis posit that emigration is a barometer of US–Soviet relations and characterize Soviet Jews as pawns in, or hostages to, the superpower rivalry. While such an argument may seem plausible, it is ultimately flawed and cannot account for the entire course of emigration because it fails to consider the domestic context.

This book differs from the existing literature on Jewish

1

emigration in both its approach and conclusions. In an attempt to identify the factors contributing to emigration policy, it relies on a broad-based perspective related to a number of policy areas. One important aspect of this methodology is the introduction of a comparative analysis. Although this study focuses primarily on Soviet-Jewish emigration, it also examines Soviet-German emigration. Fundamental questions concerning the nature of emigration policy and its relationship to other policies link the Jewish and German cases. Despite unique attributes and structural differences stemming from social, cultural, demographic and geographic distinctions, a number of conceptual issues are pertinent to both cases. Of greatest significance is the correlation between oscillations in Jewish and German emigration and the Soviet domestic scene. This relationship establishes the context in which any discussion of Soviet emigration should be framed.

The analysis presented in this study falls within an established body of scholarship on the role of groups, interests and decision-making in the USSR.[3] It explicitly rejects the totalitarian model of the USSR and the view that the Soviet Union, prior to Gorbachev, was monolithic.[4] Rather, by examining emigration policy from the perspective of a dynamic political system, with numerous competing interests, a multiplicity of goals and a large and entrenched bureaucracy, this study offers an interpretation of Soviet emigration policy that incorporates the contemporary reality of the Soviet system.

Although focusing on emigration policy, this work is not a traditional policy study. Western literature on the Soviet Union contains numerous studies of Soviet policy that address wide-ranging issues such as agriculture, criminology, education and the environment.[5] The primary importance of these studies lies in what they reveal about the Soviet policy-making process. However, they differ markedly from the analysis offered here. Some of the studies are based on Western models of decision-making; most examine issues that were the subject of protracted debate conducted through specialized journals and newspapers in the USSR. The studies benefited from access to Soviet sources and, in many cases, primary source information collected in interviews with the actors concerned. However, with the exception of the post-1986 period, information on emigration decision-making could only be gleaned from the few public statements Soviet officials made about emigration, *samizdat* (self-published) material, interviews with emigrants and personal accounts. After 1986, occasional articles on emigration began appearing in the Soviet press as Gorbachev's policy of *glasnost* (openness) took root. While lending some insight, the articles have been a relatively recent phenomenon and do not make up for the complete dearth of such information during the overwhelming majority of the period concerned.

The difficulties in access to reliable Soviet information in the pre-*glasnost* period and the taboo nature of emigration (which made it a subject unfit for public discussion and open inquiry) presented considerable methodological obstacles. As a result, I did not seek to test behavior against an established model but instead employed a mode of interpretation based on a low level of causality. Using this method I was able to identify and develop signposts that illuminated relevant issues and policy areas. For the most part those signposts converge on domestic aspects of emigration policy, and for that reason I focus my discussion on the domestic components of emigration policy.

Much of the analysis about emigration has been obscured by a cultural blind spot. The Soviet Union is viewed with suspicion as the 'other' superpower, and the literature has often relied on legacies of the cold war, including time-worn stereotypes that were the product of an antagonistic US–Soviet relationship. The biases inherent in the literature would make an interesting study but here I would simply observe that seeking to explain emigration by looking exclusively at international relations reflects a predisposition of many US observers to filter events in the Soviet Union through the lens of the US–Soviet relationship. Emigration policy does not exclude considerations of the international climate, but the superpower relationship is far less germane than others have argued. Indeed, it is often irrelevant. The relatively recent phenomenon of *glasnost* has shown the

Soviet Union to be a politically complex and diverse country. Emigration policy must be reexamined from this new perspective.

Discerning whether there is a single emigration policy or whether an ongoing series of *ad hoc* decisions on emigration have had the *de facto* impact of a coordinated policy is an important preliminary task. It is the first step in establishing the context in which to assess policy. Has emigration 'policy' been the same for Jews and Germans? It is also necessary to identify the components of the emigration policy. What type of issues does emigration policy encompass and how does it reflect them? Have the issues varied over time? If so, how have such changes manifested themselves in emigration policy?

Although there is a considerable degree of differentiation in its application and implementation, I argue that one broad policy governs emigration. Changes in the rates of emigration and the continued emigration of Jews and Germans (despite restrictions on emigration in general) indicate a policy rather than a haphazard or makeshift approach toward Jewish and German emigration. Because the factors involved in the emigration of Jews and Germans are not identical, aspects of the policy have been specifically tailored to each nationality. Nonetheless, general goals and principles have shaped the overall direction of policy. Moreover, emigration policy is strategic and goal-oriented; it is modified when objectives change or when a new approach for achieving goals is adopted. Despite instances, particularly in the initial years of emigration, when the policy seemed to be a response to both internal and external pressure for emigration, the longitudinal data indicate that emigration policy is not merely reactive; indeed, perspective reveals that emigration policy is aggressive and deliberate, with adjustments in the flow of emigration linked to changing political, economic and societal circumstances.

The evidence this study presents illustrates that decisions on emigration encompass a variety of interconnected issues and policy areas that form a multidimensional basis for emigration policy. Emigration policy reflects an assessment of the role emigrants play in Soviet society as well as popular and official attitudes toward them. Local politics, cadres policy, inter-ethnic relations, education and employment practices, labor policy, anti-Semitism and anti-Zionism constitute but a few of the realms emigration has the potential to affect. Emigration from the USSR raises fundamental ideological issues relating to freedom of movement, ties abroad and questions of state loyalty. It is an issue that has international repercussions as well as one that relates to Soviet cultural values, historical traditions and domestic affairs.

The Soviet census of 1979 counted 1 810 876 Soviet Jews, ranking Jews as the sixteenth largest Soviet nationality. By 1989 the Jewish population had shrunk to 1 449 117 (twentieth in size).[6] Soviet Jews are a predominantly urban nationality, characterized by a large professional class. Scattered throughout the Soviet Union, the largest concentration of Jews (based on 1989 census data) is in the Russian republic (RSFSR), where 39.6 per cent of the Jewish population reside, and in the Ukrainian SSR, where 35.3 per cent of all Soviet Jews live. The remainder of the Jewish population is distributed among the other republics as follows: Belorussia (8.1 per cent), Moldavia (4.8 per cent), Uzbekistan (4.7 per cent), Azerbaijan (1.8 per cent), Latvia (1.7 per cent), Kazakhstan (1.3 per cent), Lithuania (0.9 per cent), Georgia (0.7 per cent), Tadzhikistan (0.7 per cent), Kirghizia (0.4 per cent), Estonia (0.3 per cent), Turkmenistan (0.2 per cent) and Armenia (less than 0.1 per cent).[7]

Official treatment of Jews has been inconsistent throughout Soviet history. Though at times beneficiaries of Soviet rule, Jews have also been subjected to wide-ranging repressive measures that resulted (until changes under Gorbachev) in the disappearance of nearly all Jewish culture. The explanation for the uneven treatment rests partially with the tensions inherent in Soviet nationality policy. Capricious treatment has not been restricted to Jews alone; many Soviet nationalities have faced harsh and arbitrary measures. Examples include the experience of the Armenians, Balkars, Bulgarians, Chechens, Crimean Tatars, Estonians, Germans, Greeks, Ingushes, Kalmyks, Karachais, Khemshils, Koreans, Kurds, Latvians, Lithuanians, Meskhetians and Poles, all of whom were deported as a result of Stalin's repressions.[8]

The special nature of each case derives from unique

historical traditions, circumstances and cultural anomalies. As is true of numerous other Soviet nationalities, the factors that have influenced the treatment of Soviet Jews are complex and difficult to isolate. While it may be impossible to identify all of the relevant causes for official behavior towards Soviet Jews, nationality policy, state-imposed atheism, the effects of Stalinism, anti-Jewish and anti-Zionist policies have all, at different times and to varying degrees, been responsible for the measures directed against Jews.

Soviet Jews and Germans represent two of the more than 100 ethnic groups in the USSR.[9] In Soviet parlance, these groups are called nationalities. Conflicts between theory and practice regarding the nationalities have always existed.[10] Although founded on the principles of Soviet federalism and national self-determination, the Soviet Union has for most of its history relied on tight central control, rather than on a high degree of autonomy for its union republics (although *perestroika* (restructuring) may change this arrangement). Theoretically, the various nationalities, depending on their size and the nature and extent of their territorial ties, are guaranteed rights aimed at preserving and promoting their cultural and historical heritage. Such rights have included native language education, publications and mass media and, for the largest nationalities (those with titular union-republic status), a local Communist Party apparatus, a number of administrative rights and duties and representation in the state institutions of the USSR. In practice, however, these rights have been limited and accorded sporadically.

Numerous aspects of the Soviet 'nationalities question' bear on the emigration issue. Contradictions and inconsistencies between Soviet nationality theory and practice[11] as well as the national-territorial structure of the USSR had a dramatic impact on Soviet Jews and Germans. To a great extent, infringements on national-cultural rights spurred the rise of the emigration movements. As those movements developed, large numbers were permitted to emigrate, raising questions about the effect of ethnically-based emigration movements on emigration policy. A discussion of 'interest group' politics in the USSR is beyond the scope of this study but bears mentioning to highlight the role of the emigration movements *vis-à-vis* the Soviet political system and their implications for core issues concerning the conduct of politics in the USSR.[12]

A total of 369 385 Soviet Jews emigrated from October 1968 through December 1989. The number of emigrants has fluctuated annually, with the 1970s characterized by a general increase in the flow of emigrants and the 1980s marked by a contrasting diminution, until 1987, when emigration increased dramatically. Because emigration policy is differentiated it is necessary to analyze it with regard to its context. A periodization of emigration policy affords the most illuminating means of revealing the components that have determined policy over the years. Contemporary emigration can be broken down into four periods. The first period, 1968–73 was the period of Zionist emigration. The majority of emigrants during this phase were either Zionists or religious Jews, and for the most part they immigrated to Israel. The years 1974–79 marked the initial phase of post-Zionist emigration and saw a shift toward immigration to the United States and countries other than Israel. The third period, 1980–86, comprised the years of decline in which emigration was drastically curtailed and the current period, which began in 1987, is what may be labeled *perestroika* emigration, for it relates directly to reform in the USSR.

This book is structured in two sections. Part One focuses on emigration as a response to the treatment of the Jewish nationality. Its three chapters are devoted to Soviet Jews. Chapter 1 surveys Soviet-Jewish history and the precursors of the emigration movement. Chapter 2 examines the birth of the Jewish emigration movement and covers the period of Zionist emigration, lasting from 1968 to 1973. Chapter 3 discusses the post-Zionist emigration of the period from 1974 to 1989. Part Two introduces a comparative perspective by devoting Chapter 4 to the history of the Soviet Germans and their emigration. The book's final chapter, Chapter 5, offers a detailed analysis of emigration policy during 1968–89 and is followed by a brief Afterword. Readers should be aware that many end-notes are textual.

Part One

1 Survey of Soviet-Jewish History: Precursors of the Emigration Movement

> Whoever, directly or indirectly, puts forward the slogan of Jewish 'national culture' is (whatever his good intentions may be) an enemy of the proletariat, a supporter of all that is *outmoded* and connected with *caste* among the Jewish people; he is an accomplice of the rabbis and the bourgeoisie. On the other hand, those Jewish Marxists who mingle with the Russian, Lithuanian, Ukrainian and other workers in international Marxist organizations, and make their contribution (both in Russian and in Yiddish) towards creating the international culture of the working-class movement – those Jews, despite the separatism of the Bund, uphold the best traditions of Jewry by fighting the slogan of 'national culture'.
>
> V. I. Lenin, 1913[1]

The historical experience of Soviet Jews, the status of Judaism and secular Jewish culture in the USSR, and the position of Jews in Soviet society created the impetus for emigration. So too did the emergence of state-sponsored anti-Zionism, which was often indistinguishable from popular anti-Semitism. While some measures affecting Soviet Jewry were designed specifically to address circumstances relating to Jews, others were the consequence of broader policies regarding nationalities and of modernizing processes in the Soviet Union.

Initially, Jews played an important functional role in the transition period after the revolution.[2] But as society changed, Jews became expendable. Policies and practices that were openly discriminatory (such as hiring quotas that excluded Jews) and those that were not designed to discriminate against Jews *per se*, but had a discriminatory effect in their case (such as the decision to equalize the socioeconomic positions of the various nationalities), reflected ambivalence

11

toward Jews. Moreover, although Soviet nationality policy
permitted the development of national culture, neither religious practice nor Zionism were tolerated, for they were
considered antithetical to socialism and communism. The
ease with which distinctions between Jewish culture and
Judaism could be blurred, and the effect anti-Zionist propaganda had in discrediting not only Zionist Jews but non-
Zionist Jews as well, led over the years to limitations on both
Jewish national-cultural self-determination and the full
participation of Jews in Soviet society. Under the guise of a
nationality policy that was supposed to permit the development of national culture while leading ultimately to the
withering away of ethnic identity, Jews increasingly faced
limitations. These factors all played a role in the later
development of the emigration movement.

THE EARLY SOVIET PERIOD

The 1917 October Revolution offered the promise of a
proletarian utopia in which all people would be treated
equally and enjoy full rights and opportunities. Jews comprised between 3 and 4 per cent of the total population when
World War I broke out, but they represented almost 20
per cent of the revolutionary movement.[3] Having suffered
greatly under tsarist rule, many Jews were captivated by the
revolutionary ideals and yearned for the elimination of
anti-Semitism and discriminatory practices.[4]

   Despite its goal of creating a denationalized proletariat, the
revolution did not eliminate ethnic identity among the many
nations now under Soviet rule.[5] In fact, the relationship of
the central Party and government administration to the
various nationalities presented a complex problem that predated the formation of the Soviet federation. Early debate
over nationality policy centered on how to bridge the gap
between a strong centralized Party and government on the
one hand, and demands for national autonomy on the other.
The resolution of the issue had a dramatic impact on the
future of Soviet Jewry, as it laid the foundation for an
accelerated process of assimilation, the demise of Jewish
culture and, ultimately, the rise of the emigration movement.

During the consolidation period of the Soviet government from 1917 to 1922, the anti-Zionist (Menshevik) Jewish Social Democratic Union, known as the Bund, claimed to possess the sole right to represent the Jewish workers, as it had during the civil war. The Bundists pursued their traditional demands for the preservation and continuation of Jewish (i.e. Yiddish) culture and national autonomy. They favored a national-cultural autonomy plan originally fostered by the Austrian Social Democrats, which placed responsibility for cultural and educational life in the localities, with national councils elected by each nationality. The state was to provide political and economic unity.[6]

The Bolsheviks opposed the national-cultural autonomy platform, viewing it as separatist and divisive. Lenin favored 'proletarian and socialist internationalism', in which the state was placed above the nationalities. Separate national cultures were seen as a hindrance to the advancement of a workers' international and as an impediment to the emancipation of all peoples. Yet Lenin did not object to the preservation of national language and culture; he believed that the different cultural traditions and unique attributes of the nationalities would eventually disappear with the withering away of the state.[7] Nonetheless, he felt that the working classes were best represented by a proletarian party rather than by separate national groups.

The nationality policy that eventually emerged from the 1917–22 period was designed to address both Lenin's vision of proletarian and socialist internationalism and the demands of the nationalities for autonomy. A federation based on ethnically constituted units was created.[8] Theoretically, all groups categorized as nations were guaranteed the right to self-determination (including secession) and were granted autonomy over national culture. In actuality, however, because the nations remained politically, militarily and economically subservient to a strong central administration, their rights were to varying degrees eroded over time. Strong administrative structures, controlled from the center primarily by ethnic Russians, enabled the Party to retain tight control in the republics through its regional apparatus. The 15 nations that held union-republic status after 1923 were the greatest beneficiaries of the arrangement, for although their native élite were answerable to Moscow, indigenous élites staffed the regional Party machines.[9] Dispersed nations, or nations lacking a territory altogether, such as the Jews, were ultimately the greatest losers because they lacked a national-territorial administrative structure for ensuring their rights.

Jews were handicapped for other reasons as well. In his 1913 tract 'Marxism and the National Question' – which incorporated what became the authoritative Bolshevik definition of a nation – Stalin wrote: 'A nation is a historically evolved, stable community of language, territory, economic life, and psychological make-up manifested in a community of culture'.[10] Arguing that Yiddish was jargon rather than a language, both Lenin and Stalin, whose views carried the day, held that Jews could not be considered a nation because they lacked a common language and territory.[11] Stalin described Jews in 1921 as being among the 'various casual national groups, national minorities, interspersed among compact majorities of other nations.'[12] While, in true dialectical fashion, nations were to be granted the opportunity to flourish so that they could eventually merge (i.e. one new nation of Soviet people would emerge from among the many nations), those whose status as a nation was in question would in fact have fewer opportunities to develop. Although limited Jewish cultural autonomy was permitted within the guidelines of a policy of proletarian and socialist internationalism, and although Jewish cultural institutions and administrative organs even thrived during the early Soviet period, without consolidated territory of their own, the potential for Jewish autonomy was limited. Under such circumstances, Jews were, in theory and in practice, likely candidates for assimilation. They and others in their position were thus foreclosed at the outset from reaping the full benefits of national-cultural fulfillment within the USSR.

For Jews, limited cultural autonomy was realized in the establishment of a number of institutions during 1918–30. These included local organs of administration as well as cultural and educational bodies. Among the local administrative institutions were five National Regions, about 200 Municipal National Soviets, and a number of Yiddish-language courts and police stations.[13] Yiddish writers' organizations, professional and amateur theatrical groups, theaters, culture clubs, museums, schools and research institutes were some of the Jewish cultural and educational institutions of the early Soviet period.[14]

On the all-union (central) level, the Evsektsiya, the Jewish section of the Communist Party, was formed in 1918.[15] The Evsektsiya was to play a decisive role in Soviet-Jewish history, for its task of carrying out Party directives among the Jewish workers helped to speed both the assimilation of Soviet Jews and the destruction of Judaism within the Soviet Union. The Evsektsiya was not an autonomous organization and its duties included disseminating communist propaganda in Yiddish as it worked to eliminate Judaism and the institutions and practices considered responsible for Jewish separatism. It was also strongly anti-Zionist, primarily because its leadership consisted predominantly of former Bund members.[16] The work of the Evsektsiya embodied the spirit of a nationality policy that was designed to effect the eventual fusion of the nationalities into a new (supra-ethnic) 'Soviet' nationality.

While secular Yiddish cultural identification was permitted and even encouraged in the 1920s and through the early 1930s, Jewish religious institutions, publications, parties and educational bodies were eliminated by the Evsektsiya.[17] Until the dissolution of the Evsektsiya itself in 1930, destructive policies affecting Jews were largely confined to those designed to eliminate religion and Zionism. Such policies conformed to the general goals of promoting limited cultural expression on a national basis, while simultaneously striving to erode elements of national separatism. For Jews, this struck a particularly heavy blow, for the lines between Jewish 'national' culture and Judaism were not always clear.

A virulent attack on Judaism and the harassment of religious leaders emerged from within the general anti-religion campaign, which operated alongside the program designed to destroy remaining vestiges of national separatism. During 1922–23 alone, over 1000 Jewish schools were closed. By 1926, the several thousand synagogues that had existed prior to the civil war were reduced in number to 1103.[18] The Hebrew language, because of its connection to Judaism and Zionism, was, in the words of one commentator,

declared 'intrinsically reactionary',[19] and the last permitted
Zionist organizations were liquidated in 1928. Thus began a
process that systematically stripped Soviet Jewry of many of
its most characteristic features.

While working to eradicate Judaism and Zionism, the
Evsektsiya was also active in fostering the economic revital-
ization and Sovietization of the Jewish community, the latter
representing an important goal of nationality policy.[20] The
revolution had brought economic ruin to the Jewish masses;
although more than half a million Jews had left their
provincial homes by 1927 to seek work in cities and industrial
centers, the vast majority of the Jewish population remained
in the former Pale of Settlement, impoverished and poorly
integrated into mainstream Soviet society.[21] As a solution to
their economic difficulties, the Jews were offered an opportunity to settle remote lands. The idea for Jewish agricultural
colonization was proposed by the Komzet (Committee for
Agricultural Settlement of Jewish Workers), which, upon its
establishment in 1924, was formally assigned the task of
achieving the colonization.[22] A public organization, the Ozet
(Society for Agricultural Settlement of Jewish Workers) was
also set up to promote and facilitate Jewish colonization.[23] A
number of important leaders of the Evsektsiya were represented in the Ozet, which formed its presidium primarily
from Komzet members. Initially, the Ukraine and Crimea
were selected for the resettlement. However, competition for
land, combined with anti-Semitism on the part of the indigenous populations in those areas, prevented realization of the
original plan.

The Jews were eventually offered the sparsely populated
area of Birobidzhan, which was formally designated for
Jewish settlement in 1928. Birobidzhan was to have helped
alleviate the problem of Jewish poverty, but additional
motivations for settling the area were operative as well. For
one, the USSR was concerned with security, and accordingly
was interested in populating its far eastern borders. Birobidzhan was strategically important because of its proximity to
the Soviet–Chinese border.[24] However, beyond the strategic
consideration, the project fulfilled another agenda as well. In
seeking the financial and moral support of Western Jews
by promoting Birobidzhan as a 'Jewish homeland', Soviet

leaders hoped that Western sponsorship for the project would dissuade Zionist inclinations towards Palestine.[25]

Enthusiasm for the Birobidzhan plan was not widespread among the Jews; the harsh climate and the absence of actual familial, historical and cultural ties to the area were powerful deterrents. Although the territorial status of the area was upgraded and Birobidzhan was formally declared the Jewish Autonomous Region (*oblast*) by government decree on 7 May 1934, it remained little more than a *de jure* Jewish Autonomous Region. In 1959, Jews numbered only 14 269, or 8.8 per cent of the total Birobidzhan population of 162 856.[26] The 1970 census reflected a decrease from the 1959 totals, to 11 452 Jews, or approximately 6.6 per cent of Birobidzhan's population of 172 449.[27] The 1979 census revealed an even greater decline, showing Birobidzhan's Jewish population to be only 10 166 (5.4 per cent of the total population of 188 710) and the 1989 census showed yet a further drop to 8887 (4.15 per cent of the total population of 214 085).[28]

Instead of migrating to Birobidzhan, many young Jews moved to the cities and industrial centers throughout the USSR following the adoption of the initial Five Year Plan in 1928.[29] This migration transformed the socioeconomic composition of the Soviet-Jewish community. For the first time, large numbers of Jews began receiving higher education and entering professional fields such as education, medicine, economics, science and the arts.[30] As the traditional Jewish community broke down due to the campaign against Judaism and as a consequence of urbanization, increased education and economic integration, a new generation of young adults, largely alienated from its ethnic and religious roots, reached adulthood. The Soviet Jews of that generation, who had participated in Soviet youth organizations and been educated in Soviet schools, eagerly anticipated the realization of the revolutionary pledge to remove the barriers separating the nationalities; they spurred the tremendous upward social mobility that characterized Soviet Jewry prior to the 1940s.

Yet as Jews reached the cities in increasing numbers, their ability to compete successfully for jobs and their growing presence in administrative positions fueled popular anti-Semitism. Jewish success in the face of anti-Semitism and other barriers led to new rounds of anti-Semitism, a pattern that grew increasingly familiar as time went on. This cycle led many Jews to the conclusion that they could never become fully integrated into Soviet society, and this judgement later became a factor for some in their decision to emigrate.

STALINISM, 1930–53

Stalin's consolidation of dictatorial power led to the notorious repressions and purges of the 1930s. Soviet Jews, both individually and collectively, were targets in the campaign against nationalist deviations, left socialists and other non-proletarian influences. Stalin's paranoia, his views toward Jews and his belief in the need to stifle any expressions of national identity, formed the backdrop for his actions. Jews, by no means the only victims of Stalin's purges, suffered greatly because they were disproportionately represented in the intelligentsia and the Party – the groups most severely affected by the purges. The generation of Jewish Party members who had been actively involved in leading the Revolution was denounced as a group of spies, traitors and enemies of the people. Many of those individuals disappeared in labor camps or were killed outright as a result of the purges.

The most powerful locus of Jewish national cadres, the Evsektsiya, was eliminated in 1930. The Evsektsiya's demise signaled the beginning of a steady decline (accelerated during 1948–53) in Yiddish publications, the destruction of youth groups and communal organizations, and the erosion of virtually everything associated with Jewish cultural life.[31] The purges affected all national cadres. But for the Jews, the purges, which were coupled with the liquidation of Jewish institutions, were a pivotal event for they brought an end to organized Jewish life in the Soviet Union. Although the Evsektsiya had grossly damaged Jewish religious life in the Soviet Union, its dissolution left the Jewish community with no official representation in the Party. And despite the role it had played in furthering the assimilation of Soviet Jews, paradoxically, it had also helped to strengthen Jewish national consciousness by promoting Yiddish culture in the

USSR.[32] In 1938 the Ozet and the Komzet were dissolved, bringing the last remaining official Jewish organizations to an end.

World War II caused still further changes for Soviet Jewry, creating geographic dislocation and social alienation. As a result of the annexation in 1939 and 1940 of the eastern sections of Poland, Bessarabia (Moldavia), North Bukovina, and the Baltic states of Latvia, Lithuania and Estonia, the size of the Jewish population in the USSR was increased by approximately 60 per cent, bringing it to between 5 and 5.2 million when the war between Germany and the Soviet Union began.[33] Jews from the annexed areas had been less affected by the assimilatory processes that had eroded the Jewish community in the heartland of the Soviet Union (i.e. areas east of the 1939 Soviet–Polish border), and of course they had not been touched at all by Soviet nationality policy between the two World Wars. However, when the Germans invaded the Soviet Union, those areas were occupied along with parts of the Ukraine, Belorussia and the Russian Republic (RSFSR); the majority of the Jewish population living there were killed.[34]

The Jews who managed to survive did not, for the most part, return to their former homes because of heightened anti-Semitism and because many found it too difficult to live where their families had been killed. It was well known that in parts of the Ukraine and Belorussia the Germans were welcomed, leaving many Jews uneasy about the prospects for resuming their former lives in an environment free of open hostility. As a result, instead of returning to their villages, many Jews moved to urban areas. The war thus accelerated the trend that had begun in the Soviet heartland more than a decade earlier, and helped to transform Soviet Jewry from a village to an urban population. Yet despite the disappearance of traditional Jewish community life, official neglect of the Jewish nature of the Holocaust and increased anti-Semitism among part of the population left Soviet Jews acutely aware of their Jewish identity and their position as outsiders in the USSR.[35]

Beginning in 1946 and lasting until Stalin's death in 1953, a campaign was waged against 'nationalist deviations' (or 'bourgeois nationalism') and foreign influences ('cosmopoli-

tanism'). This crusade, which was linked in part to the desire
to create an 'international' society in which national distinctions would have no meaning, became thoroughly anti-
Jewish from 1948 onward. Stalin's increasing paranoia and
suspicion of dual loyalties, fueled no doubt by the creation of
the State of Israel in 1948 and a general mistrust of Jews
(whom he feared had ties to relatives living abroad), played a
role in spurring the post-1948 crackdown. The targeting of
Jews may have been related to a belief that Judaism could be
destroyed more rapidly than other religions,[36] and that its
demise would help to bring about the elimination of the
Jewish nationality. Indeed, Jews who wished to identify as
Jews by, for example, continuing to write in Yiddish, fared
worse than Jews who adopted Russian norms and culture.[37]

A broad-ranging attack, which reflected Stalin's insecur-
ities and thus could no longer be explained merely by the
goals of nationality policy, was launched not only against the
remaining vestiges of Jewish culture, but also against individual Jews involved in intellectual and artistic pursuits.[38] In
November 1948 the Yiddish publishing firm Der Emes was
shut down, and in 1949 the Jewish State Theater in Moscow
was closed. The Jewish Anti-Fascist Committee, formed as a
Soviet propaganda tool in 1942 to garner support for the war
effort among Western Jews, was disbanded in 1948. It had
served as a rallying point for Soviet Jews, for it gave them a
centralized body much as the Evsektsiya had done in earlier
years. Jewish authors, artists, composers, scholars and poets
were labeled 'bourgeois nationalists' and 'cosmopolitans'.
Many who were arrested or internally deported died in
prison camps; some of the more prominent people were
shot.[39] The elimination of Jewish institutions and organizations along with their leadership inevitably helped to speed
the assimilation of Jews, reducing their national cohesion
and weakening any autonomy they had achieved.

One of Stalin's final anti-Jewish acts was his accusation in
January 1953 of nine doctors, six of whom were Jewish, of
the assassination of several high Soviet officials and the
attempted assassination of others. He charged that the
doctors were acting under orders from American and British
intelligence agents and the American Joint Distribution
Committee (a Jewish philanthropic organization).[40] The

'Doctors' Plot' was the culmination of Stalin's campaign against bourgeois nationalism and cosmopolitanism, i.e. against the Jews, for Stalin apparently was planning to use the trial as a way of laying the groundwork for the wholesale deportation of Soviet Jewry.[41] Stalin's death in March 1953 brought to an end a period that has been termed the 'Black Years' of Soviet Jewry (1939–53). The so-called Doctors' Plot was exposed as a fabrication and the accused were released from prison and exonerated in April 1953.[42]

THE ROOTS OF ANTI-ZIONISM AND ANTI-SEMITISM IN THE POST-WAR PERIOD

Despite ideology supporting the equality of nationalities and denouncing anti-Semitism, officially supported policies of anti-Zionism and/or anti-Semitism have been present during most periods of Soviet history.[43] Starting with the crackdown on bourgeois nationalism and cosmopolitanism in 1948, the post-World War II period has been characterized by increased anti-Semitism, cyclical periods of repression and, particularly since 1967, by government-sponsored production of anti-Zionist propaganda. The existence of an official policy of anti-Zionism creates confusion over whether anti-Semitism is generated at the grassroots level or as a result of state policies; moreover the distinctions are sometimes deliberately blurred. While the reasons for anti-Semitism and anti-Zionism are complex and require a full-scale study, ideological, cultural, economic, religious, social and psychological factors must be counted among the forces at play.

During Khrushchev's tenure, an anti-religion campaign ran simultaneously with an anti-Zionist campaign, further blurring distinctions between Judaism and Zionism. Khrushchev launched the anti-religion campaign as a way of ridding the Soviet Union of 'reactionary elements'. The desire to sever the links between Judaism and Jewish nationalism once and for all also motivated his action. As part of the campaign, propaganda was used to discredit Jews by (1) depicting Judaism as immoral (for example, by alleging that money is the god of the Jewish faith), (2) declaring that Judaism breeds hatred of others since it calls Jews the 'chosen people', and (3) charging that Judaism demands allegiance to another state (i.e. Israel). The campaign resulted in both the closing of synagogues and restrictions on Jewish religious observance. Khrushchev's anti-religious policies were not directed exclusively against Jews, but Judaism was among the religions subjected to exceptionally harsh treatment.[44]

In the same period, the economic trials of 1961–64 were held with the intention of exposing and eliminating corrupt activities such as blackmarketeering, bribery, speculation and other 'economic crimes'. Punishment for individuals convicted of those crimes was death. Of the approximately 250 people executed as a result of the trials, nearly 55 per cent were Jews. Because the trials of Jews were widely publicized, the impression created among the general population was that the crimes were committed mainly by Jews. This distortion appeared deliberate, readily exploiting anti-Semitic feelings among parts of the populace. The unusually high proportion of Jews among those executed led many observers to suggest that Jews were being used as scapegoats in the campaign against corruption.[45]

Bias against Jews during the Khrushchev years was further manifested in the exclusion of Jews from Party and government posts, security positions, upper level army ranks and the foreign service.[46] This was a direct example of an anti-Jewish 'policy' operating under the guise of nationality policy. Barriers to Jewish representation in the aforementioned professions have continued to the present day. They have been facilitated by the Soviet passport system, which requires citizens to show an internal passport (identification document) in connection with practically all local and national bureaucratic procedures. Because the passport designates nationality (*natsionalnost*) in its fifth entry (commonly referred to as the 'fifth point'), one's nationality is easily ascertained.[47] Since the term 'Jewish' refers in the Soviet Union to both a nationality and a religion, the ability to identify nationality expedited the policy of restricting (or removing altogether) Jews from various positions and professions regardless of whether or not the individuals affected considered themselves Jews.[48]

By the outbreak of the Arab–Israeli War in 1967, much of the Soviet-Jewish community had become assimilated as a consequence of deliberate policies and as a result of modernizing processes. Yet there were still significant numbers of Jews, primarily those living in areas west of the pre-World War II borders, who retained strong attachments to Judaism and Zionism despite, or perhaps because of, assimilative trends. Particularly for this latter group of Jews, the anti-Jewish measures were devastating.

Anti-Zionist propaganda was expanded after Israel's victory in the 1967 war. The anti-Israel, anti-Zionist media campaign has had the effect of being anti-Semitic. Although historical 'evidence' is presented as new and definitive, it employs the familiar model of Jews as agents of a Zionist world conspiracy. Repeatedly evoking stereotypic characterizations reinforces whatever popular prejudices may exist, and in turn, allows those prejudices to be utilized as justification for harassment and discriminatory treatment of Soviet Jews.[49] Zionism, officially labeled reactionary and imperialistic, is considered an ideological threat. Depicted as a racist, international counter-revolutionary movement, which purportedly has gained control of Western mass media as part of a plan of global domination, Zionism has also been regularly equated with fascism and Nazism, and Soviet history books have been altered to show Zionist 'collusion' with the Nazis.[50] The propaganda questions the loyalty of Jews as Soviet citizens, which indicates that the campaign is not solely for external consumption but also serves a domestic purpose. The late Leonard Schapiro wrote: 'the nature of the immoderate language and drawings can only have one effect at home [in the USSR] – that of stimulating hatred and contempt for the Jew; not the Zionist, not the Israeli, but the ordinary, probably assimilated Jew who lives next door'.[51]

In addition to blatant discrimination, scapegoatism as a means of placing blame or deflecting attention from the true sources of problems has often been manifested in anti-Semitic and/or anti-Zionist attitudes and actions. Anti-Semitism and anti-Zionism have also been used as rallying points around which to forge pro-government solidarity, by using the traditional tactic of identifying a common 'enemy'. Exploiting latent anti-Semitism strengthens alliances with segments of the population that traditionally have been chauvinistic or hostile toward Jews. Although popular support is not needed for official policy *vis-à-vis* the Jews, the propaganda facilitates the proffered rationale for continuing anti-Jewish measures. Not only are Soviet Jews made to feel like outsiders, but they are also constantly reminded by the propaganda that they are perceived as such. Despite a high level of assimilation among most Soviet Jews, time-worn stereotypes advanced by the propaganda impede their complete integration into Soviet society.

CONTEMPORARY STATUS OF JEWISH CULTURE

The legacy of the destructive measures against Judaism and the Jewish nationality has been the continued erosion of Jewish life in the USSR and the acceleration of a natural assimilatory process resulting from increased education, economic integration and urbanization. Restraints on public access to Jewish cultural (and religious) materials remained tight in the post-Khrushchev period and were not loosened until after Gorbachev came to power. Although the 1979 census revealed that 83.3 per cent of Soviet Jews used Russian as their native tongue,[52] prior to 1988 no Russian-language Jewish journals, radio programs, theaters or other cultural facilities existed. Two professional Yiddish theaters (the Birobidzhan Chamber Music Theater, established in 1967, and the Moscow Dramatic Ensemble, established in 1962) and a number of amateur theater companies constituted the most visible and widely available sources of Jewish cultural activity before 1988. For many years after Stalin's death, occasional lectures on Jewish literary subjects represented one of the only other sources of approved Jewish cultural activity. Likewise, prior to the Gorbachev period, no Jewish museums or sections of larger museums dealing with Jewish history, culture or folklore existed in the USSR, with the exception of the Sholom Aleichem Museum in Pereyaslav-Khmelnitsky (the writer's birthplace), and a permanent exhibition of works by Jewish painters and sculptors at the offices of *Sovetish Heimland* (a Yiddish literary review started in 1961).[53] The Hebrew language was taught in some theological seminaries and universities, but outside those fora, remained inaccessible to the vast majority of Jews.

In a sense, Jewish culture was doomed from the start because the federal structure of the USSR was linked to territorial-administrative units based on nationality. Lacking their own land, Jews and other territorially dispersed minorities could expect little in the way of real national-cultural autonomy. This ultimately was an important factor in the loss of Jewish ethnic identity. More importantly, the 'Black Years' and later discriminatory acts that impeded or totally denied Jews access to various professions and educational institutions were profoundly destructive to the future development of all of Soviet Jewry. The actions taken against the Jewish religion alienated some Jews and those designed to eliminate Jewish culture distanced still others. Most importantly, discrimination and anti-Semitic events such as show trials created common ground for Jews who might otherwise have shared only their nationality. The message unmistakably sent to Soviet Jewry was that Jewish 'nationalism' and the practice of Judaism could not be condoned, yet complete assimilation would also be impossible for those who desired it.

In a society in which Stalin's acts were not to become a subject of open discussion for another 20 years, Jews living in the Soviet Union in the 1960s found themselves in an uncomfortable but all too familiar situation: they were criticized for being outsiders, but prevented from becoming insiders. Life as a practicing Jew in the Soviet Union was impossible. Popular anti-Semitism and official anti-Zionism aided discrimination and thwarted full assimilation. In light of those circumstances, when emigration became a viable alternative in the late 1960s, it presented for many Soviet Jews the only feasible solution to their dilemma.

2 The Birth of the Jewish Emigration Movement

> There exist in our country anti-Semitic feelings. These are survivals of a reactionary past. It is a problem which is complicated by the situation of the Jews and their connections with other peoples. At the beginning of the Revolution there were many Jews in the management of the Party and state. They were better educated, perhaps more revolutionary than the average Russian. Afterwards, we created new cadres.... If now the Jews wanted to occupy the top jobs in our republics, they would obviously be looked upon unfavorably by the indigenous peoples.... But we are not anti-Semitic.... I myself have a half-Jewish grandson. We are struggling against anti-Semitism.
>
> Nikita Khrushchev, 1956[1]

POST-WAR REVIVAL OF JEWISH NATIONAL CONSCIOUSNESS

The endurance of Zionist sentiments and Jewish national consciousness in the USSR confounded Marxist theory on the nationalities, according to which class unity would erode national distinctions.[2] The horrors of the Holocaust and the 'Black Years' under Stalin had stimulated a reawakening of Jewish identity in the Soviet Union. Many Jews felt betrayed by their country's lenient treatment of Soviet citizens who had perpetuated the anti-Semitism of the Nazis, and by the failure of the Soviet Union to recognize and commemorate the suffering of Soviet Jews in World War II.[3] The purges and show trials had also left a devastating mark. The resulting discontent and alienation among Soviet Jews were manifested in a consolidated drive for emigration when a variety of international events and domestic trends converged in the late 1960s.

Following the end of the war, two types of Zionist groups arose. The first consisted of individuals in the annexed areas – the eastern sections of Poland, Bessarabia (Moldavia),

North Bukovina and the Baltic states of Latvia, Lithuania
and Estonia – who had formerly (before the annexations)
been involved in Zionist activity. They sought to locate
relatives dispersed by the Holocaust and war-related deportations and immigrate to Palestine. 'New' Zionist circles
formed in the Ukraine, Moldavia and the Baltic Republics.
Comprised of younger Jews, the members of these groups
viewed emigration as a solution to their discontent.[4] For old
and new Zionists alike, the creation of the State of Israel in
1948, the USSR's support for Israel's statehood, and the
arrival of Golda Meir, the first Minister of the Israeli legation
in Moscow, brought great pride.[5]

However, it was also during this period that the campaign
against bourgeois nationalism and cosmopolitanism was
waged, resulting in arrests of Zionists and other Jews. The
campaign was part of Stalin's effort to create the 'new Soviet
man' by removing what he considered to be vestiges of a
bourgeois society. But as Stalin grew obsessed with the
campaign, it was transformed into an outright attack against
the Jews.

During the thaw that followed Stalin's death in 1953, some
of the Zionists who had ceased their activities during the
1948–53 'Black Years' renewed their commitment to Israel.
For the most part their efforts consisted of forming small
circles that met to celebrate Jewish and Israeli holidays. By
1957, these circles had expanded to include younger Jews
whose support for Israel grew in response to the 1956 Sinai
Campaign. In Moscow, the presence and propaganda efforts
of Israelis at the 1957 International Youth Festival fostered
additional interest in Israel. Even secular Jews began to use
synagogues as a place to meet, exchange information and
express their solidarity. Throughout the 1960s, contacts
between Israeli tourists and Soviet Jews, circulation of *samizdat* (self-published) works about Israel, Jews and Jewish
history, and *samizdat* translations of classic Hebrew and
Yiddish literature into Russian grew more frequent.

Although many of the leading Zionist activists were
arrested during 1957–66, the arrests only served to spur the
creation of new leaders, adding momentum to the burgeoning movement.[6] This was a cycle that was to recur through-

out the history of interaction between Jews and the Soviet authorities. It was a pattern Soviet authorities did not initially seem to recognize.

EMIGRATION POLICY PRIOR TO 1968

A small amount of emigration did take place during 1948–67 for the purpose of reuniting divided families. Approximately 6900 Jews left the Soviet Union during the period on that basis.[7] While the actual number was small, application of the principle of reunification of families established a precedent for emigration after 1967.

Statements on emigration to Israel during the Khrushchev period (1956–64) supported the idea of reunification of families as a viable option for Jews. Most remarks were predictable for their negative characterization of Israel, yet they were significant because they hinted at the possibility of additional future emigration.[8] One of the most important indications emerged early in the Brezhnev era during Chairman of the Council of Ministers Alexei Kosygin's December 1966 visit to Paris. Kosygin stated at a press conference:

> If there are some families divided by the war who want to meet their relatives outside the USSR or even to leave the USSR, we shall do all in our power to help them. The way is open to them and will remain open to them and there is no problem.[9]

Kosygin's statement was all the more notable because it was reprinted in the Soviet press.[10] The Soviet papers omitted the phrase, 'we shall do all in our power to help them' as well as the pledge that the door would remain open in the future. Nonetheless, many Soviet Jews and members of other nationalities interpreted the statement as a signal that they were free to explore the option of emigrating.[11] Indeed, from 1966 to the outbreak of the Arab–Israeli War in June of 1967, 3437 Jews emigrated.[12] However, when the war started, all emigration to Israel was halted.

The 1967 war spelled the end of Soviet–Israeli diplomatic relations. The USSR had been producing quantities of anti-Zionist propaganda virtually continuously since 1949 (when the short honeymoon phase following the creation of the State of Israel ended), but during the 1967 war, the propaganda was marshaled into an aggressive campaign.[13] The continuation of the anti-Zionist campaign after the war, and the Soviet Union's vehement condemnation of Israel and strong support for the Arab states, disturbed increasing numbers of Soviet Jews.[14] Some concluded that a viable Jewish life in the Soviet Union would be elusive at best. Others, as they saw options dwindling, became concerned about future opportunities for their children, worrying that still greater hostility toward Jews would ensue.

Indeed rapid industrialization and modernizing processes in the USSR had increased competition along national lines, altering the social stratification of nationalities and encouraging an influx of people to urban areas. These changes were often accompanied by heightened popular anti-Semitism and anti-Jewish discrimination. They also had the additional unwelcome effect of eroding the security Jews had enjoyed in professional and educational access. Ironically, although these processes had sped Jewish assimilation, they also had created a backlash against Jews who had integrated successfully and benefited from new opportunities. Despite natural assimilatory trends and the personal attempts of Jews who did their best to blend in, complete assimilation was made impossible; policies that in effect were detrimental to Jews and resentment toward Jews who were considered to have achieved their success at the expense of others prevented full integration.

Also contributing to this sense of unease was the impact of limitations on Jewish admission to institutes of higher education that began to be felt by the younger generation, whose parents had been educated and employed prior to the onset of discriminatory admission and hiring practices. During 1958–68, the percentage of Jewish scientific workers declined from 10.2 per cent to 7.4 per cent of the total number of scientific workers,[15] and the percentage of Jews in institutions of higher education dropped from 4.2 per cent in the 1956–57 academic year to 2.5 per cent in the 1968–69 academic year.[16] This discrimination was not reserved merely for Jews; the development of national cadres and a nationality policy aimed at equalizing the distribution of professional jobs according to each nationality's proportion of the total population affected other groups as well. Indeed, like the Jews, 14 nationalities with 'national'-territorial units outside the boundaries of the USSR (who were also viewed with suspicion because of their links abroad) experienced drastic reductions in both admission to educational institutions and representation in various professions.[17]

In addition to limitations on higher education, the exclusion of Jews from the diplomatic and civil services, high military posts, foreign trade positions, and senior and administrative positions in institutions of higher learning, specialized research institutes and the Party, remained operative after Khrushchev's demise. For the group of Jews who had maintained a commitment to Zionism, dissatisfaction with the quality of Jewish life in the Soviet Union and policies that were anti-Jewish or anti-Zionist became increasingly important concerns. Likewise, among Jews who had been adversely affected by job competition and/or discrimination on the basis of nationality (including restrictions on admission of Jews to institutes of higher education), a sense of ethnic identity developed.

THE BIRTH OF THE CONTEMPORARY EMIGRATION MOVEMENT AND THE SOVIET RESPONSE

By 1968–69, significant international events – principally the 1967 Arab–Israeli War, officially-sponsored anti-Semitism in Poland, and the 1968 Soviet invasion of Czechoslovakia – provided the external stimuli that caused Soviet-Jewish Zionist, cultural and religious leaders to conclude that domestic reform would be impossible. The creation of the State of Israel, family ties in the West, previous exposure to emigration primarily as a result of the Soviet–Polish Repatriation Agreement (effective from 1957–59) and the impression that new opportunities for emigration seemed possible all contributed to the emerging view that emigration offered a solution.

At the initiative of the Ministry of Internal Affairs' Department of Visas and Registration (OVIR) some emigration, the first since the Six-Day War, was permitted starting in September 1968.[18] Observers have speculated that this emigration was intended to enhance the Soviet Union's international image in the aftermath of the 1968 invasion of Czechoslovakia.[19] Although the 379 visas issued by the year's end did not constitute a widespread development,[20] renewed emigration encouraged a group of strongly committed Soviet-Jewish Zionists. By 1969, Zionists and others began organizing strategies aimed at achieving their goal of emigration.[21] As communication between them and coordination of activities improved throughout the country, the demand for emigration became consolidated and the movement was born.[22]

Soviet Jews were emboldened by the example the various dissident movements had set in their campaigns for greater human rights, democracy and religious and other freedoms in the Soviet Union.[23] Following the dissidents' lead, many Soviet Jews became vocal and aggressive in openly calling for their right to emigrate. However, unlike the dissident groups, the Jewish emigration movement did not strive for internal reform. Indeed, emigration was the goal for those who had lost hope for living in the Soviet Union as Jews (in the broadest sense of the word) as well as for those who were convinced that as Jews they would never be able to integrate fully into Soviet society. Using the framework of international human rights principles to champion their demands, Jewish activists based their campaign for emigration on the universal right of freedom of movement, incorporated in the 1948 Universal Declaration of Human Rights (UDHR)[24] and the 1966 International Covenant on Civil and Political Rights (ICPR).[25]

The Jews' campaign to leave raised thorny issues since the USSR did not permit free emigration. Soviet practice rejected the notion that individuals could elect to leave the USSR for permanent residence elsewhere; the USSR allowed limited emigration only within the context of reunification of divided families. Such emigration was permitted primarily in the case of Jews, Germans and Armenians. Voluntary (free) emigration was objectionable not only for the potential consequences it could have among dissatisfied ethnic groups throughout the USSR, but also because the exercising of individual free will in a country committed to an ideology that placed the needs and rights of the collective above those of the individual, was not well received.[26]

Soviet authorities responded to the push for emigration with a two-pronged approach designed to constrain the growing movement. Under the mistaken impression that demand for emigration would quickly exhaust itself, controlled emigration was permitted while expectations that free emigration or a more relaxed policy toward existing emigration would be forthcoming were strongly discouraged.[27] As this policy developed after 1970, increasing numbers of exit visas were issued,[28] although the authorities simultaneously set up a number of obstacles that made the emigration process difficult.

Punitive actions against would-be emigrants indicated that despite the decision to allow a restricted flow of emigration, the scope would remain narrow; the ability to emigrate was not to be taken for granted. In the late 1960s and early 1970s, policies were focused on diluting and weakening the emigration movement by allowing the leadership and the most committed Zionists to leave in the hope that doing so would reduce and eventually exhaust future demand.

The emigration option represented a departure from previous approaches to the Jewish 'national question'. Although attempts to undermine Jewish national consciousness were not diminished, the most persistent and intractable segments of the Jewish community were simply removed by virtue of their emigration. Several factors point to why the Soviet authorities experimented with emigration as a method of addressing the Jewish question.

As discussed in Chapter 1, considerable ambivalence toward Jews, as manifested in the vociferous anti-Zionist campaign and the persistence of popular anti-Semitism in the USSR, had not diminished. Zionist aspirations, Jewish national consciousness and the resistance of significant segments of Soviet Jewry to assimilatory tendencies, suggested that, contrary to Marxist–Leninist–Stalinist theory on national groups, ethnic sentiments had not disappeared. National cleavages among the Soviet nationalities remained strong and had not withered away.

In the case of the Jews, ethnic identity was heightened

because of the very policies designed to weaken and eventually eliminate it. Stalin had used drastic measures to address the Jewish question, but despite the lasting damage his actions had inflicted on Jewish culture and Judaism, Jewish identity, like the national identity of various other ethnic groups, was resistant to the Stalinist goal of creating new *Soviet* people from an amalgamation of the nationalities in the USSR. Moreover, in the eyes of the Soviet authorities, Zionism promoted Jewish separatism through its emphasis on Jewish national statehood and was thereby antithetical to Marxist–Leninist ideology and Soviet nationality policy. By 1968, when Stalinist tactics were no longer in use, limited emigration became an option for dealing with unassimilable Jews. The possibility of an extra-territorial solution for the Jews (in Israel) and the existing precedents provided by earlier emigration elevated the viability of emigration as a solution to the situation.[29]

The emigrant pool during the first period of mass emigration (1968–73) dovetailed with Soviet policy objectives. The group of emigrants consisted largely of Jews from the areas annexed during World War II, the Georgian SSR and Central Asia, where there was a lower level of assimilation. Although the majority of Soviet Jews reside in the Soviet heartland (defined here as the RSFSR and the eastern part of the Ukraine and Belorussia), heartlanders constituted only 10.6 per cent of the total emigration in 1971, 14.6 per cent in 1972, and 19.6 per cent in 1973.[30] Instead, the bulk of the 1968–73 emigration was from regions in which less than 20 per cent of Soviet Jews lived. While this was deliberate on the part of the authorities responsible for granting visas – given their objective of removing the most pro-Zionist Jews – it also reflected the strongly held Zionist commitment of Jews living in those areas.

Jews of the periphery (the southern republics and the annexed territories), who had retained a greater attachment to Jewish culture, Zionism and/or Judaism, were less 'Sovietized' than the more assimilated Jews from the heartland. When questioned, they indicated that Zionism was the greatest motivating factor for immigration to Israel. Family reunification and religious considerations were also important determinants, particularly among the elderly.[31]

But Soviet policy-makers were unprepared for the massive response the opportunity to emigrate would bring. The procedural and bureaucratic deterrents the Soviet authorities mounted in their effort to discourage additional emigration galvanized the activists and their international supporters. Despite obstacles, the example set by growing emigration encouraged individuals to apply while the opportunity to leave was available. The sense that some restrictions had been lifted was supported by hard evidence: the number of visas issued in 1972 was greater than the combined number for 1968–71. A total of 13 022 Jews emigrated in 1971, rising to 31 681 in 1972 and to 34 733 in 1973.

Expanding emigration levels not only heightened Soviet-Jewish demand for further emigration, but also enlarged the international spotlight on Soviet Jewry, which became an unyielding irritant for Soviet negotiators dealing with the United States on issues ranging from arms control to export matters.[32] As the movement's momentum increased, the Soviet-Jewish activists directed growing attention toward garnering international support and publicity. Emulating dissident groups, they employed tactics such as demonstrations, hunger strikes, press conferences with foreign journalists, petitions, letters of protest, telegrams and declarations to Soviet and international bodies, *samizdat* writings and official complaints made personally to authorities responsible for emigration. The objective of such public actions was to inform Western sympathizers and fellow Soviet Jews of the activists' situation.

In the belief that international pressure on the Soviet leadership was the key to continued emigration, Soviet Jews also relied on supporters in the West to publicize their situation. Soviet Jews concluded that emigration was tied to the US–Soviet détente of the early 1970s because it had increased in tandem with the warming of US–Soviet relations. Western supporters of the emigration movement called for the linking of a range of issues under negotiation between the US and the Soviet Union to continued and increased emigration.[33]

The activists' assumptions regarding the connection between increased emigration and improving US–Soviet relations were only partially correct. The Soviet decision to permit greater emigration represented a *realpolitik* assessment, a calculated decision as to the most expedient way to handle a domestic problem. It also reflected a new twist in Soviet policy toward the nationalities. Significant emigration of Soviet Jews had begun before the USSR started receiving pressure from the West, indicating that the role of the West, at least initially, was not decisive.[34]

But the Soviet authorities had seriously underestimated both the activists' ability to garner international support and the willingness of their supporters to campaign tirelessly for them. They did not expect the emigration issue to reach the highest levels of US–Soviet relations, as it did in the Jackson–Vanik amendment to the Trade Act of 1974, which linked trade and investment benefits and guarantees to free emigration. Nor did they anticipate that the issue would play a dominant role in the Conference on Security and Cooperation in Europe (CSCE).[35] However, Soviet policy-makers soon realized that while Jewish emigration represented an effort to alleviate a domestic problem, it could also be packaged as a concession to the US,[36] serving both a domestic and international agenda at once.[37]

Jews (and the Soviet Germans and Armenians who also were allowed to emigrate) held a unique position because their efforts to emigrate were successful. Others with family ties in the West, such as Ukrainians, Russians and the various Baltic nationalities, for instance, were not permitted to emigrate, indicating that permissible emigration was not simply a matter of fulfilling the humanitarian objective of reuniting divided families. On the contrary, emigration of Jews represented a deliberate strategy for handling an ethnic problem. The large-scale emigration of specific ethnic groups underscored the nationality component in emigration decisions superficially based on reunification of families. Yet even the decision to permit the emigration of particular nationalities was not devoid of important restrictions. Not only was emigration limited to a select group of nationalities, but within those groups it was tightly controlled and circumscribed. The decision to create obstacles to emigration through cumbersome and difficult application procedures on the one hand, and, on the other, to deal with activists in a repressive manner, indicated the restricted nature of emigration.

As increasing numbers of Jews applied to leave, a variety of intimidating tactics were used in an effort to exercise control over the growing movement. Threats, house searches, disruption of postal and telephone service, public denunciation in the work place, interrogations, short-term detention, military call-ups, incarceration in psychiatric hospitals and 'show' trials, often followed by prison, labor camp or terms of exile, grew more common over time.[38] Soviet Jews sentenced on political grounds became known in the West as 'prisoners of Zion'.[39] Possession of Hebrew-language materials, open involvement in the campaign for realization of the right to emigrate, teaching or studying Hebrew, or pursuing the furtherance of Jewish cultural or religious life in the Soviet Union, carried wide-ranging criminal charges.[40] Prosecution was intended to crush the activity of the Jewish activists and deter Jews from contemplating emigration. Such treatment also represented a new and aggressive initiative aimed at intimidating Jews who wished to identify with their cultural or religious traditions by equating Jewish consciousness with criminal behavior. All expressions of Jewish national identity, whether through cultural avenues, Hebrew study or Zionism, were deemed anti-state activity by Soviet authorities.

The earliest criminal case of a Jewish activist widely reported in the West was that of Boris Kochubievsky. In May 1968 Kochubievsky had written a *samizdat* piece entitled, 'Why I am a Zionist' and applied to emigrate in November of that year. He was granted permission to leave but shortly before he was due to depart, Kochubievsky was arrested and charged under Article 187-1 of the Ukrainian SSR Criminal Code with 'Dissemination of Knowingly Slanderous Fabrications, Defaming the State and Social System of the USSR'; he was convicted and sentenced to 3 years in a labor camp. Kochubievsky's conviction initiated a series of trials for people accused of possessing material relating to Jewish themes, written in Hebrew, or considered 'Zionist' in content.[41]

A second case that received great attention in the West

during the early stages of the movement was the 1970 trial of a group of 11 activists (nine Jews and two non-Jews) who planned to hijack an airplane to Sweden. The hijackers were arrested at Smolny Airport in Leningrad before they boarded the plane. In addition to being charged under the RSFSR Criminal Code with 'Responsibility for the Preparation of a Crime and for Attempted Crime' (Article 15) and 'Stealing of State or Social Property in Especially Large Amounts' (Article 93-1), all the defendants were charged with 'Treason' (Article 64-a). Seven of the eleven defendants were also charged under Article 70 – 'Anti-Soviet Agitation and Propaganda' – and Article 72 – 'Organizational Activity Directed Toward Commission of Especially Dangerous Crimes Against the State and Likewise Toward Participation in an Anti-Soviet Organization'. Initially, two defendants, Edward Kuznetsov and Mark Dymshits, were given the death penalty but their sentences were commuted to harsh terms in a labor camp. These commutations appeared to be a response to worldwide condemnation as well as criticism by the British, French and Italian Communist Parties.[42]

Contrary to their desired effect, both trials – of Kochubievsky and of the unsuccessful hijackers – took on symbolic proportions and became focal points for greater protest inside as well as outside the USSR.[43] An example of the broad-based support organized in the West was the First World Conference on Soviet Jewry, which was held in Brussels in February 1971 and drew delegates from 38 countries. Conscious of its international image in the era of détente, the Soviet government launched a press campaign to discredit the conference. It also sent a group of 'official' Jewish representatives to Brussels, headed by Colonel-General David Dragunsky (a well-known Jewish representative of the official Soviet viewpoint) to present the Soviet perspective to the media during the conference.[44]

THE ANTI-ZIONIST CAMPAIGN OF THE 1970s

As time went on, the anti-Zionist campaign was used increasingly to vilify Israel, not only because of Soviet support of Arab states, but also as a means of discouraging immigration to Israel. The Soviet media tried to dissuade prospective emigrants by depicting Israel as a militaristic state; it highlighted the difficulties of finding employment in Israel and reported that many immigrants were disillusioned by their experience. Anti-Israel propaganda helped contribute to the image of Jews as betrayers, for the general public was led to believe that anyone choosing to live in Israel was suspect, unworthy of Soviet citizenship and a disgrace to the Soviet people.[45]

The dual themes of Jews as traitors and Jews as naive innocents duped by Zionist propaganda and therefore not fully responsible for their decision to leave the Soviet Union were deliberately linked to anti-Zionism by a complex group of factors. Portraying some Jews as traitors reinforced the notion that only the most unworthy Soviet citizens would emigrate. Depicting other Jews as unwitting victims also served to create the sense that Jews were responding to forces outside the USSR rather than electing to emigrate because of circumstances in the Soviet Union.

Criticism of Israel and Israeli propaganda not only discredited the Jewish state, but also reflected a deeper issue. Emigration implied rejection; the decision of Jews to emigrate was an implicit disavowal of the Soviet system and society. The rebuff was considered insulting and opportunistic, and threatened a value system that placed the collective above the individual. Since it was politically unacceptable to acknowledge that Soviet citizens might actually emigrate voluntarily, it was necessary to establish external causation. Anti-Zionism provided a convenient means of addressing the ideological implications of the emigration movement.

PROCEDURAL DETERRENTS

The Soviet Exit Visa Application Process

The major procedural obstacle to emigration throughout the 1970s and most of the 1980s was the application process. In addition to the repressive crack-down on would-be emigrants, the application procedure was part of the effort to

restrict the scope of emigration. The cumbersome requirements and numerous bureaucratic hurdles designed to deter
emigration were promulgated by the USSR Council of
Ministers' regulations on entry to the USSR and exit from
the USSR, which established the legal procedure for the
application process.[46] For prospective emigrants over the age
of 16, the basic requirements for filing an application consisted of submitting to the Department of Visas and Registration (OVIR) a *vyzov* (letter of invitation from a relative living
abroad), a declaration of one's intention to leave, a curricu-
lum vitae, permission from one's parents and former
spouse(s), a certificate from one's place of residence indicating the number and relationships of family members, copies
of certificates of birth, marriage, divorce and death of
relatives, diplomas from educational institutions and
photographs.[47]

Until 1976, a *kharakteristika* (reference) from one's place of
employment or study had also been required. The *kharakteristika* requirement was particularly objectionable to prospective emigrants because their ability to emigrate could easily
be jeopardized by an employer who refused to supply the
reference.[48] In 1976 the *kharakteristika* was replaced by the
spravka (work certificate), which required the employer's
signature and information on the length of service at each
place of employment, but did not include a character reference. Another problematic requirement (prior to 1987) was
that the *vyzov* be delivered by post from abroad. This raised
difficulties because in some cases deliberate postal disrup-
tions were used to prevent prospective applicants from
receiving international mail, thus rendering it impossible for
them to initiate the process. Consent from parents, former
spouses and others created additional difficulties in situa-
tions where relatives withheld permission without cause.[49] In
1988, as part of the process of reform under Gorbachev,
some procedures surrounding emigration were loosened.[50]

Implementation of the application regulations, relegated
to local level administrators, was not uniform.[51] In some
regions bureaucratic details were more strictly enforced than
in others.[52] For example, although the instructions on how
to apply were said in the 1970s to be posted on the wall

of each OVIR office,[53] an average of 77 per cent of emigrants surveyed reported that they were never shown official instructions.[54]

Various fees, modified over the years,[55] were required in connection with obtaining an exit visa. In 1970, a significant monetary distinction was created between fees charged for immigration to socialist countries and those levied for emigration to non-socialist countries.[56] Aside from the emigration fees, individuals emigrating with visas to Israel were required to relinquish their Soviet citizenship (for which there was a fee), although no Soviet statutes or ministerial directives required renunciation of Soviet citizenship upon emigration.[57] Individuals who immigrated directly to other non-socialist countries such as Great Britain, the United States and West Germany were not compelled to renounce their Soviet citizenship and thus did not pay additional fees in that connection.[58] This practice remained one of the mysteries of Soviet emigration policy. Its roots probably lay in hostility toward Israel and the absence of diplomatic relations between Israel and the USSR.[59]

Compulsory renunciation of Soviet citizenship was for some an important deterrent, for it underscored the permanence of immigration to Israel. Indeed, emigrants inevitably left friends and family behind, not knowing if they would be permitted to see them again.[60] Mandatory relinquishing of Soviet citizenship signified the 'disowning' of Jewish emigrants, in effect a final rejection – although they themselves were perceived as rejecting their Soviet homeland – of Jews who chose to emigrate. For propaganda purposes, Jews forced to renounce their citizenship could also be depicted as having been denied Soviet citizenship. This created an altogether different impression about Zionist emigration than did the notion of voluntary emigration.[61]

The 'Education Tax'

In 1972 procedural deterrents to emigration were for a short time upgraded in an attempt to stem the potential for an unwelcome by-product of emigration: the departure of increasing numbers of highly educated specialists. Jewish activists had been enormously successful in mobilizing support and accommodating growing interest in emigration. About 140 000 invitations were sent from Israel to prospective emigrants during 1969–72.[62] One-third of the invitations in those years were sent to families having at least one member with university-level education.[63] The high concentration of well-educated Jews in the Soviet population meant that inevitably the Soviet authorities would have to confront the possibility of some of their most talented citizens applying to emigrate. To forestall such a 'brain drain', the USSR Presidium of the Supreme Soviet issued a decree on 3 August 1972, entitled 'On Reimbursement by Citizens of the USSR, Leaving for Permanent Residence Abroad, of State Expenditure for Education'. The decree stated:

> Citizens of the USSR who leave for permanent residence abroad (except for those moving to socialist countries) are required to repay government expenditures for their training in an institution of higher education, postgraduate studies, medical internship and advanced military education and for the award of corresponding academic degrees.[64]

The decree became effective on 14 August and was applied retroactively to all those who had received permission and were preparing to emigrate.[65]

The tax was designed to curb the emigration of well-educated Jews. It also sought to discourage prospective emigrants from enrolling in institutes of higher education, thereby diminishing the economic and intellectual impact of emigration. If Jews chose not to pursue higher education, such a decision would also have had the ancillary effect of facilitating a more or less self-regulating *numerus clausus* (quota), which could only have had a welcome reception in universities and other institutions attempting since the late 1950s to address the uneven representation of ethnic groups in their ranks.[66] The tax also sought to deter the emigration of highly-educated Jews.

The reimbursement charges ranged from 12 200 rubles for graduates of Moscow State University and 6000 rubles for graduates of other universities, to 4500 rubles for graduates of economics, law, pedagogical, historical–archival and cultural institutes. In addition to the reimbursement of state expenditures by graduates of higher educational institutions or those in their final year of study, supplementary payment was required in three cases, the largest amount being a further 7200 rubles for individuals awarded a Doctor of Science degree.[67] The payment scale also included a schedule of fees based on the number of years of higher education actually completed for individuals who had been enrolled but were not graduates of universities or other institutions of higher education.

The charges outlined in the decree often exceeded the actual costs of higher education in the USSR, which reportedly amounted to an average of 4500 rubles for $4\frac{1}{2}$ years of university education, and 1700 rubles per year for postgraduate training.[68] The justification for the tax was based on the notion that the state deserved to be reimbursed for its investment in the education of individuals who decided to emigrate. Yet in the case of emigrants who had for many years been employed, statements, such as a respected Soviet demographer's, that individuals with 5–6 years' work experience had repaid their debt, cast considerable doubt on the official Soviet explanation for what had become commonly known as the 'education tax'.[69] Moreover, from 1940–56 higher education was not free, therefore individuals educated during that period had already paid for their education.[70]

The education tax was severely restrictive because the sums required were beyond the means of most Soviet citizens. At the time the tax was imposed, the average monthly salary was between 130 and 140 rubles,[71] making it virtually impossible to amass the necessary funds to emigrate. According to one report, an official of the Soviet Ministry of Finance told a group of Soviet Jews on 15 August 1972, 'We are not so naive as to suppose that you have as much as this [to pay for exit visas]. But you know where to get it.'[72]

Western Jewish organizations, which were purportedly expected to supply the funds for the tax, refused to pay, labeling the new measure a 'ransom tax'. In response to the tax, Soviet Jews signed petitions and staged protest demonstrations; Western scientific and academic communities also condemned the tax. In the United States Congress, the introduction of legislation linking emigration to trade with the Soviet Union was partially motivated by outrage at the education tax.[73]

In April 1973 the tax was suspended. Selective enforcement of the tax during the period it was in effect suggests that Soviet leaders were unsure of the soundness of the tax policy.[74] While the US government claimed responsibility for suspension of the tax,[75] the decision to halt the tax probably reflected more than mere concern about the US position. The tax had proven to have little effect.[76] Although the education tax was intended as a deterrent, not only did the number of emigrants rise during the period of its application, but most of the emigrants at that time were not, for reasons having little to do with the tax, highly educated.

Pre-1974 emigration was primarily Zionist in nature. Most of the emigrants during the period were from the periphery areas of the USSR; they did not emigrate for greater opportunities in the West, but rather left the Soviet Union to live in Israel and to be reunited with family members. The radical socioeconomic transformation of Soviet Jewry that had occurred through industrialization, urbanization and higher education had not benefited those Jews as greatly as it had the Jews living in the Soviet heartland. Therefore, the tax was probably of remote concern to the vast majority of the emigrants at the time. The concentration of highly educated emigrants did not emerge until the following period, when not only the motivations for emigration had changed but so too had the destination of the emigrants. Had the tax been in force in the post-1973 period, its impact probably would have been greater.

CONCLUSION

The Zionist phase of contemporary Soviet emigration, so named for the predominance of Zionism as a factor galvanizing the emigrants, constituted the opening chapter in the history of Soviet-Jewish emigration. Soviet authorities developed a strategy of controlled emigration whereby some Jews were permitted to leave while others were harassed in an attempt to discourage expressions of Jewish identity and demand for emigration. This plan had the unintended effect of stiffening rather than weakening resolve. Indeed, the course of history reveals that Soviet authorities were never successful in quelling the desire to emigrate, although they used harassment and repressive tactics to discourage emigration.

The ambivalence reflected in emigration policy mirrored the ambiguous relationship toward Jews generally. At an initial level, harassment of Jews, a complicated application process and the criminalization of activities associated with Jewish emigration represented an attempt to discourage emigration and to further assimilation. While this effort backfired, harassment and discrediting of would-be emigrants did serve to bolster Marxist–Leninist ideology because they neutralized criticism of the system implicit in the act of emigration. However, utilizing anti-Zionist allegations as a deterrent to emigration doomed nationality policy *vis-à-vis* the Jews. The alienating and isolating nature of the propaganda, whose message was that Jews were outsiders who could not be trusted, contravened the reputed assimilatory goal of nationality policy. It also assured the continuation of the existential disquiet Jews felt in the Soviet Union, a feeling reinforced by the powerful realization that as Jews they could never be full members in Soviet society.

As discussed in Chapter 3, tensions inherent in the clash between Soviet nationality policy and Soviet attitudes toward Jews, and in emigration policy itself, continued to be seen in every period of Jewish emigration. Not until President Gorbachev's *novoye myshleniye* (new thinking) created a context in which emigration could be understood as a component of civil society did this conflict begin to recede.

3 Post-Zionist Emigration

There is no social basis for emigration in the USSR. We have no unemployment, there is no poverty in the country. The Soviet constitution guarantees all citizens vital social rights. Living standards are constantly rising. The Leninist nationalities policy ensures the equal development of all nations and nationalities in our country.

Boris Shumilin, USSR Deputy Minister of
Internal Affairs, 1976[1]

Young Jewish mathematicians are not accepted in many universities and graduate schools; they find it difficult, at best, to obtain appropriate work.

The problem is increased a hundredfold because, like some shameful disease, one cannot discuss it openly. One cannot speak of something which ought not to exist. If I do, I risk everything – my work, my profession, my family, even my life.

Grigori Freiman, 1978[2]

As the emigration movement matured, both domestically and internationally, the Soviet leadership faced an expanding campaign. The attempt in the 1968–73 period to bifurcate policy toward growing Jewish ethnic identity by permitting the most pro-Zionist and religious Jews to emigrate while simultaneously discouraging emigration among the remaining (majority) segments of Soviet Jewry was unsuccessful. Permitting Zionists and religious Jews to leave not only failed to weaken pressure for emigration, but among mainstream Soviet Jewry, it actually stimulated further demand. Once it became clear that emigration presented a viable alternative for Soviet Jews, growing numbers chose to take advantage of it. By 1974 a new phase in emigration, which was to last until the end of the decade, had begun.

Active Western support for Soviet Jews plus a Jewish homeland outside Soviet territory meant that the Jewish emigration issue could not escape the international agenda. Soviet authorities were aware that the departure of large numbers of Jews could have political benefits abroad. But the USSR considered the emigration of its citizens to be an internal affair, and domestically, emigration was a double-edged sword: although it alleviated a variety of pressures and provided a convenient way of dealing with the 'Jewish problem', it also heightened the risk of fostering parallel demands by other nationalities. To deter other ethnic groups and control the number of Jewish emigrants, the USSR impeded emigration not only by mounting increasingly repressive attacks against prospective emigrants but also by developing a sophisticated application of international human rights doctrines concerning freedom of movement. Narrow interpretation of those doctrines enabled the Soviet Union to deny exit visas on grounds relating to domestic considerations permissible under international agreements.

The second period of mass emigration, 1974–79, was characterized by fluctuating emigration levels and the diminishing importance of Zionism as the chief factor motivating emigration. Affirmative action in employment and education, competition from other nationalities and anti-Semitism had, by the 1970s, made difficulties in professional advancement and admission to universities commonplace for Jews. These factors, in combination with the realization by many Soviet Jews that they could not escape being associated with Israel and the dominant themes of the anti-Zionist campaign, established a growing impetus for emigration. But in response to greater numbers of Soviet Jews requesting permission to emigrate, controls on opportunities for Jews became tighter and anti-Zionist propaganda increased. These actions produced a further counter response, which in an escalating spiral, resulted in still more Jews seeking to emigrate. The full impact of what is known as the 'drop-out' phenomenon – opting, once outside the Soviet Union, to emigrate to countries other than Israel – was felt during this period as increasing numbers of Soviet-Jewish emigrants chose to go to the United States and, to a much lesser degree, to Canada, Western Europe, Australia and New Zealand.

The growing number of emigrants demonstrated Jews' continued interest in leaving the USSR but it also reflected a decision by Soviet policy-makers to permit a large exodus. While the upgrading of repressive tactics as the years went on signaled one message to Soviet Jews and their Western supporters, large-scale emigration sent an altogether different one. By the end of the decade, a total of 228 701 Jews had emigrated.[3]

What prompted these seemingly conflicting postures? In the latter part of the 1970s, exploding emigration levels on the one hand and hostility and punitive actions toward would-be emigrants on the other, were to a great degree an exaggeration of the policy started a decade earlier. The strategy was designed to address a problematic nationality issue, but neither of its components was wholly successful. The 'Jewish question' did not disappear. Jewish activists became more committed to expressing their cultural and religious identity, and demand for emigration was not curtailed.

In 1980 a dramatic reversal in emigration policy emerged. Reduced annually and eventually dropping below 1000, emigration fell from the 1979 total of 51 320 to 21 471 (1980), 9447 (1981), 2688 (1982), 1314 (1983), 896 (1984), 1140 (1985) and 914 (1986). The shift away from large-scale emigration was accompanied by new heights of repression, marked by a huge increase in the number of 'refuseniks' (Jews refused permission to emigrate) and an expanded campaign against Jewish activists and Jewish cultural activities.

Harassment of visa applicants during 1980–86 represented a broadening and acceleration of the tactics used in the previous decade, but the intent was no longer to allow limited emigration while containing the overall growth of the movement. The idea of permitting emigration as a means of addressing a problematic nationality situation ceased to be operative. Instead the goal became ending emigration altogether, resulting not only in the rapid curtailment of Jewish emigration but also of German and Armenian emigration. The reasons for the abrupt policy about-face were complex, involving a combination of domestic and international concerns that related to the Soviet economy, socio-demographic considerations, a new approach to particular nationality questions and other issues, which are discussed fully in Chapter 5.

With Gorbachev's rise to power, yet another shift in emigration occurred. *Perestroika* (restructuring) and democratization within the Soviet Union heralded the arrival of 'new thinking' on many issues, including emigration. Starting in 1987, emigration increased markedly, although the initial surge appeared to signal only a decision to resolve outstanding refusenik cases. As the new policy progressed, it became clear that a significant trend toward renewed large-scale emigration had begun. Yet the rationale of the late 1970s did not return with this shift; instead, emigration increasingly came to be viewed as an important sign of the USSR's commitment to fulfill its international human rights commitments as well as a reflection of the growing liberalization of Soviet society.

Changes in emigration policy during the 20-year period beginning in 1968 reflect the ways in which emigration has been exploited and controlled by Soviet authorities. A complex issue, emigration has been linked to nationality in a number of ways. For one, the restricted nature of emigration ensured that only members of certain nationalities had the ability to emigrate.[4] Moreover, Soviet authorities themselves used emigration as a means of addressing longstanding and intractable issues concerning the Jewish nationality. Emigration trends were not only subject to the policy directives of Soviet authorities, but also to the goals of the emigrants themselves and to the changing composition of the emigrant pool. Shifts in the international climate had little direct effect on emigration, but deserve mention for the role they played in providing an overall context in which decisions were taken.

THE DROP-OUT PHENOMENON: CAUSES AND EFFECTS

By 1974, 18.8 per cent of the Jewish emigrants who left the Soviet Union elected to immigrate to Western countries other than Israel. This decision was formally made when the emigrants reached Vienna, their first transit point after leaving the USSR.[5] The proportion of drop-outs represented an extraordinary increase over the complete absence of drop-outs during 1968–69, and the 2.7, 1.6, 0.1 and 3.6 per cent drop-out rates of 1970–73 respectively.[6] The initial rise of immigration to destinations other than Israel was in part motivated by fears about Israel's security in the immediate aftermath of the 1973 October War in the Middle East. Emigration and requests for visas had decreased during 1974 and 1975, probably because of uncertainty about life in Israel. Letters sent from recent emigrants residing in Israel to friends and family remaining in the Soviet Union detailed negative experiences resulting from absorption difficulties, high inflation, competition for professional jobs similar to those held in the USSR and the personal cost of living in a country surrounded by hostile neighbors. The news had greatest impact upon those who lacked a strong Zionist commitment and therefore did not feel particularly drawn to Israel.

The drop-out trend became more pronounced when emigration began to increase again in 1976 having dropped from 34 733 in 1973 to 20 628 in 1974 and to 13 221 in 1975. In 1976 emigration rose to 14 261.[7] By 1979, as emigration reached a peak of 51 320, the majority chose not to go to Israel, suggesting that additional considerations were at play.

The decision to immigrate to the United States and other Western countries rather than to Israel underscored the declining importance of the Zionist factor to emigrants after 1973. The post-1973 emigrants were mostly educated urban professionals whose high level of assimilation reflected the predominance of heartlanders in the emigrant pool. As the group of emigrants began to correspond more closely to the geographic distribution of Soviet Jews,[8] considerations prompting the decision to emigrate changed. Factors that were not principally important to earlier emigrants grew increasingly significant among the later group.

Surveys of emigrants revealed that discrimination on the basis of nationality, cultural or political motivations, economic considerations and family reunification were the chief factors motivating emigration.[9] The survey findings indicated that the most assimilated Soviet Jews left the USSR for cultural and political reasons, while those from the annexed areas, who reported stronger Jewish identification, attributed their emigration to nationality-based discrimination, Zionism and economic factors. The lesser educated, rural Jews were motivated primarily by economic considerations.[10]

These results reflected the views of the majority of emigrants after 1976.

In one sense, the absence of strong Zionist and/or religious motivations pointed to the success of Soviet nationality policy, although some assimilation would have occurred in any case through urbanization, economic integration and increased education. Yet despite considerable assimilation, heartland Jews were unable to escape their Jewish 'nationality' completely for nationality was entered in all domestic passports (identity papers). From hiring policies to the anti-Zionist campaign, Jews were constantly reminded that they were excluded from opportunities because of their nationality. The inability to assimilate fully intensified the feeling of separateness among the heartland Jews and the ostracism and sense of 'otherness' prompted many of them to emigrate.[11] They felt that an anti-Jewish bias in Soviet policies and attitudes left them no other choice. In effect, many Jews sensed that they were indirectly being encouraged (or forced) to leave through hiring policies that increasingly barred them on the grounds that Jews were unreliable employees precisely because they might emigrate.[12] This was reinforced by anti-Zionist propaganda. The inherent contradictions in nationality policy with respect to Jews, namely that on the one hand it had encouraged assimilation yet on the other it had denied Jews the possibility of melding completely into the fabric of Soviet society, represented the failure of Marxist–Leninist–Stalinist ideology toward the nationalities.

This failure was all the more palpable because it was most pronounced among that part of the Soviet-Jewish population least influenced by Zionism, Judaism or Jewish cultural values; a group of people who were not only objectively likely to assimilate, but who often affirmatively identified as Russians rather than Jews. To foster ethnic identity among those Jews, a profound force that would alter the social fabric of their everyday lives would have been required. The accelerated anti-Zionist campaign, coupled with discriminatory actions and a policy of co-opting national élites throughout the USSR, accomplished this task. Economic 'pull' factors in the West only reinforced it.

While the *numerus clausus* (quota) reflected anti-Semitism, it was also an integral part of an affirmative action plan intended to create educated élites and equalize educational disparities among the nationalities. It was particularly beneficial to titular nationalities with union-republic status because they were best represented in the union-republic apparatus and thus able to compete most successfully for jobs and benefit readily from policies designed to privilege local élites.

The *numerus clausus* formed a constituent component of Soviet nationality policy.[13] As discussed in Chapter 2, it had contributed to the uneasiness Jews felt about their place in Soviet society. Their disquiet grew in the late 1970s as opportunities continued to dwindle. The emigrants of the latter half of the 1970s were, unlike their predecessors in the first phase of emigration, largely educated urban professionals. They pointed to the systematic policy of reducing the professional prominence Jews held (within the circumscribed professions open to them) as an important reason contributing to their decision to emigrate. Limited future opportunities for a generation of youth became a serious concern of many Soviet-Jewish intellectuals.[14] The percentage of Jewish students in Moscow higher educational institutions dropped from 3.16 per cent in 1970–71 to 1.82 per cent in 1978–79 (and fell further to 1.57 per cent in 1980–81).[15] While the reductions may in part be explained by natural demographic processes and emigration, the absence of Soviet data makes it impossible to determine the extent to which a deliberate anti-Jewish quota was responsible for the decrease. Regardless of the precise reasons for the decline, a general perception that past options were either disappearing or had already vanished became commonplace, greatly troubling a segment of the Soviet-Jewish intelligentsia.[16]

Responding to the negative situation they perceived, many Jewish professionals chose to leave the USSR. However, Soviet authorities viewed the exodus of a large number of highly educated and highly skilled Jews as proof of their claim that Jews were unreliable and therefore appropriately excluded from opportunities for higher education and professional advancement. Although a *numerus clausus* precipitated large-scale emigration, the departure of Soviet Jews was used as justification for limitations placed on the professional positions they held. Once emigration escalated, it was difficult to break this cycle, which Jews charged Soviet authorities with creating and which Soviet authorities claimed Jews had forced upon them.[17]

Whether intended or not, the *numerus clausus* worked its way into the emigration question by the 1970s. In the absence of any documentation, it is difficult to ascertain whether Soviet authorities hoped to encourage emigration through the policy of élite co-optation and integration and anti-Jewish quotas. Most likely, they did not. Emigration did present a new option for resolving the Jewish question, but the authorities' ambivalence toward the growing size of the emigration movement indicated that they were unlikely to have used the *numerus clausus* to promote additional emigration. It is more likely that greater desire to emigrate was a by-product to be tolerated and sometimes channeled when, as discussed in Chapter 5, increasing emigration served other policy objectives.

Most Soviet Jews who immigrated directly to the United States were granted conditional entry and refugee status as persons fleeing a communist state. When the refugee quota was filled during years of large-scale Soviet-Jewish emigration in the 1970s, the remaining Soviet Jews were admitted to the United States on an *ad hoc* basis through use of a provision granting the Attorney General parole authority to extend the ceiling on admission of refugees.[18] Immigrants entering the United States as refugees (but not as parolees) are eligible for limited resettlement assistance, funding for transportation and access to subsidized medical care, but those who receive asylum first in other countries, which they later choose freely to leave (such as Israel), are not. These re-emigrants are accorded the same treatment as other non-refugees wishing to immigrate to the United States, and do not receive special benefits. Because all Jews are entitled, under the Israeli Law of Return, to immigrate to Israel at will and become Israeli citizens (and receive government resettlement assistance), a number of emigrants may have chosen to go to the United States first, while retaining the option to immigrate to Israel at a future date.[19]

As time went on, the drop-out phenomenon became an increasing source of consternation to the Israeli government, which believed that emigrants leaving the Soviet Union on Israeli visas had an obligation to immigrate to Israel. However, it was not until 1988, when relations between the USSR and Israel had thawed somewhat,[20] that an arrangement was made for individuals bearing Soviet exit permits to claim their Israeli visas in Bucharest, Romania.[21] The plan, if it had been enforced, would have circumvented the drop-out phenomenon (during a time when worldwide immigration to Israel was low) by guaranteeing direct immigration to Israel. The policy was intended to ensure that once in Bucharest, where there was no access to US relief organizations, individuals granted permission to exit the USSR based on invitations from Israel would have had no opportunity to obtain permission to enter the US as refugees. The emigrants not wishing to use the Bucharest route rendered the Bucharest to Israel.[22] Israeli acquiescence to the Dutch Embassy's refusal to withhold Israeli entry visas from emigrants not wishing to use the Bucharest route, rendered the policy inoperative. The drop-out issue lost significance when in 1989 the US adopted a rigorous interpretation of the requirement that refugees demonstrate a well-founded fear of persecution and determined that many Soviet-Jewish applicants could not meet that standard. After 1 October 1989, when the American Embassy in Moscow began receiving applications from Soviet Jews for direct immigration to the United States, Jews who did not meet the requirement for US refugee status found that immigration to Israel was virtually the only viable means of exiting the USSR.[23]

DETERRENTS TO EMIGRATION

The rigorous application process and the waiting period during which decisions on applications were made were a means of deterring applicants. In the 1970s and 1980s until Gorbachev came to power, applying to emigrate brought immediate and often irreversible repercussions. Submission of an application often resulted in job demotion or dismissal or at least in sustained harassment. In some cases an applicant voluntarily left her or his job in order to avoid unpleasant consequences (such as ostracism by co-workers or superiors). Difficulties with neighbors and local authorities were not unusual. All of these obstacles represented the continuation and escalation of the restraints initiated in the first phase of emigration (1968–73).

While the growing number of emigrants in the late 1970s indicated that a decision had been reached to let the Jews go, action against Jews who attempted to exercise the option of leaving suggested that local administrators responsible for implementing emigration policy were in many instances hostile to the idea. Jews were resented for being able to emigrate but they were also criticized for wanting to leave at all.[24] A certain amount of harassment (by employers, OVIR officials and neighbors) might simply have been vindictive, intended to give the Jews one last hard knock before they left. Some of the obstacles might have been more policy-oriented, designed to prevent a 'brain drain', which was considered to be a problem as more and more educated Jews decided to leave. Additional factors unrelated to the Jews, including issues of power and departmentalism within institutions such as the KGB and local offices of OVIR might have been played out over the emigration issue, resulting in contradictory treatment of Soviet Jews.[25]

The potential impact of the Jewish emigration movement on other nationalities could not be ignored either. Obstacles were also intended to deter emigration movements from developing in the general population. The erratically enforced emigration procedure, plus the secretive nature of the decision-making process added to the sense that the possibility of emigrating was not to be taken for granted. This message was intended not only for Jews but also for other disgruntled nationalities who might demand that they too, be permitted to emigrate. Requiring that emigration of Jews be tied to both Israel and family reunification was an additional means of ensuring that other nationalities would not view emigration as an alternative for themselves as well.[26] So too was the policy of repeatedly denying visas to particular individuals.

Although emigration increased, indefinite refusal in response to emigration applications became more common in the 1970s. Official figures were never made public, but there were said to be approximately 3000 refuseniks at the end of

1979,[27] a number of whom had first applied to leave as early as 1970.[28] Refusing permission to emigrate was meant to have a deterrent effect, but it had an additional, unexpected result as well. Many of the refuseniks formed the core of the movement's leadership and their repeated refusal meant that the leadership remained fairly stable. The refuseniks were often bold, with little to lose, having already called attention to themselves and risked their jobs and standing in the community by applying to emigrate. Their resolve was hardened by their having been refused as well as by the precariousness of their situation. As a result, they were generally not afraid to engage in activities such as hunger strikes, demonstrations and meetings with foreign tourists and journalists. When some refuseniks faced punitive detentions or prison terms, their status as leaders and heroes was further augmented in the refusenik community and abroad.[29]

VISA APPLICATION DENIALS UNDER INTERNATIONAL LAW

While Soviet Jews relied on the body of international human rights instruments to claim the right to emigrate, Soviet officials responded by narrowly interpreting the clauses regarding restrictions on freedom of movement. The most common reason for refusal of an emigration application in the 1970s was protection of state secrets. Knowledge of state secrets is one of the grounds for restrictions on free movement permitted by the most relevant international human rights instrument, the 1966 International Covenant on Civil and Political Rights (ICPR). The ICPR is legally binding, but its guarantee in Article 12-2 that '[e]veryone shall be free to leave any country, including his own', is restricted in Article 12-3 as 'provided by law',[30] and as 'necessary to protect national security, public order (*ordre public*), public health or morals or the rights and freedoms of others'.[31] A broad interpretation of ICPR Article 12-3 restrictions can provide international sanction for Soviet policy on the free movement of its citizens. However, even within the context of permissible Soviet emigration – family reunification – only restrictions formulated in Article 12-3 of the ICPR are acceptable reasons for denying permission to emigrate.

Soviet practice has been to misuse the state secrets provision by withholding permission to emigrate for indefinite periods on the ground of alleged knowledge of classified information[32] and by using state secrets as an all-purpose explanation for denying permission to emigrate, even in cases where there was no exposure to state secrets.[33] The sole legal definition of state secrets in Soviet law is contained in a 1956 decree on classified information, which, though broadly constructed, does provide a statute of limitations for certain secrets.[34] Thus, the misapplication of the state secrets argument deviated not only from international norms but from Soviet statutory provisions as well.[35]

A corollary to denial on the basis of national security is refusal on the basis of Soviet national interest. It is difficult to make distinctions between the categories. For instance, the claim that emigration of highly trained individuals could result in a 'brain drain' might fall into either category. Although on its face the fear of a 'brain drain' may seem reasonable, practice showed that virtually all visa applicants faced job demotion or loss of work outright because of harassment; re-employment prospects were dim. In many cases would-be emigrants were forced to take menial jobs rather than those for which they were trained. Consequently, professionals who found themselves unemployed or under-employed no longer served the state interest, making the 'brain drain' argument suspect and at best a pretext for continued refusals.

Harassment of would-be emigrants, including disruption of their postal and telephone service, short-term detention, prosecution and prison sentences became more frequent as the 1970s progressed.[36] Those who lost their jobs and remained unemployed risked the criminal charge of Parasitism and/or Hooliganism (under Articles 209 and 206 respectively of the RSFSR Criminal Code and the equivalent articles of the criminal codes of the other union-republics).[37] A protracted review process left some unemployed applicants in serious financial difficulties. A number of students were expelled from their universities as a result of their families' attempt to emigrate; in several instances they were subsequently called for military service. Some of those students refused conscription (and thus risked further penalty), claiming that military service would preclude emigration for some period of time after discharge on the basis of exposure to state secrets.[38] Not only did such treatment contravene the ICPR and other UN provisions on freedom of movement, but it also directly contradicted pledges the USSR made as a signatory to the 1975 Helsinki Final Act of the Conference on Security and Cooperation in Europe (CSCE).[39]

THE HELSINKI FINAL ACT

The CSCE was a diplomatic conference originally conceived as a forum for discussing security matters and the status of post-World War II borders as well as commercial, economic and scientific exchanges.[40] However, as the negotiations for the conference agenda progressed, human rights were brought increasingly to the fore by Western states. Although opposed to the section in the Final Act eventually entitled 'Co-operation in Humanitarian and Other Fields' (commonly known as Basket Three), the USSR reluctantly agreed to the incorporation of the human rights issues in order to ensure the inclusion of the security and economic provisions it desired. The Final Act resulted in commitments of the 35 signatory states in three broad categories ('Baskets'): 'Questions Relating to Security in Europe' (Basket One), 'Co-operation in the Field of Economics, of Science and Technology and of the Environment' (Basket Two), and 'Co-operation in Humanitarian and Other Fields' (Basket Three). Legally, the Final Act is non-binding on the signatories.[41] Nonetheless, such non-binding status affects only the legal responsibilities of the participating states, and does not imply that they are absolved of their duty to comply with the agreement.[42]

In interpreting the Final Act pledges regarding freedom of movement, it is necessary to distinguish between statements intended for immediate application and those merely expressing a policy goal. For instance, the preamble of the 'Human Contacts' section of Basket Three includes the statement that the signatories will *'[m]ake it their aim* to facilitate freer movement' of individuals and groups. This language exemplifies a policy goal. However, the instrument also contains a number of subsections that make pledges intended for immediate application. The preface to the subsections of the 'Human Contacts' section declares that the participating states '[e]xpress their intention *now to proceed* to the implementation of the following' [emphasis added]. Among the provisions included in the list intended for immediate application are increased contacts and regular meetings on the basis of family ties, reunification of families and reunification of spouses separated as a result of marriage to a citizen of another participating state. No right of general emigration or free movement is established; the subsection on reunification of families merely proclaims that the signatories will 'deal in a positive and humanitarian spirit with the applications of persons who wish to be reunited with members of their family.'

The position the USSR maintained was that because all Soviet citizens enjoyed full social and economic rights, there was no 'social basis' for emigration.[43] The Final Act skirts the freedom of movement issue, however, for it merely reflects commitments to facilitate *freer* movement, referring to reunification of divided families, including cases of marriage between citizens of different states, but not to emigration in general. Nonetheless, in the international arena, the USSR recognized the right to emigrate in the International Covenant on Civil and Political Rights; its own domestic law also recognizes the possibility of leaving.[44]

In signing the Final Act the USSR also pledged to fulfill its obligations under the international human rights declarations and agreements (including the ICPR) and to act 'in conformity with the purposes and principles' of the Universal Declaration of Human Rights (UDHR) and the United Nations Charter.[45] The participating states also committed to uphold the commitments they previously made in other international treaties and agreements, as well as obligations incumbent upon them from generally recognized principles of international law.[46]

It is clear that the USSR has endorsed the body of international human rights law in principle. However, in practice the Soviet Union has utilized a domestic jurisdiction argument to dilute those guarantees. Soviet authorities have consistently held that questions of alleged human rights violations fall within a nation's domestic jurisdiction and are therefore not subject to international evaluation or regulation.[47] Although the USSR has signed the international human rights instruments, it has done so maintaining that the principle of respect for national sovereignty must never be challenged and that decisions relating to a country's own nationals rest solely with the particular state concerned.[48] This application of the human rights instruments enabled the USSR to cloak its abusive use of the restrictive clauses in international doctrine.

The Final Act provided for a series of follow-up meetings, thus creating the mechanism for an ongoing review process.[49] Over the years the human rights pledges received mixed treatment in the follow-up meetings. Strained negotiations and an inability to reach a consensus at the first follow-up meeting in Belgrade resulted in the absence of human rights statements in the short Belgrade Concluding Document.[50] The lengthy Madrid follow-up meeting produced both new and revised provisions in Basket Three and served to reconfirm the legitimacy of human rights in the international arena. The participating states reiterated their agreement to implement a number of pledges originally made at Helsinki regarding family reunification, contacts and regular meetings on the basis of family ties, and binational marriages. The important addition to these pledges was the inclusion of the word 'favorably' in the statement, 'The participating States will *favorably* deal with applications relating to' these areas [emphasis added].[51] These new measures did little to modify Soviet compliance, which remained poor until mid-1987, when changes in the USSR signaled the beginning of a new approach to human rights.

When the third follow-up meeting, held in Vienna from November 1986 to January 1989, issued its Concluding Document, significant advances to the human rights component of the Final Act were formally pledged by the participating states. Far more specific than in the past, the agreement detailed extended provisions in the area of 'human contacts', including freedom of movement. It explicitly addressed particular issues connected with the exit visa application process, provided for official notification of decisions in writing and outlined time limits for review of application materials and decisions, to name just a few of the specific provisions.[52] The far-reaching human rights provisions of the Vienna Concluding Document were reflective of the Soviet Union's new commitment to human rights and the rule of law under Mikhail Gorbachev.

THE SECOND DECADE: THE HALTING OF EMIGRATION, 1980–86

As the USSR turned inward in the early part of the 1980s, the formation of the Anti-Zionist Committee, coupled with a growing trend toward heightened repression throughout Soviet society induced an anti-emigration atmosphere. In addition to Soviet Jews, Soviet Germans and Armenians also experienced diminished emigration during 1980–86.[53] Limited emigration in conjunction with measures to deter widespread calls for further emigration had ceased to be an operative policy. Experience had shown that as long as some emigration was possible, demand remained strong. As a new policy was put into effect during 1980–86, would-be emigrants across the nationality spectrum were given the clear message that emigration was no longer a solution to their grievances, nor an option among the choices available to policy-makers concerned with nationality issues.

One of the first indications of the new policy came in 1979, when Soviet authorities tightened the application process by limiting emigration to those Soviet Jews who could demonstrate a 'close' degree of kinship between themselves and their relatives in Israel extending an invitation (*vyzov*). In the past, an invitation from anyone able to show a familial relationship was accepted. However, the new kinship requirement limited the range of acceptably close relatives to spouses, parents, children or siblings. The practice was expanded in the 1980s and codified in the 1 January 1987 amendments to the Council of Ministers' Regulations on Entry into the USSR and on Exit from the USSR.[54] Additionally, many applicants who presented invitations from first-degree relatives were told that unless they could demonstrate that they were economically dependent on one another, there was no reason to unite immediate family members.[55]

Beginning in 1983 refusal to grant permission to individual members of a family on the grounds that emigration of those individuals would divide, rather than reunite families, became prevalent.[56] This justification for refusal was known as 'balance of family ties'. Denial of permission to emigrate in order to protect family unity was a new tactic in the effort to curtail emigration. It grew out of the realization that unifying families without creating further divisions is virtually impossible, and was thus intended to turn the family reunification argument on its head. The 'balance of family ties' rationale went beyond the traditional categories used in the past to impede emigration, such as protection of national security, duty of care owed to relatives and other requirements of Soviet law. It reserved for the state not only the right to ensure that various responsibilities for one's relatives were met but also permitted the state to designate which adults in a given family constituted its integral components. In so doing the new rationale brought the relationship between state and society in the USSR into stark relief.

Other difficulties with the application process were also noted during the 1980–86 period. 'Access to state secrets', a common justification for refusal in the 1970s, was widely used in the 1980s. OVIR offices were reported to have substantially reduced their hours of operation, particularly in Baku, Chernovtsy, Kharkov, Kiev, Kishinev, Minsk, Odessa and Samarkand.[57] In certain cities (such as Minsk) OVIR officials began rigorously enforcing the rule necessitating parental permission to emigrate, even when the applicants were adults. These difficulties were reminiscent of those in the early years of emigration, when there was considerable regional inconsistency regarding the application process.[58] However, during 1980–86, these measures were part of a deliberate attempt to crush the emigration movement rather than simply a matter of an inefficient bureaucracy.

Problems with mail delivery were widely reported in the early 1980s as well. Many Soviet Jews had difficulty initiating the application process because invitations, which had to be sent to them through the mail, were intercepted. While interruption of mail service as a means of interfering with the application procedure was not new to the 1980s, like other measures, its scope was increased in the first years of the decade.[59]

Soviet treatment of its citizens in general, and not just with respect to Jews, became more repressive during the first part of the 1980s, as the USSR erected barricades against the West. The reactionary stance was brought on by a deepening Soviet involvement in the Afghanistan war (which the Soviet Union entered in December 1979), ailing political leaders and severe economic crisis. An overall tightening of internal controls, including heightened attacks on Western lifestyles, the August 1980 resumption, for the first time since 1973, of jamming British Broadcasting Corporation (BBC) and Voice of America (VOA) broadcasts,[60] and severely reduced telephone communications between the USSR and the West,[61] marked the Soviet retreat inward. So too did the reduction in emigration. Along with other citizens who had ties to the West, Soviet-Jewish activists were affected by revisions to the criminal code that broadened the scope of punishable offenses.[62] As conditions deteriorated, the number of arrests and punitive detentions of Soviet-Jewish activists and dissidents rose.[63]

The formation of the state-sponsored Anti-Zionist Committee of the Soviet Public (AKSO in its Russian acronym) on 21 April 1983 was for Soviet Jews the most ominous measure of the early 1980s, for it signaled the upgrading of the anti-Zionist campaign by directly linking it with the halting of emigration. While the anti-Zionist campaign had been used in the past to deter emigration by vilifying Israel and Jewish emigrants, the formation of a public committee to spearhead anti-Zionist activities was new.

The Committee's stated purpose was to 'intensify scholarly research, giving reasoned criticism of the reactionary essence of the ideology and aggressive character of the policies of Zionism'.[64] Yet AKSO's early statements pointed to a deliberate policy to slow or altogether halt future emigration.[65] At a press conference of the Anti-Zionist Committee on 6 June 1983, AKSO First Deputy Chairman Samuil Zivs stated: 'For a number of years after the war [World War II], reunification [of families divided by the war] was the chief motive prompting Soviet citizens of Jewish nationality to emigrate. . . . By now, however, most families have been reunited and the number of those who leave is naturally diminishing.'[66]

Zivs's statement carried considerable weight because, reminiscent of the Anti-Fascist Committee of the 1940s,[67] AKSO's leadership included several Soviet Jews well known for their close alliance with Party and government officials.[68] But while the Anti-Fascist Committee had given Jews a central rallying point, the Anti-Zionist Committee was not a unifying body for Jews nor was it designed to serve the Jewish community. It simply represented a new tactic in the upgraded efforts to halt emigration.

The new strategy was successful, for emigration dropped precipitously from 1980 to 1986. There was no doubt that a major policy reversal rather than a change of heart on the part of Soviet Jews had caused the number of emigrants to plummet. Despite official statements that all who wanted to leave had done so, many Jews remained interested in emigrating. This was clear from the continued protests and other activities the refuseniks organized.[69]

The reinvigorated anti-Zionist campaign accompanied a climate of open hostility toward manifestations of Jewish national consciousness. More vigorous harassment of Jewish cultural activists and Hebrew teachers resulted in arrests, convictions and, in some cases, physical brutality.[70] By the end of 1985 there were an unprecedented 26 Soviet Jews serving prison or labor camp terms for their practice of Judaism, study of the Hebrew language or activities connected with their campaign to emigrate. This was the highest number since the start of emigration in 1968.[71]

The number of refuseniks reached approximately 11 000 by 1986,[72] as emigration dropped to 914. In prior years, refuseniks of several years' standing had been permitted to leave the USSR. However, during 1980–86 the visas that were granted were issued predominantly to new applicants rather than to veteran refuseniks. Several long-term refuseniks were told that their cases were closed, that they were 'refused for life' and that they could face punitive action if they attempted to reapply.[73] This practice was first reported in Kharkov, where refused applicants were required to sign statements acknowledging that their refusal was permanent.[74] The early 1970s' policy of allowing the leaders and the most determined individuals to emigrate had been reversed. The existence of a large group of refuseniks helped to discourage others from filing applications to leave. But it was to become clear, as evidenced by the surge of applications beginning in 1987, that desire to emigrate had not been quelled.

Although prospects for emigration were limited, Jews seemed prepared to wait until possibilities for emigration would again be expanded. Not surprisingly, limited opportunities for emigration and heightened repression created a backlash within part of the Jewish community and, particularly among younger Jews, Jewish national consciousness sparked anew. This response was reminiscent of earlier periods in Soviet history in which hostility toward Jews only stimulated a keener sense of Jewish identity, underscoring yet again the failure of Soviet nationality policy to erode national consciousness.[75] Some of the Jews who had a strong sense of Jewish national consciousness began focusing on improving and gaining access to Jewish culture within the USSR; unofficial circles promoting the study of Hebrew and Jewish history and culture were reportedly organized in at least 30 cities throughout the USSR.[76] Such activities, in addition to acts of protest in the form of hunger strikes, international appeals and the signing of petitions, continued both in spite of, and in response to, the increase in repressive measures.

A NEW BEGINNING: *PERESTROIKA* EMIGRATION DURING 1987–89

Beginning in 1987 a new policy shift emerged as major changes in the USSR unfolded. Soviet-Jewish emigration jumped dramatically from the previous low levels of the decade, to an annual total of 8155. The increase was all the more striking since it followed one of the worst years for emigration, in which the total number of Soviet-Jewish departures was only 914. In addition to the policy turn-around regarding emigration, the release of Jewish political prisoners began in February 1987.[77] By September 1987, all

Soviet-Jewish political prisoners had been released and most of them were permitted to emigrate during 1987 and 1988.

Changes in emigration policy were directly related to reform in the Soviet Union. Indeed, increased emigration reflected but one facet of a complex process.[78] Burgeoning democratization in the USSR resulted in greater liberalization in a wide range of areas. The opportunities for public debate, the formation of associations reflecting a broad range of interests, the relaxation of repressive controls, increased access to information, greater accountability based on the rule of law and a renewed interest in the West marked new thinking (*novoye myshleniye*) in the Soviet Union. These developments generally had a beneficial impact on Soviet Jewry.

As emigration increased, the drop-out situation continued: 74.6 per cent of the emigrants who left the USSR in 1987 chose destinations other than Israel. This trend was furthered in 1988, when 88.6 per cent of the emigrants dropped out, but due to US policy changes it was reversed in late 1989. By mid-1990, more than 90 per cent of those who left on Israeli visas arrived in Israel. This was not a reflection of widespread renewed interest in Zionism, but rather a result of diminished possibilities for immigration to the United States.[79]

As in past years, the number of emigrants was correlated to the number of invitations issued. Historically, requests for invitations have increased when the possibility of emigration has seemed likely. In 1987 Israeli invitations were sent to 20 068 individuals (6777 families). Only 4682 of those invitations (1598 families) were sent to first-time applicants.[80] This was a significant development for it reflected a move toward resolving the outstanding refusenik cases. Indeed, during 1987 and the first quarter of 1988 approximately two-thirds of the departing emigrants were refuseniks and one-third were first time applicants, indicating that the remaining refuseniks actively trying to emigrate would eventually be permitted to do so.

The number of refuseniks was in fact reduced to 2788 individuals (700 families) by April 1989. There were 1894 refuseniks (486 families) who had been attempting to emigrate for 5–10 years, and 894 (214 families) who had been waiting to emigrate for over 10 years. Israeli data showed that approximately 50 per cent of the total refusenik population was actively engaged in trying to emigrate. According to data from the Soviet Union, 1556 refusenik cases were settled positively (i.e. the refuseniks were permitted to leave) during May–October 1989, but as late as January 1990, approximately 1500 refuseniks – some of them new – were still waiting for permission.[81] By keeping the number of refuseniks limited to a fraction of the total emigrants, Soviet policy-makers acknowledged that the benefit of maintaining a large group of refuseniks had run its course.

Very little was done to deter emigration in the post-1986 period. The Anti-Zionist Committee was downgraded, yet despite reports that it would be disbanded, it was still functioning at the time of this writing.[82] Although the 1987 amendments to the Decree on Entry to and Exit from the USSR had established a mechanism for legally restricting emigration, not all aspects of the rules and practices codified in the 1987 amendments, such as the requirement that invitations be extended by first-degree relatives, were strictly administered. Beginning in mid-February 1988 it was evident that the approach toward enforcement of emigration regulations had become more lenient as Jewish emigration was permitted to expand. This was the case regarding Soviet-German and Armenian emigration as well, which, particularly in the German case, reached astounding levels in 1988: Soviet-German emigration was 46 572 and Armenian emigration was 10 981.[83] The updated codification of the rules on entry and exit in 1987 was reflective of the new Soviet interest in developing a law-based society, but the lax implementation of the regulations indicated once again (as in the 1970s) both the privileged position of Jews, Germans and Armenians in terms of their ability to emigrate and the emphasis on nationality in emigration policy. It also demonstrated that emigration was itself a component of a broad nationality policy.

Some of the new ease in emigrating reflected compliance with agreements reached at the November 1986–January 1989 Conference on Security and Cooperation in Europe meeting held in Vienna. Regarding freedom of movement, the Vienna Concluding Document contained far-reaching provisions that addressed issues not previously considered.[84] For the first time in the CSCE process, a provision was included requiring the rendering of decisions on applications relating to family reunification in three months or less. In the past, no concrete time designations were made for application reviews. Other provisions addressed procedural arbitrariness, which in the Soviet case had been commonplace.[85]

The Vienna Concluding Document also included provisions concerning abuses of denial of permission to emigrate based on knowledge of state secrets or on lack of permission from relatives, the two most frequent grounds for refusal. Many applicants were impeded by their relatives' groundless refusal to release them from their duties and obligations.[86] The Vienna Document obligated participating states to 'ensure that acts or omissions by members of the applicant's family do not adversely affect the rights of the applicant'. Another provision explicitly addressed refusals on the basis of protection of national security. It provided for a review of an individual's secrecy designation after 6 months and thereafter at regular intervals, and called for 'strictly warranted time limits' on state secrets and formal notification of if and how work involving national security could affect future applications for travel abroad. The Vienna Concluding Document also stipulated in the preamble to Basket Three (Cooperation in Humanitarian and Other Fields) that the participating states would implement 'the provisions concerning co-operation in humanitarian and other fields in the framework of their laws and regulations, [and that] they will ensure that those laws and regulations conform with their obligations under international law and are brought into harmony with their CSCE commitments'. Toward this end, the Soviet Union drafted a law on emigration that codifies the provisions stipulated in the Vienna Document. At the time of this writing, the law was still under consideration.[87]

In a number of ways, 1988 signified the full blossoming of *glasnost* with respect to Soviet Jews. Public demonstrations by Soviet Jews, hunger strikes, petitions, meetings with high-level officials in the Soviet government and seminars in private homes on topics concerning Jewish culture, religion and emigration were, for the most part, permitted to take place from 1988 forward.[88] The broad-ranging seminars were reminiscent of those held during the 1970s, the heyday of the emigration movement.[89] Jewish cultural activity in the Soviet Union was markedly expanded, and many of the new opportunities were extraordinary by previous standards. The developments reflected the opening of Soviet society, which was coupled with an attempt to de-Stalinize the collective psyche. Such far-reaching goals were predicated on the exposure and correction of historical inequities, as well as a declared commitment to democratization and *glasnost*.

For Jews, *novoye myshleniye* translated into cultural changes such as new Jewish publications, schools and organizations, as well as official acknowledgement of historical anti-Semitism,[90] the rehabilitation of the members of the [Jewish] Anti-Fascist Committee, and the use of Jewish themes in literary, theatrical and other artistic genres. The changes were reflective not only of *glasnost* but also of yet another approach to the question of national consciousness within the USSR. For the first time since the 1930s, expressions of Jewish national consciousness outside of approved Yiddish culture were recognized.

The Hebrew language continued to lack official recognition as the language of the Jewish nationality, but private Hebrew study groups convened without interference from 1988 onward. Permitted Hebrew teaching varied from city to city and within localities, ranging from private study groups to state-sponsored Hebrew classes and schools, all of which suggested that the official position on Hebrew was undergoing revision.[91]

Officially sanctioned Jewish cultural associations that sought to develop Jewish national culture and establish international links with similar associations abroad were formed in many cities. Other indications of change included the 1989 opening of the first academy of Jewish learning (*yeshiva*) in the Soviet Union in 60 years, as well as the establishment of the Judaic Studies Center, Jewish sports clubs, religious organizations, publications and branches of Zionist groups, to name just a few of the manifestations of the new climate. Most of the developments that were taken for granted by 1990 only two years earlier had been considered radical and as late as 1986 had been forbidden altogether.[92]

These changes encouraged some Jews about the prospects for a viable Jewish life within the USSR, but the escalating number of emigrants (18 965 in 1988 and 71 196 in 1989) suggested that many Jews were taking advantage of the opportunity to emigrate while it existed. Uncertainty about Soviet reform, the future stability of the USSR and a deteriorating economy, plus overt anti-Semitism and a fear that Jews would be blamed for past problems and current crises in the USSR, kept demand for emigration high.[93]

Anti-Semitism has always been, at the very least, a latent problem in Russia and the Soviet Union. Historically, it has surfaced during times of change and transition. Therefore, reports of heightened anti-Semitism and increased threats against Jews, many of which were linked to so-called 'patriotic', i.e. Russian nationalist groups, such as Pamyat (Memory), Otechestvo (Fatherland), and Rossiskaya Narodnaya Partia (Russian National Party), were not surprising.[94] What was significant about the rise of anti-Semitism in the Gorbachev period was that its open and public manifestation was tied to the very hallmark of the Gorbachev era: *glasnost*.[95] Although anti-Semitism in the Soviet Union is officially condemned, in the past it was cloaked in the guise of anti-cosmopolitanism (under Stalin) and, as some Soviet Jews argue, anti-Zionism and anti-intellectualism (under Brezhnev). However, freedom of expression in the Gorbachev period enabled anti-Semitism to surface. While Jews worried that they would be made scapegoats for problems associated with *perestroika*[96] they were also concerned by suggestions that Pamyat's activities (including mass rallies and public dissemination of information), though condemned in some circles, were supported by at least part of the leadership.[97]

Other factors which may have contributed to the strong demand for emigration were more benign, relating to changes affecting tourism. In the past, emigrants were not able to visit the USSR, and the Soviet Union did not permit travel to Israel. As tourism became possible, Soviet Jews who had previously hesitated to emigrate may have had their fears allayed by new possibilities for returning as visitors to the USSR and for inviting friends and relatives to visit them abroad.[98] These considerations, along with the relationship among Soviet policy objectives, Jewish national consciousness, the position of Jews in Soviet society and emigration in the *perestroika* period are fully treated in Chapter 5.

Part Two

4 Soviet Germans: A Brief History and an Introduction to Their Emigration

One would have thought that the War had clearly shown who was who, and that the groundless accusations made against Soviet Germans, along with the legal restrictions, would have faded of their own accord. However, these hopes were not borne out. . . .

A certain segment of Soviet citizens of the German nationality, people, who, as a rule, have only a very remote notion of what life is like in the FRG, are setting off on trips thousands of kilometers long to their 'historic homeland' in search of a 'better lot'. We won't hide the fact that their choice is sometimes influenced by the negative experience of the past and the unresolved state of some of our current problems.

V. Auman and V. Chernyshev, 1988[1]

GERMAN IMMIGRATION TO RUSSIA

The majority of contemporary Soviet Germans are ancestors of agricultural settlers invited to Russia by Catherine the Great and Alexander I.[2] During 1763–1862, approximately 100 000 Germans migrated to Russia and founded over 3000 colonies. These so-called 'German Russians' consisted both of the Volga Germans, who arrived as early as 1763 and formed agricultural communities principally along the lower Volga River, and the Black Sea Germans (or Ukrainian Germans), who came to Russia in the early nineteenth century and settled in towns, cities and rural areas near the Black Sea. Other German immigrants joined German communities in the Caucasus, Bessarabia and Volhynia.

A third group of German settlers, the Baltic Germans, became part of the Russian Empire in the eighteenth century after territorial annexations carried out under Peter the

Great. Their history is distinct from the German colonists and they are unrelated to the people commonly referred to today as 'Soviet Germans'. The Baltic states, which had become independent in 1918, were re-annexed by the USSR during World War II. However, by 1939 most of the Baltic Germans had already been 'resettled' in Germany by the Nazis. The few Baltic Germans remaining in the USSR were, for purposes of identification, merged into the general category of *nemtsy* (Germans).[3] In addition, some non-Baltic Germans became part of the Soviet Union as a consequence of the territorial annexations of World Wars I and II. These other migrants notwithstanding, the Germans living in the USSR today are predominantly descendants of the Volga and Black Sea Germans.

EARLY NATIONALITY POLICY AND THE SOVIET GERMANS

The history of the Germans under Soviet rule has paralleled that of most Soviet nationalities in that the years of greatest national-cultural autonomy preceded the Stalin era and the period of sharpest decline and destruction came with it. But despite broad trends and prevailing policy, some nationalities fared worse than others and the Germans, like the Jews, experienced periods of particularly harsh treatment. Reflecting early Soviet nationality policy of the 1920s, limited cultural autonomy was granted within the framework of proletarian and socialist internationalism. German cultural and religious facilities were permitted and at times flourished in the German communities. Primary and secondary schools, several institutions of higher education, republican and community newspapers and periodicals, a thriving publishing industry, a national theater and hundreds of German church schools represented the pinnacle of German culture in the USSR in the late 1920s.[4] Soviet Germans also enjoyed regional territorial autonomy: the Workers' Commune for the Volga, set up in 1918, was elevated to the Volga German Autonomous Soviet Socialist Republic (ASSR) in 1924; German National Districts were designated in areas where there were large concentrations of Germans.[5]

Stalin's policy of forced agricultural collectivization during 1928–32 and the purges of the 1930s signaled the end of a thriving Soviet-German culture. Soviet Germans, like Jews and others, were stripped of many of the institutions that had enabled them to express their identity. Most German churches were closed by 1939 and all German-language schools located outside the Volga German ASSR were converted to Russian-language schools by 1938.

WORLD WAR II AND ITS AFTERMATH

Any remaining favorable attitudes towards the Soviet Germans were destroyed by the Nazi invasion of the USSR during World War II. On 28 August 1941, Stalin, fearing the potential of a Soviet-German 'fifth column', ordered that Germans living in the Volga German area be deported to Siberia, Central Asia and Kazakhstan.[6] A follow-up decree of 7 September 1941 dissolved the Volga German ASSR and the National Districts.[7] Although the deportation decree specifically mentioned only the Volga Germans, it was also applied to Germans from the Black Sea area. The Germans from villages near Ufa, Orenburg and New Samara, those from the 553 German settlements east of the Urals and those living between the Dniester and the Bug rivers, were the only ones exempted from resettlement.[8] Soviet Germans were purged from the Party and civil service, their land and livestock were confiscated, and their remaining churches and cultural institutions were closed.

As a result of the deportation order, 855 674 Soviet Germans from European Russia joined roughly 369 000 of their compatriots already living in Siberia and Central Asia. Among the latter were a number who had previously been deported during the collectivization campaign and the purges.[9] The Soviet Germans were placed in special settlements and a large number of them were assigned to harsh labor. Many did not survive.

In 1945, 250 000 of the approximately 350 000 Black Sea Germans the Nazis had evacuated during the German retreat, resettled in the Warthegau and granted German citizenship, were taken back to the Soviet Union.[10] But those individuals were not, as promised, returned to their original homes. Instead, they were put in labor camps or special settlements in Siberia, the Komi ASSR (northern RSFSR) and Central Asia. In many cases, because they were suspected of being traitors, they were treated more harshly than the Germans who had been internally deported in 1941.[11] By the war's end, the Soviet-German death toll had risen to 500 000, due both to the difficult journey during the deportations and to the harsh conditions of resettlement.[12] Although the pretext for the deportations no longer existed after the war, the Germans were not released from the special settlements nor was there any official reference to them until 1955, when two decrees concerning the rehabilitation of the Soviet Germans were issued. The effect of the blanket of silence imposed on the Soviet Germans was that information about them had reached neither the outside world nor the rest of the Soviet Union.[13]

CHANCELLOR ADENAUER'S VISIT TO MOSCOW

West German Chancellor Konrad Adenauer's September 1955 visit to Moscow for negotiations concerning the establishment of Soviet–West German diplomatic and trade relations proved to be one of the earliest post-Stalin developments affecting Soviet Germans. Adenauer used the opportunity of the visit to discuss the German population in the USSR. Among the issues he raised were the release of Soviet Germans from internment in special settlements, the return to Germany of ethnic Germans who had at one time been citizens of the Third Reich and the repatriation of approximately 9000 German prisoners of war.[14] Although initially refuting claims about prisoners of war, Soviet negotiators ultimately acknowledged their existence and agreed to their release, thus removing the issue as an obstacle to negotiations on other matters.[15]

Following Adenauer's visit, some of the 250 000 Soviet-German evacuees who had been returned to the Soviet Union in 1945 mistakenly interpreted Soviet acquiescence to the release of the prisoners of war as an indication that their own emigration would be permitted. In the aftermath of

Adenauer's visit, approximately 80 per cent of the former evacuees (predominantly Black Sea Germans) filed applications to rejoin their families. However, they were told that despite their having been granted German citizenship, they were ineligible for repatriation because the USSR recognized only their Soviet citizenship.[16]

Although no agreement was reached on German jurisdiction over individuals who had been citizens of the Third Reich, the Adenauer visit did result in changes for the Soviet-German population. On 17 September 1955 and 13 December 1955 the Presidium of the Supreme Soviet issued two decrees concerning the rehabilitation of Soviet Germans. The September decree granted amnesty to Soviet citizens detained for wartime collaboration with the Third Reich and the December decree provided for the release of Soviet Germans from the special settlements and labor camps. The edicts made no mention of the mass treason allegations that had been the basis for the deportation of members of the German nationality.[17]

After the rehabilitation and amnesty decrees, Soviet Germans began to search for their relatives. Thousands of letters requesting help in locating family members were sent abroad to ethnic German organizations and to the German Red Cross. These letters served as the first source of information in the West regarding the post-war status and location of the Soviet Germans.[18]

In addition to the rehabilitation and amnesty decrees, German cultural life began to improve after 1955. In part, increased outlets for German culture may have related to Adenauer's visit, for other nationalities did not have similar gains. However, in general, most nationalities experienced a degree of cultural revival in the aftermath of Stalin's death. The first German-language newspaper to be published was *Arbeit*, which appeared for a short time in the Altai beginning in 1955. In 1957 two papers were started: *Neues Leben*, published by *Pravda* in Moscow, and *Rote Fahne*, published in Barnaul (Altai). *Freundschaft*, based in Tselinograd, began publication in 1966. These newspapers (dailies and weeklies) are still being published with individual circulations reportedly ranging from 3000 to 30 000.[19] German-language broadcasts on Moscow Radio began in 1956 from the RSFSR, in 1957 from Kazakhstan and in 1962 from Kirghizia.[20] German-language television programs were also introduced for the Soviet-German population of Siberia and Central Asia.[21]

In comparison with Jewish culture in the post-Stalin period, German cultural access and offerings were more plentiful. Differential treatment of nationalities has been a consistent feature of Soviet nationality policy. Although theory dictated the eventual merging of the nationalities into a new, uniquely *Soviet* ethnicity, the pace of assimilation varied considerably. Thus Soviet authorities considered urban, well-educated, non-territorial nationalities such as Jews to be among the most vulnerable to the process, while those such as Germans were thought to be less so, because of their historical territorial ties, lower educational levels and poorer socioeconomic development. Groups of the latter type were permitted greater cultural opportunities as a consequence of the theoretical precept that in order for nations to merge they should first be permitted to flourish.[22]

Despite increasing cultural opportunities in the late 1950s, the Soviet Germans were not cleared of the mass treason charge and rehabilitated politically until August 1964.[23] Their exoneration notwithstanding, they were at the time forbidden to return to their pre-war areas of residence.[24] No explanation accompanied the decision to restore the reputation of the Germans more than 8 years after their release from the special settlements. Some observers have suggested that the rehabilitation decree was intended to coincide with an effort to improve relations with the Federal Republic of Germany.[25] The events may well have been connected, but lack of sufficient evidence makes it difficult to substantiate such a claim.

Not satisfied with the terms of their rehabilitation, a delegation of 37 Germans was granted permission to meet with Anastas I. Mikoyan, Chairman of the Presidium of the USSR Supreme Soviet, in June 1965.[26] The delegation demanded complete rehabilitation, to be achieved through formal permission to return to their previous settlements and through the restoration of the Volga German ASSR. The Germans argued that they, like other dispersed nationalities such as the Jews, were likely candidates for assimilation, in part because their lack of geographical cohesion made it virtually impossible to safeguard national-cultural autonomy. Mikoyan refused to re-establish the Volga German ASSR, arguing that two-thirds of all Soviet Germans had lived in areas other than the Volga German ASSR prior to World War II. He also claimed that German labor was needed in Kazakhstan and western Siberia. What Mikoyan did not openly state was that the area of the former Volga German ASSR had been fully resettled. Restoring the land to the Germans would have created a new set of problems because it would have meant uprooting the inhabitants who replaced the deported Germans. However, Mikoyan did agree to improve Soviet-German cultural offerings and investigate charges that anti-German discrimination was still rampant.[27] Such discrimination was a vestige of both the wartime hostility and animosity toward Germans and the psychological impact of the deportations on the general population.

THE SOVIET-GERMAN EXPERIENCE SINCE 1965

Despite a number of improvements, overall cultural life for the Soviet Germans has been disappointing.[28] In part, underlying social forces have been influential in eroding Soviet-German culture. Post-war Soviet Germans, educated in Soviet schools and raised without the traditional influences of the closed German communities, have become well assimilated. Incidence of German as a native language has dropped sharply.[29] The Soviet Germans have also evolved from a predominantly rural nationality to being almost evenly divided between the urban and rural sectors.[30]

Although the possibility for German-language instruction exists,[31] the number of students studying in German has steadily declined. This decrease is due to several factors. Since upward mobility in the USSR was dependent upon mastery of Russian, many parents were reluctant to place their children at a disadvantage by requesting German-language instruction. In some instances, a lack of enthusiasm for German-language study could be traced to parents' inability to speak German. In cases involving people who had been interned because they were German, negative associations with German culture have persisted. A dearth of German-language instructors and teaching materials, bureaucratic impediments and the geographic dispersal of German settlements also contributed to the decreasing number of German-language students.[32]

Native language erosion and assimilation reflected not only the force of modernizing processes but also the success of Soviet nationality policy. While a degree of assimilation was an inevitable outcome of increased urbanization, education and economic integration, the policy designed to blur national distinctions by limiting cultural access, privileging the Russian language and cultural norms and, in the case of the Germans, physically destroying ethnically constituted communities, could not help but speed the dissolution of national cultures. Like the Jews, the Soviet Germans suffered setbacks during the Stalin period that were never fully overcome.

The tradition of German communal life organized around religion was destroyed as a result of the deportations and was not permitted to redevelop. Although religious groups have made considerable gains since the 1970s, and particularly under Gorbachev, the language of worship has been shifting gradually from German to Russian, leaving the future of German-speaking congregations in question.[33] The declining importance of religion itself in the daily lives of most Soviet Germans also accompanied the process of assimilation.

Economically, the Soviet Germans have been successful, for their labor is highly valued and well rewarded. On the whole, they hold blue-collar positions. Many are *kolkhoz* (collective farm) or *sovkhoz* (state farm) directors, factory managers or high technical administrators – all signs of political acceptance. They are, however, under-represented in fields such as medicine, science, law and the arts due to the lingering effects of post-war deprivations and discrimination, as well as to their traditional occupational patterns. In the political arena, Soviet Germans have significantly increased their numbers in local soviets since their 1964 rehabilitation, but they have not been well represented in the upper echelons of the Party or government apparatus.[34]

A COMPARISON OF GERMANS, JEWS AND
THEIR EMIGRATION

Despite their vastly differing social and occupational composition, Soviet Jews and Germans have faced many similar
problems stemming from the effects of Soviet nationality
policy. Policy priorities, including the development of a new
'Soviet' nationality that was to emerge ultimately from the
blending (*slianie*) of the various nationalities as well as trends
associated with the processes of social and economic change,
had the effect of destroying national cultures. While assimilation and the erosion of national-cultural autonomy affected
most nationalities, some, such as the Jews and Germans, were
also the targets of specific policies that had particularly
devastating effects. For Germans, the deportations and loss
of their autonomous homeland and for Jews, the anti-Jewish
attacks in the form of the campaign against bourgeois
nationalism and cosmopolitanism, stripped them of their
institutions, deprived them of their cultural heritage and
communities and, in the case of the Jews, killed much of their
intelligentsia. The particular circumstances surrounding the
two nationalities also contributed to their alienation. The lack
of a national-territorial unit in the USSR, anti-Jewish and
anti-German sentiment and the sense of being outsiders in
their own country affected the national psyches of the Jews
and the Germans.[35]

Although officially reintegrated into Soviet society, Soviet
Germans still face considerable hostility stemming from
residual popular anti-German associations developed during
World War II. The tension between the wholly unmerited
treatment of Soviet Germans during the war and the belief in
Soviet-German wartime complicity among some segments of
the Soviet population continues on various levels today.
Popular associations linking Soviet Germans to Nazis persist,
and have led to feelings of insecurity among the German
population.[36] Anti-German sentiment, plus the failure to
restore the Volga German ASSR, have had a great impact on
the Soviet-German community. The lack of territorial autonomy and its resultant limitations on Soviet-German cultural
and political development has remained a major issue for
members of the German nationality.[37] These factors within

the USSR ('push' factors), in concert with those such as greater economic opportunity and religious freedom in West Germany ('pull' factors), combined to bring about considerable demand for immigration to the Federal Republic of Germany (FRG).

Although the Jewish emigration movement may have had some effect on calls for German emigration, there is no evidence of significant contacts between the Jewish and German groups.[38] Soviet-German desire to emigrate is linked to events that predated large-scale Jewish emigration, the most significant among them being the refusal to reinstate the Volga German ASSR and the failure to restore previous levels of German cultural access.

Like Jewish emigration, German emigration from the Soviet Union has taken place within the framework of inter-state repatriation agreements and as part of a domestic emigration movement – although the Soviet authorities permitted repatriation only for those Germans who were citizens of the Third Reich. The German–Soviet Repatriation Agreement of 8 April 1958 directly applied only to individuals who held German citizenship prior to 21 June 1941, though it also served as a declaration of intent to reunite divided families.[39] On the basis of the repatriation agreement and the 1955 commitment Adenauer secured regarding the return of the German prisoners of war, 16 730 Germans left the USSR from 1955 to 1960.[40]

The emigration of Soviet Germans began falling in 1959 and dropped drastically after 1960. According to official FRG interpretation, the curtailment of emigration was a result of the deterioration in Soviet–FRG relations (initiated by the Berlin crisis) and Soviet insistence that the repatriation process had been completed.[41] In the 1960s and early 1970s, German emigration followed a pattern similar to that of Jewish emigration: in the 1960s it remained low, with a total Soviet-German exodus of only 5498 from 1961 to 1969. In 1970, 340 Soviet Germans left for the FRG on the grounds of reunification of families. In 1971 the number jumped to 1145 and rose to 3426 in 1972.[42]

A large proportion of the emigrants in the 1970s were Volga Germans whose ancestors had lived in Russia and the USSR for several generations. Because the Volga Germans were deported internally during World War II rather than evacuated by the German army, their claims to family reunification arguably were tenuous. Nonetheless, having despaired of regaining German national autonomy, it was they and not the Black Sea Germans, many of whom had external family ties as a result of the war, who initiated the emigration movement. Negative experiences had led the Black Sea Germans to assimilate more rapidly than the Volga Germans, primarily because of their desire to be well integrated into Soviet society rather than grouped together in closed communities.[43]

Soviet Germans seeking to emigrate faced an application process analogous to that of Jews.[44] Prior to the Gorbachev period, Soviet authorities responded to the Soviet-German emigration movement much as they did to the Jewish movement. Soviet Germans encountered bureaucratic obstacles in the emigration process, were improperly denied permission to emigrate on the basis of national security and knowledge of state secrets, and faced harassment, discrimination, job dismissal and demotion, military draft, arrest and imprisonment as a result of their application to emigrate.[45]

Like Jews, Soviet Germans over the years have publicized their campaign to emigrate by using activist tactics such as staging protests and sending petitions to Soviet and Western authorities. Anti-emigration propaganda, including an anti-FRG campaign, also characterized Soviet-German emigration until policy changes under Gorbachev.[46] Unlike Jews, Soviet Germans have not enjoyed strong support from Western pressure groups. Until the tremendous influx of Germans from the Eastern bloc began in West Germany in 1987,[47] the majority of West Germans knew virtually nothing about the existence of the two million Soviet Germans.[48]

For its part, the FRG has pursued a strategy of primarily quiet diplomacy in dealing with the USSR on the issue of Soviet-German emigration, preferring to use private diplomatic channels rather than public ones.[49] Before the momentous changes in Eastern Europe in the autumn of 1989 resulting, among other things, in placing the question of German reunification on the public agenda, West Germany held the position that outstanding questions concerning the possible reunification of Germany and its implications for the East German people necessitated sensitive handling of the emigration question. Prior to 1989 the FRG did follow a practice similar to that of the US government of periodically presenting Soviet officials with lists of individuals wishing to be reunited with family members, but the issue was almost never raised publicly.[50] The effect of private diplomatic efforts on Soviet policy decisions remains unclear.

By the end of 1989 a total of 255 383 Soviet Germans had immigrated to West Germany since 1955. As with Jews, German desire for emigration was not stemmed by permitting the original activists to leave; to the contrary, the initial increase only encouraged further emigration. As noted above, German demands for autonomy did not subside, and in the more liberal Gorbachev period, they were infused with renewed vigor. High-level discussions under way in the USSR at the time of this writing regarding the restoration of German national-territorial autonomy could be highly significant to the future of the German emigration movement.[51] These issues and German emigration trends during 1970–89 are discussed further in Chapter 5.

5 The Domestic Context of Soviet Emigration Policy

> It would be an oversimplification to think that only with the help of outside pressure and pressure from inter-state relations or trade is it possible to achieve certain essential concessions from a country such as the Soviet Union in the conduct of our domestic policy.
>
> Roy Medvedev, 1973[1]

The most widely held view among Western scholars and analysts is that shifts in emigration policy during the 1970s and 1980s were linked to the ebb and flow of US–Soviet relations.[2] According to adherents of this position, when US–Soviet relations are good, or the Soviet Union desires improved political or economic relations, emigration increases. Conversely, emigration decreases when relations sour or the USSR sees no foreign policy advantage accruing from it. While such reasoning, which may be called the 'barometer thesis', offers a model for explaining and projecting trends in emigration, it is flawed because by overlooking influences beyond those in the realm of foreign policy it perpetuates a narrow view of the USSR as a state that makes policy only on the basis of external considerations, a state with no domestic concerns. Further, it is ultimately ineffective as a method of interpreting Soviet emigration policy. For example, it cannot account for either the surge in Jewish emigration during 1976–79, when US–Soviet relations were deteriorating rapidly, or for the flood of emigrants after 1986, although the Jackson–Vanik amendment still remained in force. Similarly, it fails to explain trends in German emigration, especially when FRG–USSR relations improved but emigration decreased.

In order to evaluate the factors determining Soviet emigration policy, it is useful to divide them into primary and secondary categories. Primary factors are directly responsible for, or have a discernible impact on, policy decisions. Secondary factors are positive or negative results of the policy; they may be important by-products, but they do not themselves drive policy. An analysis based on primary and secondary policy determinants is effective because it examines emigration policy in light of a variety of relevant factors and seeks to encompass and classify the broad spectrum of considerations. Its application dispels the notion that emigration can be analyzed only in terms of its relationship to foreign policy and reveals that the domestic context surrounding emigration is the most significant influence on emigration policy.

FACTORS IN EMIGRATION POLICY: 1968–73

Détente with the West, specifically in US–Soviet relations, formed the backdrop for emigration during the 1970s. If viewed in isolation, the linkage the barometer thesis establishes between détente and emigration seems plausible, for Jewish emigration levels rose in the early 1970s as US–Soviet relations grew warmer. The need for Western technology and grain, the desire for a Strategic Arms Limitation Talks agreement (SALT I), and the fear of a rapprochement between the US and the People's Republic of China (PRC) were key reasons the USSR pursued détente with the United States. Soviet negotiators undoubtedly realized that increased emigration fostered good relations and a more relaxed international atmosphere, and could thus be used as a concession to advance the goals of détente.

Likewise, the sharp rise in Soviet-German emigration during the first half of the 1970s corresponded with improved relations between the Soviet Union and the Federal Republic of Germany (FRG). The Soviet–FRG treaty of 12 August 1970 formally initiated the Brandt–Scheel *Ostpolitik* and led the way to improved bilateral relations during the decade.[3] Warmer ties fostered a climate that appeared conducive to a liberalized emigration policy.

Yet détente was not the primary element determining emigration policy. While an improving relationship with the West signaled a more favorable atmosphere for emigration, it is unlikely that emigration was orchestrated as part of a grand Soviet scheme to curry favor with the West. Like détente, emigration served a number of Soviet objectives and reflected a situation in which primary (domestic) and secondary (international) objectives complemented one another and converged to result in a more liberal policy. Notwithstanding any advantages emigration might have brought to Soviet dealings with the United States and West Germany, analysis reveals that emigration policy should not be divorced from its domestic milieu.

In the case of Soviet Jews, the initial decision to permit emigration was a response to the Jewish demand for emigration. Indeed, emigration began before détente became a significant factor in US–Soviet relations. For a small price, emigration afforded domestic social, economic and political benefits. These were the primary reasons for allowing emigration. In the first years, Soviet authorities calculated that they could curtail the emigration movement by permitting its leadership and a relatively small group of Jews who did not want to be assimilated to leave before their activities became an example to others who might be inclined to make similar demands. In particular, the desire to reduce the prospects for a growing movement motivated the decision to permit the emigration of Georgian, Latvian and Lithuanian Jews, whose departure would eliminate potentially destabilizing elements in areas of the Soviet Union where national identity traditionally had been strong. Between 1968 and September 1977, 52.4 per cent of Jews from the Georgian SSR, 41.9 per cent of the Lithuanian-Jewish population, and 23.0 per cent of Jews from Latvia emigrated.[4]

A secondary aspect of Jewish emigration in the early 1970s was its furtherance of a new Soviet approach to managing politically sensitive issues in the international arena.[5] Increasing emigration in the early 1970s enabled the USSR to appear to be acceding to international pressure to improve its human rights performance while in actuality it was pursuing its own objectives and responding to domestic dynamics. This view is borne out by the Soviet authorities' reaction against the Soviet-Jewish emigration movement as it became a common feature in the Western media. Perhaps unprepared at first for the magnitude of Western concern about human rights issues, Soviet policy-makers quickly rejected foreign intervention in an area they considered entirely a domestic prerogative. As if to underscore that emigration served Soviet goals and not an international agenda, harassment and repression directed at the broad spectrum of dissidents intensified as the number of emigrants increased. No amount of pressure, applied in the spirit of détente or tied to concessions in other areas, succeeded in moderating the treatment of Jews involved in activities designed to bring attention to their calls for emigration (or of dissidents whose activities touched on broader human rights questions). The Soviet posture indicated that détente was not determining the domestic agenda for human rights, including emigration. While Soviet policy-makers recognized that emigration appeased Western critics, their actions demonstrated that the Western response was at most a secondary component in setting policy.

But, as discussed in Chapter 2, Soviet policy-makers did not anticipate that the decision to permit emigration would expand rather than shrink the size of the movement. As greater numbers of Jews were granted permission to leave, still more filed applications for emigration.[6] The initial decision to let Jews leave was made when the proportions of the movement were not yet clear; as pressure for emigration continued to build, Soviet authorities could no longer count on easily containing the movement, nor could they expect its imminent demise.

FACTORS IN EMIGRATION POLICY: 1974–79

As the decade progressed, both the domestic and international parameters of emigration changed. Within the Jewish emigration movement, the most significant development was the declining importance of a Zionist motivation for emigration. A corollary to the diminishing relevance Zionism held for emigrants was an increase in the proportion of highly educated Jews from the Soviet heartland.

A reduction in the number of emigrants during the first 2 years of the period (Jewish emigration fell from 34 733 in 1973 to 20 628 in 1974 and dropped further to 13 221 in 1975) has been variously interpreted. Advocates of the barometer thesis suggested that emigration decreased in response to the passage by the US Congress of the Jackson–

Vanik amendment to the Trade Act of 1974.[7] Others, arguing a minority view, held that dynamics within the emigration movement were responsible for the decline in emigration.[8] While the evidence for the latter position is stronger, and will be discussed fully below, it is instructive to focus briefly on the Jackson–Vanik amendment because it provides an essential backdrop to the barometer thesis.

Two years before the passage of the Jackson–Vanik amendment to the Trade Act of 1974,[9] the US and USSR formally agreed in the 1972 US–Soviet Trade Agreement that the Soviet Union would be granted most-favored-nation (MFN) status (a non-discriminatory tariff classification) and Export–Import Bank credits in return for Soviet payment of its World War II Lend-Lease debt – which was to be reduced from $11 billion to $722 million. Because the US Constitution requires a congressional grant of authority to empower the President to carry out pledges such as those outlined in the US–Soviet Trade Agreement, the agreement was presented for consideration by the Congress as part of the Omnibus Trade Reform Act, which was later passed as the Trade Act of 1974.[10]

The Jackson–Vanik amendment to the Trade Act of 1974 requires that non-market economy countries not previously granted MFN tariff status be refused such status as well as trade credits, credit guarantees and investment guarantees if those countries deny their citizens the right or opportunity to emigrate, impose excessive taxes on emigration documents, or charge other fees as a consequence of a citizen's stated desire to emigrate.[11]

The passage of the Jackson–Vanik amendment illustrated the high level to which the issue of emigration had risen in the American political arena, yet its actual impact on Soviet-Jewish emigration levels remains a subject of debate. The view that the Soviet Union would be willing to increase emigration in exchange for Western technology and trade benefits formed the foundation for the Jackson–Vanik amendment.[12] By positing a relationship between emigration levels and US–Soviet relations, the adherents of the barometer thesis concluded that the decrease in emigration during 1974 and 1975 was an angry Soviet response to the enactment of the Jackson–Vanik amendment.

The Jackson–Vanik amendment not only had little, if any impact on emigration, but also proved to be a poor vehicle for applying pressure on the Soviet Union. After it was passed, lack of support for the Jackson–Vanik initiative on the part of other Western nations diluted its impact. The Soviet Union was able to turn to other countries for the technology and additional needs the United States would not satisfy. France, Great Britain, Japan and West Germany did not link trade with emigration and were willing to conduct business as usual with the USSR.[13] As a result, the Soviet Union was able to fulfill its requirements elsewhere without modifying its policy.

A more plausible explanation for the mid-decade slump focuses on the domestic emigration movement rather than on external events. As the emigrant pool became less Zionist in composition and some Soviet Jews became fearful about living in Israel in the aftermath of the 1973 Arab–Israeli War, would-be emigrants began questioning whether they wanted to choose Israel as their adoptive country. The 1974–76 years may be considered a pioneering period for Soviet-Jewish settlement in America, much as 1968–70 had been for the first immigrants to Israel. Many Soviet Jews delayed filing emigration applications while waiting to hear news about the United States and other potential destinations. As was the case with Israel in the earlier period, letters offering advice about immigrating to the United States were an important source of information for prospective emigrants. During 1974–75 the United States was in a period of economic recession; news of the difficulties that high inflation and unemployment caused the new immigrants reached the USSR and discouraged others from choosing to emigrate at that time.[14]

Data on the composition of the emigrant pool during the middle of the decade provide evidence supporting the view that emigration declined largely because fewer applications were filed.[15] As Jews from the heartland, who were progressively less interested in immigrating to Israel but were not yet certain about where to go, considered their options, there was a lag in the number of people requesting permission to emigrate. This may be concluded from a decline in the number of invitations requested from Israel during the

period.[16] By 1977, when the economic situation had improved and growing numbers of Soviet Jews were choosing
to immigrate to the United States, requests for invitations
and the emigration level itself had begun to rise.[17]

The argument that the Jackson–Vanik amendment
prompted the USSR to decrease emigration in 1974 and
1975 does not explain why the number of emigrants began
increasing in 1976, reaching 16 736 in 1977, 28 864 in 1978
and 51 320 in 1979. This rise has been attributed to another
external variable, the 1975 signing of the Final Act of the
Conference on Security and Cooperation in Europe (CSCE).
Yet the Final Act did not bring improved Soviet cooperation
in other areas. After the Act was signed, US–Soviet relations
in fact began to deteriorate. The Soviet–Cuban action in
Angola beginning in 1975–76, the military intervention by
the USSR in the Horn of Africa by the end of 1977, the
lengthy SALT negotiations[18] and the US–PRC entente contributed to the worsening US–Soviet relationship.[19] Tension
between the superpowers escalated, reaching a breaking
point with the December 1979 Soviet invasion of Afghanistan. This action caused the Carter administration to reassess
its approach to US–Soviet relations, resulting in a partial
grain embargo, a ban on the sale of high technology and
strategic goods, curtailment of Soviet fishing rights, the
request by President Carter for withdrawal of the SALT II
Treaty from Senate consideration and the US boycott of the
1980 Moscow Olympics.[20]

If emigration were a barometer of US–Soviet relations,
these negative factors should have combined to stall or
impede emigration, yet they did not. Proponents of the
barometer thesis point instead to legislation in the summer of
1979 superseding the Stevenson amendment,[21] to rumors
that the waiver to the Jackson–Vanik amendment would be
invoked in 1979,[22] and to the signing of the SALT II Treaty
in June 1979, as factors motivating the tremendous increase
in emigration at the end of the decade. Yet the barometer
thesis analysis of emigration trends has several flaws. First, it
does not account for large-scale emigration during years of
tense relations (1976–79): the number of Soviet-Jewish emigrants rose during the last 4 years of the 1970s despite the
deterioration of US–Soviet relations. Second, in the context

of poor relations, the barometer thesis does not satisfactorily explain why the Soviet Union would pay the price of what was then record emigration for improved relations with no guarantee of a positive return. Third, the direct correlations the barometer thesis establishes between annual emigration levels and significant events in US–Soviet relations are methodologically unsound. They offer neither a consistent accounting for time-lags between changes in US–Soviet relations and emigration trends nor any consideration of policy implementation in the USSR.

The pattern of Soviet-German emigration during these same years further underscores the weakness of the barometer thesis as a model for analysis of Soviet policy. As détente began to crumble and East–West relations became increasingly polarized, the US and FRG positions on the linkage of human rights questions to other policy areas diverged. Unlike the US, West Germany did not experience a cooling of its relations with the USSR in the late 1970s. As a result of re-evaluating its trade relationship with the USSR, West Germany adopted a policy that de-coupled FRG–USSR trade and political relations. One of the reasons guiding this decision was that East–West trade had become an important economic consideration for West Germany.[23] The election debates of 1976 (during a time of growing unemployment in the FRG) had called attention to the dependence of West German industry on East–West trade.[24] Differences in other aspects of the FRG attitude towards the USSR, primarily as a result of the desire for continued trade, also led West Germany (from the late 1970s through the election of Chancellor Kohl in 1983) to follow an increasingly independent course from the US in its relationship with the USSR.[25]

Despite improvements in West German–Soviet relations during the late 1970s, Soviet-German emigration was curtailed after 1976.[26] Thus, on the one hand, while US–Soviet relations deteriorated, Jewish emigration increased, and on the other, while West German–Soviet relations grew warmer, German emigration was reduced. These trends suggest that the international climate was not a primary factor determining the flow of emigration. Moreover, fluctuations in the number of Soviet-Jewish emigrants and inverse levels of

Jewish and German emigration during 1976–79 indicate that emigration was not used to attain Soviet international goals in the late 1970s.

In the case of Soviet Germans, specific demographic considerations were likely to have been important factors in the decision to reduce emigration. The majority of Soviet Germans were laborers and semi-skilled workers, predominantly concentrated in the Kazakh SSR and the RSFSR. At a time of declining population growth rates among Slavic nationalities, the titular (Kazakh) nationality was experiencing large population growth. According to the 1979 census, the proportion of Kazakhs in the total population of the Kazakh SSR increased from 30.0 per cent (1959) to 32.6 per cent (1970) to 36.0 per cent (1979). These figures may be contrasted with those for the RSFSR, in which the proportion of the titular (Russian) nationality decreased from 83.3 per cent (1959) to 82.8 per cent (1970), to 82.6 per cent (1979).[27]

Because Germans were associated with 'European' (in this case, Slavic) nationalities, they may have been identified as able to serve – at least psychologically – as a counterweight to the growing ethnic Kazakh population. Although the number of Soviet Germans was small compared to the large Kazakh presence (Soviet Germans comprised 6.13 per cent of the population of the Kazakh SSR in 1979), they constituted the third largest nationality group in the republic.[28] Soviet Germans (and other non-Asian nationalities) were readily identified by their physical characteristics, language (in 1979 35.3 per cent of Soviet Germans living in Kazakhstan spoke Russian as their first language and 58.2 per cent spoke Russian as their second language),[29] and style of dress. In Kazakhstan, the 'local' population was identified as 'black' or 'Asian', whereas the 'Russian' population in the republic was considered 'white' or 'European'.[30] As local nationalism, social mobility and demands for education policies more favorable to the indigenous (Kazakh) nationality increased along with the Kazakh growth rate, maintaining a physical presence of Soviet Germans and other 'European' nationalities presumably assumed greater significance; reliance on Russians (or Europeans) to safeguard against regional ethnic tensions has been a traditional feature of Soviet nationality policy. The key element was the perception of a European presence, a subtle but important consideration in light of a diminishing Slavic/European birthrate and an increasing Central Asian (and predominantly Moslem) population.

Additionally, the reduction in Soviet-German emigration may have signified adjustments in the emigrant pool itself. As with Soviet Jewry in the middle of the decade, the diminution may have reflected decreased demand by Soviet Germans. Feedback from friends or family who had already immigrated to West Germany or other personal considerations might have played a significant role.

In contrast to the Soviet-German case, Soviet-Jewish emigration policy in the second half of the 1970s was conditioned primarily by the same issues that drove it in the beginning of the decade: nationality policy, the uneasy position of Jews in Soviet society and the necessity of confronting the demands of a significant segment of the population that could no longer be quieted by imprisoning outspoken critics. The familiar dilemma regarding the Jewish nationality – policies that forbade expression of Jewish identity and simultaneously the societal obstacles that prevented their full assimilation – was played out in emigration policy. The decision to let Jews emigrate removed individuals who would not accept their lot in Soviet society, but it also satisfied those who felt that the Soviet Union was better off without its Jews. The rapid escalation of Jewish emigration in the last years of the decade demonstrated the USSR's multifaceted approach to the situation.

In the Soviet Union promotion, upward mobility and access to key positions generally have been based on one's ability to master Russian cultural norms and language. The process of industrialization brought an influx of technically and administratively skilled members of the Russian and other Slavic nationalities to urban areas lacking properly trained personnel. Because Soviet Jews generally assimilated to the Russian (rather than indigenous republican) culture, except perhaps in the Georgian SSR, they often have been perceived in the non-Russian republics as agents of russification. As tension between the indigenous populations and Slavic settlers flared over issues such as jobs and housing, emigration in combination with official anti-Zionism and popular anti-Semitism offered an escape valve for some of the pressure. Competition for jobs, particularly in fields where Jewish professionals predominated, was often waged along ethnic lines and local officials benefited from more jobs, and in turn more housing, being available for distribution.[31]

Moreover, the anti-Zionist campaign proved to be a convenient way of helping to deflect negative feelings resulting from the presence and preferential treatment of Slavic settlers in non-Slavic areas. Presented as a political and ideological campaign, anti-Zionism enabled the inciting of anti-Jewish feelings without the appearance of blatant anti-Semitism. When combined with emigration, anti-Zionist propaganda enabled Soviet authorities to appear as if they were actively addressing problems of ethnic favoritism. The propaganda discredited Zionists (read 'Jews') and implicitly suggested that the USSR would be better off without them.[32] Furthermore, by attacking Zionism and Zionists, rather than Jews *per se*, Soviet authorities may have hoped to avoid alienating the most assimilated Jews, whose professional contributions, particularly in the technical and scientific realms, were important.[33]

In the heartland, emigration relieved other social pressures. Proportionally, Jews were the most highly educated Soviet nationality, and this made them well qualified for the jobs open to them. Yet as increasing numbers of Jews requested to leave, a perception that Jews were unreliable employees because they were likely to emigrate became a self-fulfilling prophecy.[34] At the same time expectations grew that the emigration of Jews would remove impediments to the advancement of others in jobs and education.[35] While social strains were partially a by-product of rapid industrialization, urbanization and uneven economic advantage, they were aggravated by the legacies of nationality policy. Permitting the emigration of urban Jews enabled Soviet authorities to respond to some of these tensions.

FACTORS IN JEWISH AND GERMAN EMIGRATON: 1980–86

Beginning with the December 1979 Soviet invasion of Afghanistan, the US response in the form of sanctions and withdrawal of the SALT II Treaty from Senate consideration and the signing of a US–PRC bilateral trade agreement,[36] US–Soviet relations soured quickly. The United States accused the Soviet Union of complicity in the December 1981 declaration of martial law in Poland and responded by denying several United States firms the licenses needed to export technology to the USSR, banning US participation in the Siberian natural gas pipeline to Western Europe,[37] postponing new long-term grain purchase negotiations[38] and closing the US offices of the Soviet Purchasing Committee. The shooting down of a South Korean passenger jet by a Soviet fighter-plane over the island of Sakhalin in September 1983, the deployment of US Pershing II and Cruise missiles in Western Europe at the end of 1983, Soviet suspension of the START negotiations in response to the deployments and the Soviet boycott of the 1984 Summer Olympics in Los Angeles, characterized the continuing deterioration of US–Soviet relations.

The barometer thesis would suggest that the progressively deteriorating superpower relationship in the early 1980s led to the diminished emigration levels in the first half of the decade. Yet strained relations, while unquestionably harmful to a range of US–Soviet dealings, were not the primary determinant of emigration in the 1980s. For one, the monthly number of exit visas for Soviet Jews had begun decreasing as early as November 1979, casting doubt on claims that the reduction was a direct outcome of the actions undertaken by the United States in response to the December 1979 Soviet invasion of Afghanistan. The decline in Soviet-German emigration during the early 1980s was the continuation of a process that had begun during a period of relatively good Soviet–FRG relations in the 1970s. The experience of the 1970s indicated that a cordial atmosphere was neither a prerequisite nor a determinant of emigration, a lesson bolstered by the patterns of the 1980s. While an anti-emigration policy was not inconsistent with the progressive deterioration of US–Soviet relations, the primary mechanism driving emigration policy was the maturing of several domestic problems of the 1970s into full blown-crises in the 1980s.

Economic, demographic and leadership uncertainties posed considerable challenges to the Soviet Union by the beginning of the new decade. The effect of changing circumstances in the USSR prompted a re-evaluation of prior policy and diminished the attractiveness of using emigration to serve the same purposes as it had in the 1970s. Emigration in the 1970s represented a response to Jewish national consciousness, provided a new option for channeling anti-Jewish sentiment, offered a mechanism for resolving nationality tensions and signaled an attempt to purge the country of unwanted citizens whose demands for emigration could incite disaffection among others. The cumulative effect of internal Soviet developments on emigration was a drastic limitation during 1980–86. Jewish emigration fell to 21 471 in 1980, 9447 in 1981, 2688 in 1982, 1314 in 1983, 896 in 1984, rose somewhat to 1140 in 1985, and fell again in 1986 to 914. German emigration also plummeted, dropping from 6954 in 1980 to 460 in 1985 (and rising only slightly in 1986). Both trends spelled the virtual cessation of emigration.

By 1980 the diffusion of power and attendant paralysis of the system caused by Leonid Brezhnev's weakening grip sharpened the fault lines within the leadership. The lack of consensus over policy had a negative impact on emigration, and the perception that events were spinning out of control led to increased restraints. Indeed, in the beginning of the 1980s, decreasing emigration levels went hand in hand with increasing repression. Renewed opposition to emigration was consistent with the inward-turning, isolationist position the Soviet Union assumed in the first half of the decade. Old age and conservatism in the leadership engendered a return to more traditional methods for handling demands for emigration. Notwithstanding Yuri Andropov's short tenure, there were no serious indications until after Gorbachev became General Secretary in 1985, that an end was near to the stagnation and 'muddling through' of the late Brezhnev years. With a political backdrop of uncertainty and multiplying economic, demographic, ethnic and labor problems, the Soviet Union was not prepared to countenance large-scale emigration in the early 1980s.

The proportions of actual and potential Soviet-Jewish (and German) emigration could not be ignored during a time of declining economic and population growth. Soviet statistical data indicate that the growth rate for the entire Soviet population has slowed since the 1950s.[39] The full impact of low birth rates (lower in the 1960s than in any prior period of Soviet post-World War II history) would be felt in the second half of the 1980s, as the children of the late 1960s reached working age. The departure of large numbers of individuals at a time of a growing labor deficit could not have been looked upon favorably.

As changes in the demographic situation made themselves felt, compounded by the need for wide-ranging economic reform, the predominantly Slavic leadership was forced to confront important issues regarding how to secure its own power base, manage the increased assertiveness of non-Russian nationalities, allocate jobs and resources, stimulate the economy and rectify the disparity between centers of population and regions of industrialization.[40] In light of the growing problems, policy-makers surely recognized that family reunification would be a never-ending process; indeed by the beginning of 1980 controlled emigration had led to the departure of 228 701 Soviet Jews. Uniting some family members through emigration almost invariably has the effect of creating new family separations and the leadership took measures to slow emigration with an eye toward eventually terminating it.

Finally, historical legacies (predating the Soviet period, yet characterizing it as well) and Marxist–Leninist ideology had created an entrenched mistrust of things foreign and an emphasis on the collective rather than on the individual.[41] During a stressful and uncertain period, these fundamental beliefs grew more prominent, forming a hostile environment for emigration, which even in better times was not without constraints. In a period when the Soviet leadership was unable to chart a clear course, it would have been difficult to marshal a coherent and effective pro-emigration policy.

GORBACHEV'S OBJECTIVES AND POST-1986 EMIGRATION

Although the array of domestic problems responsible for the extreme reduction in emigration during the early 1980s had not changed by the time Gorbachev became General Secretary in 1985, within 2 years a major policy re-evaluation had occurred. The result was a dramatic change in existing emigration practice. As Gorbachev began to exercise firm control over Soviet decision-making and unveiled his plans for *perestroika* (restructuring) and *glasnost* (openness), the downward spiral of Jewish and German emigration was suddenly reversed. The emigration of both groups accelerated in 1987, followed by further increases in 1988 and 1989. The number of Jewish emigrants reached 8155 in 1987, 18 965 in 1988 and 71 196 in 1989, breaking the previous record of 51 320 reached in 1979. Most surprising was that for the first time, the number of German emigrants far exceeded that of Jews, reaching 14 488 in 1987, 47 572 in 1988 and 98 134 in 1989.

In 1987 Soviet officials announced their decision to handle emigration applications in a more timely fashion and to review outstanding cases with an eye to permitting the eventual emigration of the refuseniks.[42] Increased Jewish emigration in 1987 did not stem from the thaw in US–Soviet relations, nor was its purpose simply to enhance relations prior to the December 1987 Reagan–Gorbachev summit meeting. Emigration on the magnitude of 1987 did not occur before either the 1985 summit meeting in Geneva or the 1986 summit meeting in Reykjavik. The 1987 policy turnaround can only be understood in the context of the extraordinary changes in the USSR during the late 1980s.

By and large, Jewish emigration in 1987 represented the partial resolution of the estimated 11 000 refusenik cases,[43] as opposed to a significant increase in the number of new, first-request applicants. Approximately 77 per cent of the 1987 emigrants had formerly been refused permission to emigrate.[44] Allowing the refuseniks to emigrate meant that the USSR could begin to rid itself of a large group of mobilized emigration activists whose skills were already lost to the Soviet Union (since most of the refuseniks had been dismissed from their jobs after filing emigration applications). Emigration of the refuseniks also enabled the Soviet Union to reduce the number of divided families actively seeking reunification (in the hope that newly divided family members would not choose to emigrate as well), a problem it had committed to resolve by signing the Final Act of the Conference on Security and Cooperation in Europe.

Fulfilling the obligations of the Final Act became increasingly important to the USSR after 1986 as Gorbachev sought to establish credibility at home and abroad with respect to the Soviet Union's commitment to the rule of law. Most importantly, resolving the refusenik problem would have the immediate benefit of enabling Gorbachev to put the situation behind him, rid himself of its legacy and move on to the pressing issues on his agenda. Maintaining large numbers of refuseniks was undoubtedly a liability, but whether changes in the domestic situation would be sufficient to discourage pressure for future emigration remained unclear.

Although representing a departure from past practices, Gorbachev's approach to the refusenik problem did not at first signal a fundamental change in the Soviet anti-emigration stance of 1980–86. Despite a more flexible policy toward the emigration of Jews, Germans and Armenians, restrictions persisted and free emigration (by all members of those nationalities or by the general Soviet population) continued to be impossible. In 1987, the 1 January USSR Council of Ministers' decree revising the regulations on emigration and immigration and the relatively small percentage of first-request applicants, bolstered the then prevalent view that increased emigration would be short-lived. As discussed in Chapter 3, the Council of Ministers' decree restricted the permissible grounds of emigration to reunion with first-degree family members, defined as spouses, parents or siblings. It also codified the reasons for which exit may be refused, such as knowledge of state secrets, infringement on rights and interests of other Soviet citizens, and outstanding obligations to state, cooperative or other public organizations.[45] The decree established the legal foundation for emigration, as well as the potential to impede emigration via restrictive eligibility rules.

While the predominance of refuseniks among the new emigrants and the amendments to the emigration decree in 1987 did not suggest that further emigration was likely, the composition of the emigrant pool in 1988 indicated a radical departure from previous practices. Indeed, slightly less than 50 per cent of the emigrants during the first seven months of 1988 were refuseniks (as opposed to 77 per cent in all of 1987), suggesting that a decision had been made to expand emigration. Increased Jewish emigration was accompanied (and surpassed) by German emigration, which reached record highs. Armenian emigration was also significantly expanded. The sudden and dramatic surge in the emigration of all three nationalities pointed clearly to a policy reversal.

On one level, a liberal emigration policy seemed to be contrary to the best interests of *perestroika*. Many ingredients would be necessary for successful reform, including the support of skilled professionals and the creative participation of the intelligentsia. Because of their socioeconomic standing, Jews had the potential to be important contributors to (and beneficiaries of) *perestroika*. Insofar as they may have been strategically positioned, their increased emigration would have meant a loss of valuable resources.[46] Moreover, in light of greater democratization, restricting emigration to select groups could have become increasingly indefensible and easily could have led to demands by other nationalities for the freedom to emigrate. Broadening the emigration of particular groups without providing similar opportunities for others might have invited a backlash by those passed over.

Nonetheless, other domestic considerations were at the heart of the policy reversal. While many of the concerns that caused the drastic curtailment of emigration in the early 1980s had not dissipated, Gorbachev's leadership, his vision and the dramatic reforms he sought to undertake began to affect every aspect of Soviet policy, and emigration proved no exception. Emphasis on the rule of law, the rapid and continuing expansion of the boundaries of permissible public discourse and a readiness to countenance fundamental changes in Soviet society provided an umbrella for new policies and opportunities. Increased emigration was a manifestation of the internal processes under way in the Soviet

Union and the relaxation of restrictions on emigration reflected the broad trend toward liberalization.

As *glasnost* engendered a greater willingness among Soviet citizens to engage in critical evaluation of their system, questions concerning freedom of movement and choice of residence within the USSR emerged for discussion even in circles outside the Jewish community.[47] In light of the new reality unfolding in the USSR, the Soviet leadership had only two choices for handling the ongoing demand for emigration: it could continue to impede almost all emigration, or it could permit unrestricted emigration. A middle course could no longer be tolerated. The first option held little promise, for past experience showed that pressure for emigration would not cease. Indeed, even during the highly restrictive period of 1980–86, demand for emigration remained strong albeit circumscribed by the repressive situation. During a more liberal period, such pressure could be expected to increase. Continuing a restrictive emigration policy would undermine *glasnost*, the new image of Party and government responsiveness and the fresh commitment to the integrity of international documents such as the Helsinki Final Act. On the other hand, a decision to permit greater emigration and at the same time provide incentives that might encourage people to *choose* to remain in the USSR, would embody the spirit of democratization.

Starting in 1988, popular discontent about the pace and problems of economic reform, including widespread shortages, began to plague Gorbachev, suggesting that the path to economic *perestroika* would be long and difficult.[48] Increasingly, Jews who were uncertain about the prospects for successful *perestroika* chose to leave. It was also clear from the growing numbers who have emigrated since restraints were loosened after 1986 that a sizeable group of people wanted to emigrate irrespective of any benefits *perestroika* could bring. Indeed, many decided to take advantage of the opportunity greater liberalization offered for receiving an exit visa. Still others, fearful of the rise of overt anti-Semitism and alarmed by the increasing frequency with which Jews were being blamed for the failures of the Soviet system, felt they had no choice but to leave.[49]

Like many Jews, Soviet Germans also responded to the

changed circumstances by seizing the opportunity to emigrate. Fear of losing the chance to emigrate and dwindling hopes for the realization of German autonomy within the USSR created 'push' factors for Soviet Germans, while obvious economic benefits exerted a 'pull' force toward the FRG. The astounding number of emigrants since 1986 is disproportionate to all previous levels of German emigration in the contemporary period, when the number never rose above 9704 (in 1976). The acceleration seems to indicate the beginning of a move toward genuinely free emigration, though it is still too early to tell.

The desire for joint ventures and increased trade opportunities with the Federal Republic of Germany might have motivated the surge in German emigration, but alone are insufficient to explain the inflated levels considerable resentment developed within West Germany as the number of Soviet and other German immigrants from the East surged and began to strain existing resources.[50] Unemployment and economic problems in the FRG exacerbated tensions, leaving no doubt that the West German populace had little interest in seeing emigration increase so markedly.[51] Indeed, changes in East Germany (GDR) that prompted the exodus of 344 000 Germans from the GDR to the FRG in 1989, and the removal of all travel restrictions on East Germans announced in November 1989, created a crisis with respect to absorption in West Germany. The additional emigration in 1989 of 376 975 ethnic Germans from the USSR and Eastern European countries (other than East Germany) compounded the situation.[52] Before talks on German reunification started, West Germans, who considered East Germans to be automatic citizens of the FRG, had even begun discussing the importance for Germans to remain in East Germany and work for change there.[53] West Germans were even less enthusiastic about the influx of Soviet and other East European Germans.[54]

The higher levels of German as opposed to Jewish emigration might have been a function of delays occasioned by the volume of exit visas being processed or a result of changes in US policy, or both, rather than a consequence of a particular policy directive. Reports circulated regarding tremendous processing backlogs at the US Embassy in Moscow.[55] No such difficulties were reported for German emigrants, who were automatically eligible for German citizenship.

In the past, Soviet Jews wishing to immigrate to the United States applied for visas for Israel and changed destinations in Vienna. Starting in 1989, the rigorous enforcement of US immigration law was applied to Soviet Jews. No longer were Soviet Jews permitted to enter the country as refugees, but rather they were required to apply for entry as immigrants. In part this change was a response to the tremendous increase in the number of immigrants expected as a result of the Soviet Union's relaxation of restrictions on emigration. It was also occasioned by changes in the USSR that threw into question the ability of Soviet Jews to continue to demonstrate a 'well founded fear of persecution' – a necessary requirement of US refugee policy.

Thus, as of the fall of 1989, Soviet Jews could no longer exit the USSR with Israeli entry visas and expect to drop out and immigrate to the United States. Instead, those wishing to immigrate to the US were required to apply directly to the United States. This did not preclude Soviet Jews from immigrating to Israel and later attempting to immigrate to the United States. However, once Israeli citizens, they would no longer be eligible for US refugee status. Refugees in the United States are entitled to resettlement and absorption support as well as other government benefits; as a result the US maintains an annual ceiling on the number of refugees it will admit. Once the quota is filled, an additional number may receive permission to enter with humanitarian parole status if evidence demonstrating financial support in the US can be presented. Differences in the levels of Jewish and German emigration may thus have had as much or more to do with US or German policy as with any policy decision of the Soviet government.

Ultimately, in a setting in which most who request exit visas receive them, it will be Soviet Jews and Germans who will themselves determine the flow of emigration. Their decisions will be affected by circumstances inside as well as outside the USSR. Difficulties in Germany generated by the socioeconomic implications of German unification will affect future decisions of prospective Soviet-German emigrants. Likewise, some Soviet Jews who do not want to immigrate to Israel but cannot qualify for entry into the United States will opt to remain in the USSR. So will those Jews and Germans satisfied with changes in the Soviet Union. However, Jews and Germans and their emigration are part of an overall nationality dilemma inextricably linked to the roots of ethnic discord in the USSR. The problems range from outright discrimination and open hostility (from the government and in the form of inter-ethnic animosity) to controversial language and cultural policies, questions of national autonomy, territorial rights, religious tolerance, cadres policy and regional inequalities. These concerns and others – for example, about the economy – add further complexities to the emigration question for they underscore the numerous dimensions of the issue. Like the other factors detailed above, they will also have an important impact on the future course of Soviet emigration.

CONCLUSION

The failure of the barometer thesis as a mode of appraising Soviet emigration policy can be seen on two separate levels. First, an application of the thesis as a predictive model reveals that its projections do not correspond with the course of historical events. From beginning to end, domestic issues have been the primary factors in setting emigration policy. Emigration began in the late 1960s – before SALT I, grain negotiations or the full flowering of détente – as a Soviet response to the rise of a Jewish emigration movement. Although the groundwork for détente was being laid in that period, it formed only the backdrop to emigration decisions, and thus must be counted as a secondary factor in emigration policy. By the late 1970s, when the barometer thesis would predict a lull or slackening in the flow of emigrants, the reverse occurred: Jewish emigration skyrocketed during deteriorating US–Soviet relations and German emigration decreased despite a distinct improvement in Soviet–FRG relations.

Under the premise that poor relations spawn restricted emigration, the precipitous drop of the early 1980s retains some plausibility, although only if viewed in a vacuum. But to posit the Gorbachev era shift as an elaborate ploy to obtain trade credits and a waiver of the Jackson–Vanik amendment so as to bolster the Soviet Union's crisis-ridden economy would ignore the momentous nature of internal upheaval in the USSR. It would also fail to credit the revitalizing force of Mikhail Gorbachev following the stagnation of the Soviet leadership and isolation of the USSR in the early 1980s.

The second level of failure of the barometer thesis is that it reflects an 'Amero-centric' world view, a certain hubris whereby US analysts attribute all Soviet decisions to the mood and expected response of America. In Soviet studies this view has been a particular species of the cold war perspective that saw the USSR as a menacing monolith rather than as a diverse and complex state. A consistent, almost willful, ignorance of Soviet domestic politics (other than an obsession with Kremlinology) epitomized this attitude. Change in the USSR under Gorbachev, driven by domestic imperatives, illustrates the need for a clearer understanding of Soviet politics and society and a de-emphasis on the role the United States plays in setting the Soviet domestic policy agenda.

Afterword

By 1989, when Gorbachev's *perestroika* was in its fifth year, it began to appear that for the first time the nationality component in emigration would become less important or ultimately insignificant as the USSR moved gradually toward honoring the international human rights guarantees it had made over the years. At the time of this writing, the Supreme Soviet was considering a new law on entry into and exit from the USSR that would remove the requirement of an invitation in order to initiate the application process, set strict limitations on secrecy classifications so as to prevent the arbitrary denial of permission to leave and place property claims by relatives against those desiring to leave in a court of law (rather than under the jurisdiction of the Department of Visas and Registration).

The introduction of a new US policy in 1989 requiring Jews and others wishing to immigrate to the US to apply directly to the US for an entry visa eliminated the drop-out situation. The Soviet sanctioning of emigration of Jews directly to the United States also indicated the decreased importance of the nationality component in emigration policy. Emigration remained confined predominantly to the nationalities that had experienced large-scale emigration in the past, probably because members of those nationalities had the greatest incidence of family ties abroad. But the removal of the requirement that Jews leaving the USSR emigrate on visas to Israel, underscored that a transformation had begun in which emigration was to lose its link to nationality policy and become instead a recognized human right guaranteed in international law and administered through Soviet procedures that would not be politicized or subject to arbitrary determinations.

By 1989, an additional twist in the history of emigration emerged. For the first time in 20 years, neither the United States nor the Federal Republic of Germany welcomed the influx of immigrants that Soviet policy changes made possible. The irony was that after so many years of berating the Soviet Union about its human rights violations, the US and

106

West Germany balked at receiving the flood of immigrants that inundated them when the USSR was finally prepared to permit large-scale emigration of Germans and Jews.

The USSR's current practice of allowing virtually anyone who can present the proper documentation to emigrate represents a gamble. Like the situation in East Germany in late 1989 when all restrictions on exit from that country were suddenly lifted, *perestroika* emigration seemed aimed at reducing growing pressure by letting off steam. It also signified both the move toward greater democracy in the USSR and the Soviet Union's commitment to honor guarantees it made in the international community. In the past, actions taken as a way of removing the most dissatisfied individuals in order to prevent them from influencing others backfired. Instead, a snowball effect was created in which the large number of individuals permitted to leave only produced greater numbers of applicants. By late 1990 conditions in the USSR had spurred a mass exodus and uncertainties about the direction of reform were widespread. Whether a normal process of migration would develop remained an open question.

Table 1   Annual Soviet-Jewish Emigration

Year	Number of emigrants
1965–June 1967	4 498
October 1968–1970	4 235
1971	13 022
1972	31 681
1973	34 733
1974	20 628
1975	13 221
1976	14 261
1977	16 736
1978	28 864
1979	51 320
1980	21 471
1981	9 447
1982	2 688
1983	1 314
1984	896
1985	1 140
1986	914
1987	8 155
1988	18 965
1989	71 196
Total	369 385

Source: National Conference on Soviet Jewry, New York.

Table 2   Annual Soviet-German Emigration

Year	Number of emigrants
1955	608
1956	800
1957	1 221
1958	4 681
1959	5 960
1960	3 460
1961	451
1962	927
1963	242
1964	262
1965	365
1966	1 245
1967	1 092
1968	598
1969	316
1970	340
1971	1 145
1972	3 426
1973	4 494
1974	6 541
1975	5 985
1976	9 704
1977	9 274
1978	8 455
1979	7 226
1980	6 954
1981	3 773
1982	2 071
1983	1 447
1984	913
1985	460
1986	753
1987	14 488
1988	47 572
1989	98 134
Total	255 383

Source: Deutsches Rotes Kreuz
[German Red Cross], Hamburg.

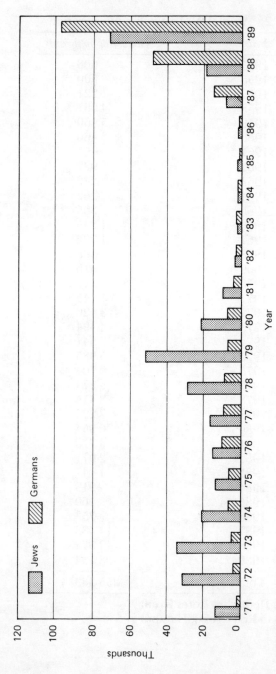

Figure 1 Comparison of Annual Soviet-Jewish and Soviet-German Emigration

Sources: National Conference on Soviet Jewry (New York), Deutsches Rotes Kreuz [German Red Cross] (Hamburg).

Notes

Introduction

1. The process of reform and democratization currently under way in the Soviet Union may result in significant changes in Soviet emigration practice.
2. One notable exception is the 1983 work by Victor Zaslavsky and Robert J. Brym, *Soviet-Jewish Emigration and Soviet Nationality Policy* (London: Macmillan, 1983).
3. See A. H. Brown, *Soviet Politics and Political Science* (London: Macmillan, 1974); Robert V. Daniels, 'Soviet Politics Since Khrushchev', in John W. Strong (ed.), *The Soviet Union Under Brezhnev and Kosygin* (New York: Van Nostrand Reinhold, 1971); Darrell P. Hammer, *The USSR: The Politics of Oligarchy*, 2nd edn, rev. (Boulder, Colorado: Westview, 1986); Jerry F. Hough, *The Soviet Union and Social Science Theory* (Cambridge, Massachusetts: Harvard University Press, 1977); Donald R. Kelley, 'Group and Specialist Influence in Soviet Politics: In Search of a Theory', in Richard B. Remnek (ed.), *Social Scientists and Policy Making in the USSR* (London: Praeger, 1977); Boris Meissner and Georg Brunner (eds), *Gruppeninteressen und Entscheidungsprozesse in der Sowjetunion* (Cologne: Wissenschaft & Politik, 1975); Alec Nove, *The Soviet Economic System*, 3rd edn (Boston: Allen & Unwin, 1986); H. Gordon Skilling and Franklyn Griffiths (eds), *Interest Groups in Soviet Politics* (Princeton: Princeton University Press, 1971); Susan Gross Solomon (ed.), *Pluralism in the Soviet Union: Essays in Honour of H. Gordon Skilling* (London: Macmillan, 1983); Jiri Valenta, 'The Bureaucratic Politics Paradigm and the Soviet Invasion of Czechoslovakia', *Political Science Quarterly* 94 (1979), pp. 55–76; Lawrence Whetten, *Current Research in Comparative Communism: An Analysis and Bibliographic Guide to the Soviet System* (New York: Praeger, 1976).
4. For classic works on (Soviet) totalitarianism see Zbigniew K. Brzezinski and Samuel P. Huntington, *Political Power: USA/USSR* (New York: Viking, 1964); Carl J. Friedrich and Zbigniew K. Brzezinski, *Totalitarian Dictatorship and Autocracy*, 2nd edn, rev. (Cambridge, Massachusetts: Harvard University Press, 1965).
5. For examples see Donna Bahry, *Outside Moscow: Power, Politics, and Budgetary Policy in the Soviet Republics* (New York: Columbia University Press, 1987); Theodore H. Friedgut, 'Interests and Groups in Soviet Policy-Making: The MTS Reforms', *Soviet Studies* 28 (October 1976), pp. 524–47; Thane Gustafson, *Reform in Soviet Politics: Lessons of Recent Policies on Land and Water* (Cambridge: Cambridge University Press, 1981); Ellen Jones, 'Committee Decision-Making in the Soviet Union', *World Politics* 36 (January 1984), pp. 165–88; Donald R. Kelley, 'Environmental Policy-Making in the USSR: The Role of Industrial and Environmental Interest Groups', *Soviet Studies* 28

(October 1976), pp. 570–89; John Löwenhardt, *Decision-Making in Soviet Politics* (New York: St. Martin's, 1981); Richard M. Mills, 'The Formation of the Virgin Lands Policy', *Slavic Review* 29 (March 1970), pp. 58–69; Sidney Ploss, *Conflict and Decision-Making in Soviet Russia: A Case Study of Agricultural Policy, 1953–1963* (Princeton: Princeton University Press, 1965); Peter H. Solomon, Jr., *Soviet Criminologists and Criminal Policy: Specialists in Policy-Making* (New York: Columbia University Press, 1978); Philip D. Stewart, 'Soviet Interest Groups and the Policy Process: The Repeal of Production Education', *World Politics* 22 (October 1969), pp. 29–50; Jiri Valenta and William Potter (eds), *Soviet Decisionmaking for National Security* (London: George Allen & Unwin, 1984); Charles E. Ziegler, 'Issue Creation and Interest Groups in Soviet Environmental Policy: The Applicability of the State Corporatist Model', *Comparative Politics* 18 (January 1986), pp. 171–92.

6. *Natsionalny sostav naselenia: Chast II* [National Composition of the Population: Part II] (Moscow: Finansy i statistika, 1989), p. 4.

7. Based on statistics in *Natsionalny sostav naselenia: Chast II*, pp. 7, 60, 63, 65, 69, 72, 78, 82, 84, 86, 88–9, 91, 93, 95–6.

8. See Robert Conquest, *The Nation Killers: The Soviet Deportation of Nationalities* (London: Macmillan, 1970; reprint edn, London: Sphere, 1972); *Argumenty i fakty* (30 September–6 October 1989), p. 8.

9. According to the 1979 census, Soviet Germans ranked as the fourteenth largest nationality, with a total population of 1 936 214. The 1989 census showed the German population to have grown to 2 035 807, placing Germans in sixteenth place in population size. The majority of Soviet Germans (according to the 1989 census) live in Kazakhstan (47.0 per cent) and the RSFSR (41.3 per cent), with smaller percentages living in Kirghizia (5.0 per cent), Uzbekistan (2.0 per cent), the Ukraine (1.9 per cent), Tadzhikistan (1.6 per cent), and scattered among the other republics (1.4 per cent). Derived from figures in *Natsionalny sostav naselenia: Chast II*, pp. 8, 61, 63, 66, 70, 72, 78, 82, 84, 86, 89, 91, 93, 95–6.

10. See V. I. Lenin, *Collected Works* (Moscow: Progress, 1966), vol. 20, pp. 17–51; V. I. Lenin, *The Right of Nations to Self-Determination* (Moscow: Foreign Languages, 1947); Joseph Stalin, *Marxism and the National and Colonial Question: A Collection of Articles and Speeches* (New York: International, 1935?); Walker Connor, *The National Question in Marxist–Leninist Theory and Strategy* (Princeton: Princeton University Press, 1984); Robert C. Tucker (ed.), *The Marx–Engels Reader*, 2nd edn (New York: W. W. Norton, 1978). For further information on Soviet nationality issues see Edward Allworth (ed.), *Nationality Group Survival in Multi-Ethnic States: Shifting Support Patterns in the Soviet Baltic Region* (New York: Praeger, 1977); Hélène Carrère d'Encausse, *Decline of an Empire: The Soviet Socialist Republics in Revolt*, trans. Martin Sokolinsky and Henry A. La Farge (New York: Newsweek Books, 1979); Zvi Gitelman, 'Are Nations Merging in the USSR?', *Problems of Communism* 32 (September–October 1983), pp. 35–47;

Erich Goldhagen (ed.), *Ethnic Minorities in the Soviet Union* (New York: Praeger, 1968); Gail Warshofsky Lapidus, 'Ethnonationalism and Political Stability: The Soviet Case', *World Politics* 36 (July 1984), pp. 555–80; Y. V. Bromlei, 'Natsionalnye problemy v usloviakh perestroiki' [National Problems in the Conditions of Perestroika], *Voprosy istorii* no. 1 (January 1989), pp. 24–41; V. Tishkov, 'Narody i gosudarstvo' [Peoples and State], *Kommunist* (1) (January 1989), pp. 49–59; Ronald Grigor Suny, 'Nationalist and Ethnic Unrest in the Soviet Union', *World Policy Journal* (Summer 1989), pp. 504–28; Paul Goble, 'Ethnic Politics in the USSR', *Problems of Communism* 38 (4) (July–August 1989), pp. 1–14; Gail W. Lapidus, 'Gorbachev's Nationalities Problem', *Foreign Affairs* 68 (4) (Fall 1989), pp. 92–108.

11. Soviet nationality policy in the post-war period called for a steady rapprochement (*sblizhenie*) and eventual fusion (*slianie*) of nationalities, while simultaneously promoting the flourishing and development of all Soviet nationalities.

12. H. Gordon Skilling's pioneering contributions on the role of interest groups in Soviet politics raised questions about what constitutes group activity in the Soviet context. See H. Gordon Skilling, 'Interest Groups and Communist Politics', *World Politics* 18 (April 1966), pp. 435–51; H. Gordon Skilling and Franklyn Griffiths (eds), *Interest Groups in Soviet Politics* (Princeton: Princeton University Press, 1971). Skilling's evaluation of the analyses that ensued from the publication of his above cited works may be found in H. Gordon Skilling, 'Interest Groups and Communist Politics Revisited', *World Politics* 36 (October 1983), pp. 1–27.

1 Survey of Soviet-Jewish History: Precursors of the Emigration Movement

1. V. I. Lenin, 'Critical Remarks on the National Question', in *Collected Works* (Moscow: Progress, 1964), vol. 20 (December 1913–August 1914), p. 26.

2. See John Armstrong, 'Mobilized and Proletarian Diasporas', *American Political Science Review* 70 (2) (June 1976), pp. 393–408.

3. Chimen Abramsky, 'Russian Jews – A Bird's Eye View', *Midstream* 24 (December 1978), p. 35.

4. For a concise history of Russian Jewry prior to the revolution see S. Ettinger, 'The Jews in Russia at the Outbreak of the Revolution', in Lionel Kochan (ed.), *The Jews in Soviet Russia Since 1917*, 3rd edn (Oxford: Oxford University Press for the Institute of Jewish Affairs, 1979), pp. 15–29.

5. The designation of an ethnic group as a nationality, a national grouping, a nation, or some other term is a debate that I do not wish to enter here. I use the Soviet designation 'nationality' to refer to the various peoples living in the USSR. However, for the purpose of this study, any of the aforementioned terms should be considered interchangeable. For a discussion of the terminological issues at play

see Walker Connor, 'A Nation is a Nation, is a State, is an Ethnic Group is a . . .', *Ethnic and Racial Studies* 1 (4) (October 1978), pp. 377–400.

6. Solomon M. Schwarz, *The Jews in the Soviet Union*, with a Foreword by Alvin Johnson (Syracuse, New York: Syracuse University Press, 1951), p. 92.

7. See V. I. Lenin, *Natsionalny vopros* [The National Question] (Moscow: Gosudarstvennoe izdatelstvo, 1936); V. I. Lenin, 'O Prave natsii na samoopredeleniye' [On the Right of Nations to Self-Determination], in *Sochinenia* (Moscow: Gosudarstvennoe izdatelstvo politicheskoi literatury, 1948), vol. 20. For a detailed analysis of Lenin's pre-1917 theory of self-determination see Richard Pipes, *The Formation of the Soviet Union: Communism and Nationalism, 1917–1923*, rev. edn (Cambridge, Massachusetts: Harvard University Press, 1964), pp. 41–9.

8. See Pipes, *The Formation of the Soviet Union*, pp. 242–93.

9. The fifteen union-republics are: the Russian Federation (RSFSR), Ukrainian Soviet Socialist Republic (SSR), Belorussian SSR, Latvian SSR, Lithuanian SSR, Estonian SSR, Moldavian SSR, Georgian SSR, Armenian SSR, Azerbaijani SSR, Uzbek SSR, Turkmen SSR, Tadzhik SSR, Kirghiz SSR and Kazakh SSR. The Central Executive Committee of the USSR formally agreed to the formation of the Union by approving the Constitution of the USSR in July 1923. The Constitution was ratified by the Second All-Union Congress of Soviets in January 1924.

10. I. V. Stalin, 'Marksizm i natsionalny vopros' [Marxism and the National Question], *Sochineniya* [Works], vol. 2, 1907–1913 (Moscow: Gosudarstvennoe izdatelstvo politicheskoi literatury, 1946), p. 296. The English translation may be found in J. Stalin, 'Marxism and the National Question' (1913), in *Marxism and the National and Colonial Question: A Collection of Articles and Speeches* (New York: International, 1935?), p. 8.

11. V. I. Lenin, *Polnoe sobranie sochinenia* [Complete Collected Works] 5th edn, 55 vols, vol. 8 (September 1903–July 1904), pp. 27, 73, 75, 313; vol. 10 (March–July 1905), p. 267 (Moscow: Gosudarstvennoe izdatelstvo politicheskoi literatury, 1958–65; Stalin, 'Marxism and the National Question', pp. 3–61. Incorporated in this document, on pp. 35–46, is a subsection entitled, 'The Bund, Its Nationalism and its Separatism'. For the Russian, see I. V. Stalin, *Sochineniya*, vol. 2 (1907–1913), pp. 332–47.

12. 'Theses on the Immediate Tasks of the Party in Connection with the National Problem: Presented to the Tenth Congress of the Russian Communist Party, Endorsed by the Central Committee (1921)', in Stalin, *Marxism and the National and Colonial Question*, p. 96.

13. Benjamin Pinkus, *The Soviet Government and the Jews 1948–1967* (New York: Cambridge University Press with Hebrew University of Jerusalem–Institute of Contemporary Jewry and Israel Academy of Sciences and Humanities, 1984), pp. 12–13.

14. Through the early 1930s, 116 libraries, 47 reading clubs, 1000 Yiddish schools, 3 teachers' colleges, 5 agricultural institutes, 16

industrial-technical schools and 18 Yiddish theaters operated in the USSR. See William Orbach, 'A Periodization of Soviet Policy Towards the Jews', *Soviet Jewish Affairs* 12 (November 1982), p. 53; Judel Mark, 'Jewish Schools in Soviet Russia', in Gregor Aronson, Jacob Frumkin, Alexis Goldenweiser and Joseph Lewitan (eds), *Russian Jewry 1917–1967*, trans. Joel Carmichael (New York: Thomas Yoseloff, 1969), pp. 253–4; Schwarz, *The Jews in the Soviet Union*, p. 142.

15. The Evkom, the Commissariat for Jewish National Affairs, was part of the state bureaucracy and was also formed in 1918. Although the Evkom and the Evsektsiya were distinct bodies, their duties were similar. The Evkom was disbanded in 1924.

16. Norman Levine, 'Lenin on Jewish Nationalism', *Wiener Library Bulletin* 33 (1980), p. 49.

17. In writing on Judaism in the USSR Rothenberg stated that the Evsektsiya was 'notorious for its efforts to outdo even official Soviet policy in uprooting Jewish religion, Jewish consciousness, and Jewish feelings'. Joshua Rothenberg, 'Jewish Religion in the Soviet Union', in Kochan (ed.), *The Jews in Soviet Russia*, p. 177.

18. Orbach, 'A Periodization of Soviet Policy', p. 50.

19. Rothenberg, 'Jewish Religion', pp. 175–6. Rothenberg notes (p. 176) that Hebrew was the only language '*condemned unconditionally* in the Soviet Union'.

20. Rothenberg suggests that the Evsektsiya's activities were partially motivated by a desire to dispel anti-Semitism by showing that Jews were treated no differently from other ethnic groups. Rothenberg, 'Jewish Religion', p. 172.

21. The area known as the 'Pale of Settlement' consisted of the northeastern Ukraine (annexed in the seventeenth century), Polish territory partitioned in the eighteenth century, and the Black Sea coast (Crimea, New Russia and Bessarabia), which was colonized by the tsarist proconsul in the early nineteenth century. Under tsarist rule, the hundreds of thousands of Jews living in the Pale were forbidden to leave the area and were subject to restrictive measures.

22. The full name of the Komzet was the Committee of the Presidium of the Councils of Nationalities for Agricultural Settlement of Jewish Workers.

23. The Ozet was established by the Council of People's Commissars in December 1924 and began its operations in January 1925.

24. For first-hand statements regarding the strategic importance of populating the Soviet far east see Schwarz, *The Jews in the Soviet Union*, pp. 175, 179.

25. See Chimen Abramsky, 'The Biro-Bidzhan Project, 1927–1959', in Kochan (ed.), *The Jews in Soviet Russia*, pp. 70–1.

26. *Itogi Vsesoyuznoy perepisi naselenia 1959 goda SSSR: Svodny tom* (Moscow: Gosstatizdat, 1962), p. 204.

27. *Itogi Vsesoyuznoy perepisi naselenia 1970 goda*, 7 vols (Moscow: Statistika, 1972–74), vol. 4 (1973), p. 76.

28. *Vestnik statistiki*, no. 7 (1980), p. 50; *Natsionalny sostav naselenia: Chast*

II (Moscow: Finansy i statistika, 1989), p. 40.

29. The 1928 Five Year Plan initiated rapid industrialization in the USSR, bringing with it massive social transformation.

30. In 1926, 23.2 per cent of Jews were non-manual workers, 19 per cent were artisans, 11.8 per cent were traders, storekeepers, peddlers, etc., and 9.1 per cent were farmers. See Schwarz, *The Jews in the Soviet Union*, p. 20. (Schwarz cites 1926 census data as computed by L. Zinger and B. Engel, in *Idishe Bafelkerung fun FSSR in Tables un Diagrames*. See Schwarz, p. 23, note 36.) Statistics show that by 1937, Jews accounted for 7.5 per cent of all professional and semiprofessional workers in the USSR. 8.8 per cent of university teachers and research specialists, 10 per cent of graduate engineers, technicians, architects and journalists, 10.7 per cent of people in the arts and theater, and 15.9 per cent of physicians were Jews. See Schwarz, p. 300 (Schwarz cites a 6 March 1949 article in *Komsomolskaya pravda*).

31. 6846 Yiddish publications appeared during 1918–40. Abramsky, 'Russian Jews – A Bird's Eye View', p. 37. However, the number fell to 194 during 1941–48 and to zero between 1948 and 1958. Victor Zaslavsky and Robert J. Brym, *Soviet-Jewish Emigration and Soviet Nationality Policy* (London: Macmillan, 1983), p. 17. See also Benjamin Pinkus, 'Yiddish-Language Courts and Nationalities Policy in the Soviet Union', *Soviet Jewish Affairs*, no. 1 (November 1971), pp. 40–60.

32. Jacob Sonntag, 'Yiddish Writers and Jewish Culture in the USSR: Twenty Years After', *Soviet Jewish Affairs*, no. 2 (1972), p. 38, note 1.

33. Mordechai Altshuler, *Soviet Jewry Since the Second World War – Population and Social Structure*, Studies in Population and Urban Demography, no. 5 (New York: Greenwood, 1987), pp. 3–4.

34. Altshuler estimates that the total number of Jewish deaths in the USSR during World War II was between 2.5 and 3.3 million. See Altshuler, *Soviet Jewry*, p. 4. Altshuler bases his estimate on data in Robert A. Lewis, Richard H. Rowland and Ralph S. Clem, *Nationality and Population Change in Russia and the USSR: An Evaluation of Census Data, 1897–1970* (New York: Praeger, 1976), p. 300. Schwarz estimates that 1.3 million Jews died in the Ukraine, Belorussia and the occupied parts of the RSFSR alone. See Schwarz, *The Jews in the Soviet Union*, p. 232.

35. For a detailed discussion of the Jewish situation during the war and in its immediate aftermath see Schwarz, *The Jews in the Soviet Union*, pp. 219–38, 309–50.

36. Walter Kolarz suggested that the harshness of the Jewish policy may have been related to Stalin's assumption that Judaism could be destroyed more rapidly than other religions with 'better preserved' sociological roots. Walter Kolarz, *Religion in the Soviet Union* (New York: St. Martin's, 1961), p. 388.

37. For an interesting discussion of official anti-Semitism and the influence of Stalin's associates and their respective ideological views see Benjamin Pinkus, *The Jews of the Soviet Union: The History of a National Minority* (New York: Cambridge University Press, 1988), pp.

217–18.

38. See Yehoshua A. Gilboa, *The Black Years of Soviet Jewry 1939–1953*, trans. Yosef Shachter and Dov Ben-Abba (Boston: Little, Brown, 1971).

39. See Benjamin Pinkus, 'Soviet Campaigns Against "Jewish Nationalism" and "Cosmopolitanism", 1946–1953', *Soviet Jewish Affairs* 4 (Autumn 1974), pp. 53–72.

40. Czech Party leaders were also accused of disloyalty during the 1952 (Soviet-instigated) Slansky trial in Prague. Party Secretary Rudolf Slansky and several others (mostly Jews) were accused of being part of an 'international Jewish conspiracy' and of acting as British and American intelligence agents. They were sentenced to execution.

41. See Pinkus, *The Jews of the Soviet Union*, pp. 178–81.

42. Candid discussion of the specifically Jewish nature of the Doctors' Plot was not forthcoming in the Soviet Union for many years. In the *glasnost* period, the memoirs of Yakov Rapoport, who was arrested in connection with the Doctors' Plot, were published in *Druzhba narodov*, no. 4 (April 1988), pp. 222–45. Additionally, a straightforward account of the Doctors' Plot was published in *Moscow News*, no. 6 (14–21 February 1988), p. 16.

43. See Leonard B. Schapiro, 'Antisemitism in the Communist World', *Soviet Jewish Affairs*, no. 1 (1979), pp. 42–52; Bernard D. Weinryb, 'Antisemitism in Soviet Russia', in Kochan (ed.), *The Jews in Soviet Russia*, pp. 300–32.

44. See Harry G. Shaffer, *The Soviet Treatment of Jews* (New York: Praeger, 1974), pp. 15–18.

45. See 'Economic Trials: Death Sentences for Jews', *Jews in Eastern Europe* 2 (December 1962), pp. 16–23; William Korey, *The Soviet Cage: Anti-Semitism in Russia* (New York: Viking, 1973), pp. 78–9; Thomas E. Sawyer, *The Jewish Minority in the Soviet Union* (Boulder, Colorado: Westview, 1979), pp. 161–2.

46. See Salo W. Baron, *The Russian Jew Under Tsars and Soviets* (New York: Macmillan, 1964), pp. 332–5.

47. The passport system was adopted in 1932, and revised in 1953 and 1974. Citizens 16 years of age or older living in urban areas must carry a passport. The passport contains the name, age, address and picture of the holder, as well as his or her nationality (the fifth entry), work history, marital status, details of military service, permission to live in a particular place and other similar information. See 'Ob utverzhdenii Polozhenia o pasportnoi sisteme v SSSR' [On the Affirmation of the Regulations of the Passport System in the USSR], Decree no. 677, confirmed by the USSR Council of Ministers on 28 August 1974, in *Sobranie postanovlenii Pravitelstva SSSR*, no. 19 (1974), item 109. See also Leon Boim, 'The Passport System in the USSR and its Effect Upon the Status of Jews', in *Israel Yearbook on Human Rights* (Tel Aviv: Tel Aviv University, 1975), vol. 5, pp. 141–68; Victor Zaslavsky and Yuri Luryi, 'The Passport System in the USSR and Changes in Soviet Society', *Soviet Union/Union Soviétique* 6 (1979), pp. 137–53; Rasma Karklins, *Ethnic Relations in the*

USSR: The Perspective from Below (Boston: Allen & Unwin, 1986), pp. 31–2.

48.   Many people felt themselves to be Jews in name only.

49.   Paul Lendvai, 'Jews Under Communism', *Commentary* 52 (December 1971), p. 68.

50.   Ruth Okuneva, 'The Position of the Jews in the Soviet School Syllabus of World and Russian History: What Soviet Schoolchildren Read about the History of the Jewish People', in Shmuel Ettinger (ed.), *Anti-Semitism in the Soviet Union: Its Roots and Consequences*, 3 vols (Jerusalem: Hebrew University of Jerusalem, Centre for Research and Documentation of East-European Jewry, 1979–83), vol. 3 (1983), pp. 68–71. For examples of anti-Zionist publications see Yuri Ivanov, *Ostorozhno: Sionizm!* [Beware: Zionism!] (Moscow: Politizdat, 1969); V. A. Semenyuk, *Natsionalisticheskoe bezumie: Ideologia, politika i praktika mezhdunarodnogo sionizma* [Nationalist Madness: The Ideology, Politics and Practices of International Zionism] (Minsk: Belarus, 1976); Tsezar Samoilovich Solodar, *Dikaya polyn* [Wild Wormwood] (Moscow: Progress, 1980); Lev Korneev, *Klassovaya sushchnost sionizma* [The Class Essence of Zionism] (Kiev: Politizdat Ukrainy, 1982); Lidia Artemevna Modzhoryan, *Mezhdunarodny sionizm na sluzhbe imperialisticheskoy reaktsii: Pravovoy aspekt* [International Zionism in the Service of Imperialist Reaction: The Legal Aspect] (Moscow: Mezhdunarodnye otnoshenia, 1984); Ivan Vasilevich Prudnik, *Sionistskoe lobbi v SShA* [The Zionist Lobby in the USA] (Minsk: Belarus, 1984). For examples of anti-Semitic propaganda, see T. Kichko, *Iudaizm bez prikras* [Judaism without Embellishments] (Kiev: Akademia nauk URSR, 1963); V. Ya. Begun, *Vtorzhenie bez oruzhia* [Invasion without Arms] (Moscow: Molodaya gvardia, 1977).

51.   Leonard Schapiro, 'Introduction', in Kochan (ed.), *The Jews in Soviet Russia*, p. 8.

52.   *Vestnik statistiki*, no. 7 (1980), p. 41. The 1989 census reported figures on native language use, listing four categories of Jews. The data presented on speakers of the Jewish (i.e. Yiddish) language as a first language were Mountain Jews (73.2 per cent), Georgian Jews (90.7 per cent), Central Asian Jews (64.6 per cent) and all other Jews (11.1 per cent). The last category comprised 95 per cent of the total Jewish population. *Natsionalny sostav naselenia: Chast II*, p. 4.

53.   For detailed information see Lukasz Hirszowicz, 'The Soviet-Jewish Problem: Internal and International Developments, 1972–1976', in Kochan (ed.), *The Jews in Soviet Russia*, pp. 387–9; Pinkus, *The Jews of the Soviet Union*, pp. 273–83; Institute of Jewish Affairs, *The Position of Soviet Jewry: Human Rights and the Helsinki Accords 1985* (published on behalf of the International Council of the World Conference on Soviet Jewry in cooperation with the Jewish Communities Concerned, 1985), pp. 36–8.

2   The Birth of the Jewish Emigration Movement

1.   'Les Entretiens entre Moscou et les Socialistes français' [Meetings
     between Moscow and the French Socialist Party], *Les Réalités*, no. 136
     (1957), pp. 64–7, 101–4. A translation of this document may be
     found in Benjamin Pinkus, *The Soviet Government and the Jews
     1948–1967* (New York: Cambridge University Press with Hebrew
     University of Jerusalem–Institute of Contemporary Jewry and Israel
     Academy of Sciences and Humanities, 1984), pp. 54–8. The quoted
     excerpt is on p. 58 in Pinkus.
2.   See Part I of Marx's 'The German Ideology', translated and re-
     printed in English in Robert C. Tucker (ed.), *The Marx–Engels Reader*
     (New York: W. W. Norton, 1978), pp. 146–200. See also Chapter 1
     in Walker Connor, *The National Question in Marxist–Leninist Theory
     and Strategy* (Princeton: Princeton University Press, 1984), pp. 5–27.
3.   See Benjamin Pinkus, 'National Identity and Emigration Patterns
     Among Soviet Jewry', *Soviet Jewish Affairs* 15 (November 1985), p. 12.
4.   Benjamin Pinkus, *The Jews of the Soviet Union: The History of a National
     Minority* (New York: Cambridge University Press, 1988), p. 310.
5.   See Yehoshua A. Gilboa, 'The 1948 Zionist Wave in Moscow', *Soviet
     Jewish Affairs*, no. 2 (November 1971), pp. 35–9.
6.   For full details see Pinkus, *The Jews of the Soviet Union*, pp. 312–14.
7.   Approximately 6934 emigration visas for Israel were granted during
     1948–67. Z. Alexander, 'Immigration to Israel from the USSR', in
     Israel Yearbook on Human Rights (Tel Aviv: Tel Aviv University, 1977),
     vol. 7 special supplement, p. 319. (Z. Alexander is a pseudonym for
     Zvi Nezer.) In the absence of statistics issued by the Soviet author-
     ities, the number of Israeli entry visas processed by the Dutch
     Embassy in Moscow (which represented Israel's interests in the
     USSR from 1967 to 1990) serves as a reliable guide to the number of
     exit visas issued by the USSR. Unless otherwise stated, all figures
     cited in this chapter for the number of Israeli visas granted to Soviet
     Jews may be found in Alexander.
8.   For example, see 'Les Entretiens entre Moscou et les Socialistes
     français', pp. 64–7, 101–4; *Jewish Chronicle* (23 August 1957); *New
     York Times* (25 September 1959), p. 14; *Pravda* (9 July 1960). When
     Brezhnev assumed power, similar statements continued to be made.
9.   Quoted in 'Many Jews are Reported Seeking to Leave Soviet', *New
     York Times* (2 January 1967), p. 8.
10. The statement was carried in *Pravda*, *Izvestia* and *Komsomolskaya
     pravda* on 5 December 1966, in *Moscow News* on 17 December and in
     various regional newspapers.
11. 'Many Jews are Reported Seeking to Leave Soviet', p. 8.
12. This figure is compiled from unpublished Israeli government
     sources.
13. The principal tenets of Soviet anti-Zionism are derived from 'The
     Protocols of the Elders of Zion', a forged manuscript that was
     allegedly adopted at the First Zionist Congress in 1897. The contem-

porary characterization of Zionism, derived from 'The Protocols', identifies Zionism as a racist, international counter-revolutionary movement that purportedly has gained control of Western mass media as part of its supposed plan of global domination. Zionism is labeled reactionary and imperialistic and is regularly equated with both fascism and Nazism. For citations to anti-Zionist writers and examples of their writing in the contemporary period see Zvi Gitelman, 'Moscow and the Soviet Jews: A Parting of the Ways', *Problems of Communism* 29 (January–February 1980), pp. 25–31; William Korey, 'The Soviet "Protocols of the Elders of Zion"', in *Anti-Semitism in the Soviet Union: Its Roots and Consequences*, 3 vols (Jerusalem: Hebrew University of Jerusalem, Centre for Research and Documentation of East-European Jewry, 1979–83), vol. 2: *Part I: Proceedings of the International Colloquium on Anti-Semitism in the Soviet Union [held in Paris, 18–19 March 1979]*, pp. 19–29. See also note 50, Chapter 1.

14. Zvi Gitelman's survey of Soviet press coverage of Zionism and Jewish topics from 1963 to 1977 reveals that the number of column inches and articles devoted to Zionism rose drastically after 1967, with Zionism comprising the subject of half, and in some years even more, of the articles on Jewish topics. See Gitelman, 'Moscow and the Soviet Jews', p. 26.

15. Scientific workers (*nauchnye rabotniki*) are those employed by universities, research institutes and the Academy of Sciences, without regard to field, i.e. in the social sciences, the humanities and the natural sciences. These percentages are based on statistics in *Narodnoe khozyaistvo SSSR v 1959 godu: Statisticheskii ezhegodnik* (Moscow: Statistika, 1960), p. 757; *Narodnoe khozyaistvo SSSR v 1968 godu: Statisticheskii ezhegodnik* (Moscow: Statistika, 1969), p. 697.

16. Mordechai Altshuler, *Soviet Jewry Since the Second World War – Population and Social Structure*, Studies in Population and Urban Demography, no. 5 (New York: Greenwood, 1987), p. 135; and derived from data in *Narodnoe khozyaistvo SSSR v 1968 godu: Statisticheskii ezhegodnik* (Moscow: Statistika, 1969), p. 694.

17. The 14 nationalities are the Germans, Poles, Koreans, Bulgarians, Greeks, Hungarians, Romanians, Kurds, Finns, Turks, Persians, Czechs, Baluchis and Slovaks. For a detailed discussion see I. Domal'skii, 'New Developments in Anti-Semitism', in *Anti-Semitism in the Soviet Union: Its Roots and Consequences*, vol. 1: *Proceedings of the Seminar on Soviet Anti-Semitism Held in Jerusalem on April 7–8, 1978*, pp. 255–71.

18. Some of the Jews who had applied to emigrate before the Six-Day War were asked by OVIR if they still wished to emigrate. Those who decided to reapply were given exit visas. See Alexander, 'Immigration to Israel', p. 286.

19. See Victor Zaslavsky and Robert J. Brym, *Soviet-Jewish Emigration and Soviet Nationality Policy* (London: Macmillan, 1983), p. 35.

20. Alexander, 'Immigration to Israel', p. 286.

21. For the tactics employed by the emigration activists see the discussion later in this chapter.

22. The term 'movement' is used loosely, for it includes divergent groups of Soviet Jews who often shared little more than the common goal of emigration.
23. For a history of the various dissident movements see Ludmilla Alexeyeva, *Soviet Dissent: Contemporary Movements for National, Religious, and Human Rights* (Middletown, Connecticut: Wesleyan University Press, 1985).
24. Article 13(2) of the Universal Declaration of Human Rights states: 'Everyone has the right to leave any country, including his own, and to return to his country'.
25. Article 12(2) of the International Covenant on Civil and Political Rights states: 'Everyone shall be free to leave any country, including his own'.
26. For an explanation of how the stress on collective interests affected attitudes toward emigration, see Alan Dowty, *Closed Borders: The Contemporary Assault on Freedom of Movement* (New Haven: Yale University Press, 1987), pp. 58–76.
27. For a full discussion of Soviet policy design and objectives regarding emigration in the early 1970s see Chapter 5.
28. Only 4235 Jews emigrated during 1968–70. The source of all figures referring to the number of Soviet-Jewish emigrants is the Soviet Jewry Research Bureau of the National Conference on Soviet Jewry (New York).
29. The notion of reducing the number of Jews in the USSR was not without precedent: Stalin's death in 1953 halted plans he was allegedly making for the wholesale deportation of Soviet Jewry. In Eastern Europe, the Gomulka regime in Poland had made Jews the scapegoat for its domestic problems and forced several thousand Jews to leave the country from July 1967 to May 1969.
30. Alexander, 'Immigration to Israel', p. 308.
31. Zaslavsky and Brym, *Soviet-Jewish Emigration*, pp. 32–4; Yochanan Altman and Gerald Mars, 'The Emigration of Soviet Georgian Jews to Israel', *Jewish Journal of Sociology* 26 (June 1984), pp. 35–45.
32. See the discussion in Chapter 5 on the Jackson–Vanik amendment.
33. The most explicit example of this sort of linkage was embodied in the Jackson–Vanik amendment, which is described in detail in Chapter 5. See also Paula Stern, *Water's Edge: Domestic Politics and the Making of American Foreign Policy*, Contributions in Political Science, no. 15 (Westport and London: Greenwood, 1979).
34. For information on the role of the West see Chapter 5.
35. The Jackson–Vanik amendment is discussed in Chapter 5. The Conference on Security and Cooperation in Europe (CSCE) process is discussed in Chapter 3.
36. The United States championed the cause of Soviet Jewry for several reasons. First, considerable domestic pressure from the activists' US supporters was exerted on the Congress and public support for Soviet Jewry impacted on the executive branch as well. Second, supporting the cause of Soviet Jewry dovetailed with the ideological agenda of the US. Third, Israeli–Soviet diplomatic relations were severed in 1967, leaving the Israeli government unable to deal

directly with the USSR on behalf of Soviet Jewry.

37. According to Adam Ulam, 'Probably no other aspect of the *rapprochement* with the US was subject to as much debate and lively disagreement within the Politburo as the question of whether and to what extent to humor the US on the Jewish question.' Adam Ulam, *Dangerous Relations* (New York: Oxford University Press, 1983), p. 80. Ulam has argued that '[w]ith mass terror no longer a viable option, the regime had every incentive to find other ways to get rid of the most vocal element among the malcontents.' (ibid., p. 81). The same view has been expressed by Shapiro, who wrote that factors occasioning Soviet policy on emigration include: 'the desire to get rid of Jewish activists and thus deprive local communities of the most dynamic and potentially dangerous elements'. See Leon Shapiro, 'An Outline of the History of Russian and Soviet Jewry 1912–1974', in S. M. Dubnow, *History of the Jews in Russia and Poland: From the Earliest Times Until the Present Day*, trans. I. Friedlaender, 3 vols (Philadelphia: Jewish Publication Society of America, 1916–20; reprint edn, New York: Ktav, 1975), vol. 3: *From the Accession of Nicholas II Until the Present Day*, p. 493.

38. See items referring to Soviet Jews in the *samizdat* journal *Khronika tekushchikh sobyty* [Chronicle of Current Events]. When this *samizdat* journal could no longer be published in the USSR, it began appearing in the West as *A Chronicle of Human Rights in the USSR*. See items referring to Soviet Jews in *A Chronicle of Human Rights in the USSR*, nos 1–6 (1972–73); 'Jewish Emigration from the USSR and the Policy of the Soviet Authorities', *A Chronicle of Human Rights in the USSR*, no. 19 (January–March 1976), pp. 38–52.

39. Imprisoned Jewish activists were generally known as 'prisoners of Zion', as opposed to 'prisoners of conscience'. The term 'prisoners of conscience' generally referred to imprisoned dissidents. In some cases, such as that of Anatoly Sharansky, individuals were imprisoned for their activities on behalf of the emigration and the dissident movements. For accounts containing information about Soviet Jewish 'prisoners of Zion', see Mark Ya. Azbel, *Refusenik: Trapped in the Soviet Union* (Boston: Houghton Mifflin, 1981); Martin Gilbert, *The Jews of Hope: The Plight of Soviet Jewry Today* (London: Macmillan, 1984); Lukasz Hirszowicz, 'The Soviet-Jewish Problem: Internal and International Developments, 1972–1976', in Lionel Kochan (ed.), *The Jews in Soviet Russia Since 1917*, 3rd edn (Oxford: Oxford University Press for the Institute of Jewish Affairs, 1979), pp. 366–409; Edward Kuznetsov, *Prison Diaries*, trans. Howard Spier with an Introduction by Leonard Schapiro (New York: Stein & Day, 1975); Philippa Lewis, 'The Jewish Question in the Open: 1968–71' in Kochan, *The Jews in Soviet Russia*, pp. 349–65; Joshua Rubenstein, *Soviet Dissidents: Their Struggle for Human Rights* (Boston: Beacon, 1980), pp. 153–85; Leonard Schroeter, *The Last Exodus* (New York: Universe, 1974); Natan Sharansky, *Fear No Evil*, trans. Stefani Hoffman (New York: Random House, 1988); Colin Shindler, *Exit Visa: Détente, Human Rights and the Jewish Emigration Movement in the*

USSR (London: Bachman & Turner, 1978); Telford Taylor, *Courts of Terror: Soviet Criminal Justice and Jewish Emigration* (New York: Vintage, 1976).

40. The charges included 'Treason' (Article 64 of the Criminal Code of the RSFSR and equivalent provision of the criminal codes of the other union-republics); 'Anti-Soviet Agitation and Propaganda' (Article 70); 'Circulation of Fabrications Known to be False Which Defame the Soviet State and Social System' (Article 190-1); 'Hooliganism' (Article 206); 'Engaging in Vagrancy or Begging or Leading Another Parasitic Way of Life' (Article 209); 'Illegal Making, Acquisition, Keeping, Carriage, or Marketing of Narcotics' (Article 224); or 'Evasion of Military Service by Self-Mutilation or Any Other Method' (Article 249).

41. Schroeter, *The Last Exodus*, pp. 39–49.

42. The Leningrad trial became an election issue in Italy, where Italian dock workers boycotted Soviet ships in protest against the harsh sentences. See Zvi Nezer, 'The Emigration of Soviet Jews', *Soviet Jewish Affairs* 15 (February 1985), p. 20.

43. For a full account of the Leningrad trial see *Exodus*, a *samizdat* journal that devotes an entire issue (number 4) to the Leningrad hijacking trial of December 1970. A complete translation may be found in *Soviet Jewish Affairs*, no. 1, supplement (June 1971), pp. 1–45.

44. See Herbert Kellner, 'Belgium', in *American Jewish Yearbook, 1972* (New York: American Jewish Committee, 1972; Philadelphia: Jewish Publication Society of America, 1972), vol. 73, p. 499; Abraham J. Bayer, 'American Response to Soviet Anti-Jewish Policies', in *American Jewish Yearbook, 1973* (New York: American Jewish Committee, 1973; Philadelphia: Jewish Publication Society of America, 1973), vol. 74, pp. 213–14; 'Dragunsky Proclaims Juridical Right of Jews to Emigrate', *Radio Free Europe Research*, USSR: Nationalities (24 February 1971). For a survey of the Soviet media reports on the Brussels Conference see 'Soviet Jews Reject the Brussels Provocation', *Soviet Weekly* (27 February 1971).

45. For example, see V. Mikhailov, 'Istoria odnogo padenia' [The Story of a Fall], *Sovetskaya Rossia* (6 October 1968); 'Soviet Jews' Disenchantment With Israel', TASS in English and in Russian for abroad (2 January 1971), in BBC *Summary of World Broadcasts* (5 January 1971), SU/3575/A4/1; 'Odessa Jews' Indignation at Letters from Tel Aviv', TASS in Russian for abroad (3 February 1971), in BBC *Summary of World Broadcasts* (5 February 1971), SU/3602/A4/5; 'Mify i deistvitelnosti sionistsky' [Zionist Myths and Realities], *Literaturnaya gazeta* (17 November 1971); 'Pravda o "zemle obetovannoy"' [The Truth about "the Promised Land"], *Literaturnaya gazeta* (12 January 1972); R. Brodsky, 'Sionistsky "rai" i deistvitelnost' [The Zionist "Paradise" and Reality], *Krasnaya zvezda* (12 September 1972); Anatoly Kurov, 'Sionistsky obraz zhizni' [The Zionist Way of Life], *Moskovskaya pravda* (17 February 1973), p. 3.

46. See 'Polozhenia o vezde v Soyuz Sovetskikh Sotsialisticheskikh Res-

publik i o vyezde iz Soyuza Sovetskikh Sotsialisticheskikh Respublik' [Regulations on Entry into and Exit from the USSR], Decree no. 660, confirmed by the USSR Council of Ministers, 19 June 1959, in *Sobranie postanovlenii Pravitelstva SSSR*, no. 13 (1959), item 80. Decree no. 660 was updated and superseded by new regulations (Decree no. 801, 22 September 1970) effective 1 January 1971, which may be found in *Sobranie postanovlenii Pravitelstva SSSR*, no. 18 (1970), item 139. Amendments to the 1970 decree are embodied in Decree no. 1064, dated 28 August 1986. Decree no. 1064 became effective 1 January 1987, and may be found in *Sobranie postanovlenii Pravitelstva SSSR*, Section One, no. 31 (1986), item 63, pp. 563–6.

47. For further details of the application process see 'Applying to Emigrate: Complicated Procedure', *Insight: Soviet Jews* 3 (June 1977); Leonard Schroeter, 'How They Left: Varieties of Soviet Jewish Exit Experience', *Soviet Jewish Affairs* 2 (Autumn 1972), pp. 9–16; United States, Congress, House, Committee on International Relations, *Implementation of the Final Act of the Conference on Security and Cooperation in Europe: Findings and Recommendations Two Years After Helsinki*, report by the Commission on Security and Cooperation in Europe, 95th Congress, 1st session, 23 September 1977, pp. 74–80; United States, Congress, House, Committee on International Relations, *Basket III – Implementation of the Final Act of the Conference on Security and Cooperation in Europe: Findings Eleven Years After Helsinki*, report by the Commission on Security and Cooperation in Europe, 100th Congress, 1st session, March 1987, pp. 33–7; Gerald F. O'Keefe, 'Soviet Legal Restrictions on Emigration', *Soviet Union/ Union Soviétique* 14 (3) (1987), pp. 301–41.

48. George Ginsburgs, 'Soviet Law and the Emigration of Soviet Jews', *Soviet Jewish Affairs* 3 (Spring 1973), pp. 10–11. Ginsburgs reported that employers feared that if they wrote a positive report they would be admonished for allowing a good worker to leave, and if they wrote a negative reference they would have to explain why a poor worker was permitted to retain his or her job. Consequently, many chose to write nothing at all.

49. Soviet emigration procedure requires prospective emigrants to secure written permission from their relatives remaining in the USSR (i.e. parents, dependants and children). In cases where maintenance obligations to family members do not pertain, absence of family consent is nonetheless one of the grounds on which permission has been denied. The 'Fundamental Principles of Legislation of the USSR and Union Republics on Marriage and the Family' (adopted by the USSR Supreme Soviet on 27 June 1968) stipulate in Articles 18 and 21 that unconditional maintenance obligations apply to parents only for children who are minors; or, in cases where the children are orphans, the obligations are transferred to the grandparents, brothers, sisters or step-parents. Spouses have an obligation to each other only if one of them is disabled or pregnant and in need of material assistance (Article 13). Parents only have an obligation to an adult child if that child is disabled (Article 18). Likewise, children

only have an obligation to parents who are incapable of working (Article 21). Obligations may be placed on other family members in the case of an adult relative in need of assistance (Article 21). See 'Osnovy zakonodatelstva SSSR i soyuznikh respublik o brake i seme' [Fundamental Principles of Legislation of the USSR and Union Republics on Marriage and the Family], adopted by the USSR Supreme Soviet, 27 June 1968, in *Vedomosti Verkhovnogo Soveta SSSR*, no. 27 (3 July 1968), item 241.

50. For instance, beginning in 1988, requirements concerning invitations were not strictly enforced. See Interview with R. A. Kuznetsov, Chief of OVIR, in *Argumenty i fakty*, no. 22 (28 May–3 June 1988), p. 8. (An English translation of this interview appears in *FBIS Daily Report: Soviet Union*, 13 June 1988, pp. 76–80.) A new draft law on entry to and exit from the USSR was under consideration by the Supreme Soviet at the time of this writing. If approved, this law would alter several aspects of the application process.

51. Until 1976 decisions on pending applications were thought to be made by the ministries of internal affairs of the union- and autonomous-republics. News reports in January 1976 indicated that decisions on emigration would henceforth be made by the local authorities responsible for internal affairs. (For example, see the interview given to Novosti Press Agency by Boris Shumilin, USSR Deputy Minister of Internal Affairs, in *Soviet News* (27 January 1976), pp. 35–6.) However, those refused permission to emigrate were told that decisions were handed down 'from above'. See *Implementation of the Final Act of the Conference on Security and Cooperation in Europe: Findings and Recommendations Two Years After Helsinki*, p. 74. See also Andrei Bezruchenko, '"Refuseniks" Still Being Refused', *Moscow News*, no. 9 (5–12 March 1989), p. 6.

52. George Ginsburgs, 'Current Legal Problems of Jewish Emigration from the USSR', *Soviet Jewish Affairs* 6 (Autumn 1976), p. 6; A. Gashunin, A. Zonis and Yu. Semenovski, 'Jewish Emigration: The Problem of Relatives', *Glasnost* (Moscow), nos 2, 3 and 4 (July 1987) [*samizdat* journal published in translation by The Center for Democracy, New York], p. 16.

53. Valery Chalidze, *To Defend These Rights: Human Rights and the Soviet Union*, trans. Guy Daniels (London: Collins & Harvill, 1975), p. 99.

54. *Implementation of the Final Act of the Conference on Security and Cooperation in Europe: Findings and Recommendations Two Years After Helsinki*, p. 179. In 1988 the Public Council, which was comprised of long-term refuseniks (Jews refused permission to emigrate), issued a list of shortcomings in OVIR's performance. According to the Public Council, the Moscow OVIR posted statutes on emigration in November 1988, but did not do so in its district offices. See *Newsbreak*, 23 January 1989 (newsletter of the National Conference on Soviet Jewry).

55. The fees documented when this book went to press were 30 rubles for exit visas to socialist countries, and 200 rubles for visas to non-socialist countries. If an emigrant forgoes her or his Soviet

citizenship the fees are increased to 50 rubles for persons emigrating to socialist countries and 500 rubles for those emigrating to non-socialist countries. See 'Getting an Exit Visa. . . . How are Human Contacts and the Reunification of Families to be Facilitated?', interview with Rudolf Kuznetsov, Chief of OVIR, in *New Times* (Moscow), no. 28 (20 July 1987), p. 26. In a 1988 interview Kuznetsov stated that fees, payable to the state only if permission to depart is granted, had been halved. See 'Interview with R. A. Kuznetsov, Chief of OVIR', *Argumenty i fakty*, no. 22 (28 May–3 June 1988), p. 8. A translation of this interview may be found in *FBIS Daily Report: Soviet Union*, 13 June 1988, pp. 76–80. See also 'Poshlina po delam, rassmatrivaemym organami Ministerstva vnutrennikh del SSSR i Ministerstva inostrannykh del SSSR' [Customs Duties Applicable to Cases under Consideration by Organs of the USSR Ministry of Internal Affairs and the USSR Ministry of Foreign Affairs], in *Byulleten normativnykh aktov Ministerstv i vedomstv SSSR*, no. 7 (July 1977), pp. 24–7. In addition to the customs duties, emigrants incur a variety of additional costs (e.g. transportation) and face restrictions on what they may take with them. The total cost of emigrating for each adult family member has reportedly ranged from 1300 to 1500 rubles, while the average monthly wage has ranged from 130 rubles in 1972 to 212 rubles in 1988. See *Narodnoe khozyaistvo SSSR v 1972 g.: Statisticheskii ezhegodnik* (Moscow: Statistika, 1972), p. 515; *Narodnoe khozyaistvo SSSR v 1988 g.: Statisticheskii ezhegodnik* (Moscow: Finansy i statistika, 1989), p. 81; *Implementation of the Final Act of the Conference on Security and Cooperation in Europe: Findings and Recommendations Two Years After Helsinki*, p. 84; Konstantin Zotov, 'Human Contacts After Helsinki: The USSR's Contribution', interview in *Soviet News* (17 June 1980), p. 183. (Zotov was head of OVIR at the time the interview was conducted).

56. There has been small-scale emigration from the Soviet Union to some East European countries, such as the former German Democratic Republic.

57. Fees assessed in connection with relinquishing Soviet citizenship also differed based on whether one's destination was a socialist or non-socialist country.

58. According to Sawyer, renunciation of Soviet citizenship was required in connection with some non-socialist countries Soviet authorities labeled 'fascist', including Israel, Spain, Portugal and South Africa. See Thomas E. Sawyer, *The Jewish Minority in the Soviet Union* (Boulder, Colorado: Westview, 1979), p. 191; 'Soviet "Education" Decree', *Jews in Eastern Europe* 5 (November 1972), pp. 55–6.

59. In a March 1989 interview, Yuri Reshetov, Chief of the USSR Ministry of Foreign Affairs, Office for International Humanitarian Cooperation and Human Rights, made the following comments: 'In fact, in a departure on an Israeli visa, the loss of Soviet citizenship does occur. Such a regulation of this question was adopted in the 1960s. This was influenced by an attempt to take into account the geopolitical feature associated with the fact that Soviet citizens who

on coming to Israel could be fighting the very next day after their arrival, with weapons in their hands, against the Arab people, which we could not allow. But, on the other hand, the resolution of this question was influenced by the psychology of stagnation and an acute reaction to the very fact of leaving the USSR, which we now view more calmly and in a more civilized way.' *Argumenty i fakty*, no. 12 (23–31 March 1989), p. 7 (as translated in *FBIS Daily Report: Soviet Union*, 4 April 1989, p. 6).

60. Beginning in 1987 tourism from the USSR to Israel based on family visits was made possible as a result of improved Soviet–Israeli relations. Soviet-Jewish emigrants were also permitted to visit the USSR as Israeli citizens.

61. Similarly, many dissidents forcibly expelled from the Soviet Union were issued visas for Israel in an effort to discredit the emigration movement and disgrace the dissidents. See Joshua Rubenstein, *Soviet Dissidents: Their Struggle for Human Rights* (Boston: Beacon, 1980), p. 183.

62. This figure is compiled from unpublished Israeli government data. Although invitations are generally sent in response to requests by Soviet Jews themselves, 'phantom invitations' were reportedly sent to Soviet Jews who had not requested them. In cases involving Soviet Jews who wished to emigrate but had no relatives in Israel, invitations were sent by people posing as their relatives. See Arthur Jay Klinghoffer with Judith Apter, *Israel and the Soviet Union: Alienation or Reconciliation?* (Boulder, Colorado: Westview, 1985), p. 110.

63. Samuel C. Oglesby, 'Soviet Emigration Policy: Exit Visas and Fees', Congressional Research Service, Library of Congress, E 190 FOR USSR 73-83F (11 April 1973), p. 6.

64. 'O vozmeshchenii grazhdanami SSSR, vyezzhayushchimi na postoyannoe zhitelstvo za granitsu, gosudarstvennykh zatrat na obuchenie' [On Reimbursement by Citizens of the USSR, Leaving for Permanent Residence Abroad, of State Expenditure for Education], in *Vedomosti Verkhovnogo Soveta SSSR*, no. 52 (27 December 1972), item 519. According to Alexander, a precedent for this action dates to the 1930s when Jews in the West were asked to pay from £130 to £150 for each Soviet-Jewish family emigrating to Palestine. See Alexander, 'Immigration to Israel from the USSR', p. 292, note 11.

65. A Council of Ministers order detailing the fee schedule and exemptions was printed in January 1973, in *Sobranie postanovlenii Pravitelstva SSSR*, no. 1 (1973), item 4.

66. For a discussion of the *numerus clausus* see Chapter 3. See also the discussion above in this chapter on limitations on Jewish admission to institutes of higher education.

67. The other instances were an additional 5400 rubles for a Candidate's degree and an additional 1700 rubles for each year of study in a graduate school (in cases where a dissertation was not defended).

68. Zev Katz, 'A New Soviet Export – Jews', *New York Times* (11 September 1972), p. 36; William Korey, *The Soviet Cage: Anti-Semitism in Russia* (New York: Viking, 1973), p. 317.

69. See B. Urlanis, 'Vozrast cheloveka: ekonomichesky aspekt', [A Person's Age: The Economic Aspect] *Literaturnaya gazeta* (29 July 1970), p. 10. This comment was made in connection with the financial effect of pensions on the state economy.
70. 'A Historical Aside on the New "Education Tax"', *Radio Liberty Research*, CRD 232/72 (4 September 1972). For a well documented and highly detailed discussion of the 'education tax' see 'The Soviet "Diploma Tax"', Institute of Jewish Affairs *Background Paper*, no. 24 (November 1972).
71. *Narodnoe khozyaistvo SSSR v 1972 g.: Statisticheskii ezhegodnik*, p. 515.
72. Cited in Korey, *The Soviet Cage*, p. 318. See also M. Alexandrovski, 'The Emigration of Jews from the USSR', *Radio Liberty Research*, RL 87/73 (19 March 1973), p. 4.
73. This legislation, known as the Jackson–Vanik amendment, is discussed in Chapter 5.
74. For details on how the tax was enforced see George Ginsburgs, 'Soviet Law and the Emigration of Soviet Jews', *Soviet Jewish Affairs* 3 (1973), p. 14; Hedrick Smith, 'Soviet Jews Say Exit is Still Restricted', *New York Times* (23 March 1973), p. 4; Hedrick Smith, 'Soviet Implies it Has Ended Exit Fees', *New York Times* (22 March 1973), pp. 1, 3.
75. Then Secretary of Treasury George Shultz stated that he had convinced General Secretary Leonid Brezhnev during meetings held on 11–14 March 1973 of the need for improvements in emigration if the Soviet Union expected favorable trade concessions from the US. Oglesby, 'Soviet Emigration Policy', p. 7.
76. Records on revenue from the tax during 15 October 1972 to 31 March 1973 showed that a total of 6 759 821 rubles were paid by only 1435 Soviet Jews, during a period when a total of more than 30 000 Jews emigrated. Alexander, 'Immigration to Israel from the USSR', p. 294.

3 Post-Zionist Emigration

1. 'Emigration from the USSR: Interview with Deputy Minister of Internal Affairs', *Soviet News* (27 January 1976), p. 35.
2. Grigori Freiman, 'A Soviet Teacher's "J'Accuse"', *New York Times Magazine* (25 November 1979), p. 122. This article was adapted from a longer *samizdat* piece.
3. The sum includes the total number of emigrants with Israeli visas during October 1968 through December 1979.
4. An exception to nationality-based emigration has been the emigration of the Pentecostals, who have emigrated because of religious persecution.
5. Z. Alexander, 'Immigration to Israel from the USSR', in *Israel Yearbook on Human Rights* (Tel Aviv: Tel Aviv University, 1977), vol. 7, special supplement, p. 333. (Z. Alexander is a pseudonym for Zvi Nezer.) During the years 1968–87 (with the exception of the period from October 1972 to October 1973), the first point of destination

for virtually all emigrants leaving the Soviet Union on Israeli visas was Vienna. In Vienna Jews were no longer under the auspices of the Soviet government and were free to continue on to Israel or to elect to go elsewhere. Starting in 1988 (and for the first time since 1973), several hundred Jews (723 in 1988) elected to emigrate via Bucharest, Romania, rather than through Vienna. The Israeli government announcement in June 1988 that it would issue Israeli entry visas exclusively from the Israeli Embassy in Bucharest in order to ensure that Soviet Jews immigrate to Israel, was ignored by the Dutch Embassy in Moscow (which represented Israel's interests in the USSR, including the administering of visas, from the time USSR–Israeli ties were severed in 1967 until the reopening of the Israeli Consulate in Moscow in January 1991). Israel did not obligate the Dutch Embassy to withhold Israeli visas from people wishing to fly to Vienna rather than to Bucharest. See *Jews in the U.S.S.R.* 17 (5 May 1988), p. 1. The Israeli decision was controversial because, if it had been enforced, it would have forced emigrants to go to Israel. The decision crystallized a split within the international Jewish community between those who believed that Jews should immigrate to Israel and those who argued that the issue was about freedom of movement, without regard to destination. By 1989, changes in US policy had made the debate moot. For further information, see the discussion later in this chapter on the reintroduction of the Bucharest transit facility in 1988 and on the elimination of the US as a drop-out option in 1989.

6. These statistics are from the World Conference on Soviet Jewry.
7. Proponents of the barometer thesis explain the drop in the number of emigrants during these years as a reaction to the passage of the Jackson–Vanik amendment. For a full discussion of this point see Chapter 5.
8. See the Introduction for the regional distribution of the Jewish population.
9. See 'Leaving the Soviet Union: The Emigrant's Experience', in United States, Congress, House, Committee on International Relations, *Implementation of the Final Act of the Conference on Security and Cooperation in Europe: Findings and Recommendations Two Years After Helsinki*, report by the Commission on Security and Cooperation in Europe, 95th Congress, 1st session, 23 September 1977, p. 183; Victor Zaslavsky and Robert J. Brym, *Soviet-Jewish Emigration and Soviet Nationality Policy* (London: Macmillan, 1983), pp. 49–51; James R. Millar, 'History, Method, and the Problem of Bias', in James R. Millar (ed.), *Politics, Work, and Daily Life in the USSR: A Survey of Former Soviet Citizens* (New York: Cambridge University Press, 1987), pp. 19–20.
10. Zaslavsky and Brym, *Soviet-Jewish Emigration*, pp. 61–2. Similar results were reported by Gitelman in a survey conducted in 1976 among 244 recent Soviet immigrants in Detroit. Gitelman reported that the heartlanders indicated they left the USSR for reasons of political alienation and anti-Semitism, while the *zapadniki* (wester-

ners) were motivated by family and economic considerations. See Zvi Gitelman, 'Soviet Jewish Emigrants: Why Are They Choosing America?', *Soviet Jewish Affairs* 7 (Spring 1977), pp. 41–3.

11. See the statement by the writer Vyacheslav Kondratyev, quoted in note 49, Chapter 5.

12. Theodore H. Friedgut, 'Soviet Jewry: The Silent Majority', *Soviet Jewish Affairs* 10 (May 1980), pp. 17–19.

13. For example, a *numerus clausus* policy was outlined in a 1970 book by Soviet ideologist V. Mishin. Mishin called for the reduction of 'overrepresented' specialists with higher education and an equalization in the development of all peoples and nations in the USSR based on the principle of proletarian internationalism. Vasilii Mishin, *Obshchestvenny progress* [Social Progress] (Gorky: Volgo-Viatskoye, 1970), cited in William Korey, 'The Legal Position of Soviet Jewry: A Historical Enquiry', in Lionel Kochan (ed.), *The Jews in Soviet Russia Since 1917*, 3rd edn (Oxford: Oxford University Press for the Institute of Jewish Affairs, 1978), p. 102.

14. Aleksandr Voronel, 'The Aliyah of Russian Intellectuals', *Midstream* 22 (April 1976), pp. 29–30.

15. *Moskva v tsifrakh (1966–1970 gg.): Kratkii statisticheskii sbornik* (Moscow: Statistika, 1972), p. 132; *Moskva v tsifrakh 1980: Statisticheskii ezhegodnik* (Moscow: Statistika, 1980), p. 172; *Moskva v tsifrakh 1981: Statisticheskii ezhegodnik* (Moscow: Finansy i statistika, 1981), p. 186.

16. For a personal account on the restricted admission of Jews to mathematics faculties see Grigori Freiman, 'A Soviet Teacher's "J'Accuse"', *New York Times Magazine* (25 November 1979), pp. 122–7. See also Boris Smolar, *Soviet Jewry Today and Tomorrow* (New York: Macmillan, 1971), pp. 71–7.

17. Zvi Gitelman, 'Moscow and the Soviet Jews: A Parting of the Ways', *Problems of Communism* 29 (January–February 1980), p. 32.

18. The Refugee Act of 1980 omitted the ideological and geographical restrictions that previously favored conditional entry for refugees from Communist-dominated areas and the Middle East, and instead considered a refugee to be a person with a 'well-founded fear of persecution'. The definition of 'refugee' incorporated in the Refugee Act of 1980 basically conforms to that of the United Nations Protocol Relating to the Status of Refugees and the United Nations Convention Relating to the Status of Refugees. See United States, Congress, *Refugee Act of 1980*, Pub. L. 96–212, in *United States Code Congressional and Administrative News*, vol. 1 (1980), pp. 94, Stat. 102–18.

19. David Harris, 'A Note on the Problem of the "Noshrim"', *Soviet Jewish Affairs* 6 (Autumn 1976), p. 110. ('*Noshrim*' is the Hebrew word meaning 'drop-outs'.) The decision of several thousand Soviet Jews to re-immigrate to another country after first immigrating to Israel also influenced subsequent emigrants in their choice of adopted country; Israeli sources put the number of Soviet Jews who first immigrated to Israel and subsequently chose to re-immigrate elsewhere at 10 000 (3.8 per cent) for the period from 1968 to 1985. In a

1985 article Pinkus estimated that 12 000–18 000 (4.5–6.8 per cent) of Soviet Jews had left Israel. See Benjamin Pinkus, 'National Identity and Emigration Patterns Among Soviet Jewry', *Soviet Jewish Affairs* 15 (November 1985), p. 25.

20. The first Soviet consular mission to Israel in 20 years arrived in July 1987 and the first Israeli consular mission to the USSR in 21 years arrived in July 1988. Although the official reason for the Israeli mission to the USSR was to inspect the Israeli consular office that the Dutch Embassy had managed on its behalf since Soviet–Israeli ties were severed in 1967, it was reported that Soviet officials unofficially disclosed that they viewed the visit as an opportunity to improve the Soviet Union's influence with Israel and relations with American Jews. See Bill Keller, 'Israelis in Moscow: A Bit of Banter, and Prayers', *New York Times* (30 July 1988), p. A4.
21. For further details see note 5 above.
22. See for example, 'Israeli Seeks to Control Emigrés' Destination', *New York Times* (20 June 1988), p. A14. Only a small number of strongly Zionist Jews elected to emigrate via Bucharest. Numbers of Jews emigrating through Bucharest are available from the National Conference on Soviet Jewry (New York).
23. For information on the debate over the destination of the emigrants see Robert Pear, 'Closing the Door Halfway for Emigrant Soviet Jews', *New York Times* (24 September 1989), sec. 4, p. 3; Yoram Dinstein, 'Free Entry To All Comers', *Jerusalem Post* (16 January 1989), p. 4; 'A Rift in the Making', *Jewish Week* (13 January 1989). The change in US practice is discussed at length in Chapter 5.
24. See Gitelman, 'Moscow and the Soviet Jews', pp. 32–3.
25. Additional reasons for large-scale emigration despite increasing harassment in this period and a full discussion of Soviet emigration policy in general may be found in Chapter 5.
26. The only numerically significant exceptions involving other nationalities (religious and bi-national marriage cases notwithstanding) are the emigration of Armenians and Soviet Germans.
27. 'The Decline of Soviet Jewish Emigration in 1980', Institute of Jewish Affairs *Research Report*, no. 17 (October 1980), p. 2.
28. The number of refuseniks had risen to approximately 11 000 by the end of 1985. Of this number there were approximately 1196 refuseniks who by June of 1986 had been waiting 10 years or more for exit visas. *The Position of Soviet Jewry 1983–1986: Report on the Implementation of the Helsinki Final Act since the Madrid Follow-Up Conference* (London: Institute of Jewish Affairs on behalf of the International Council of the World Conference on Soviet Jewry in Cooperation with the Jewish Communities Concerned, 1986), p. 11, and compiled from data in the aforementioned source on pp. 64–77. Emigration in 1987 and 1988 significantly reduced the number of refuseniks. For complete information on refuseniks after 1986 see Chapter 5.
29. For information on refuseniks see, for example, Mark Ya. Azbel, *Refusenik: Trapped in the Soviet Union* (Boston: Houghton Mifflin,

1981); Martin Gilbert, *The Jews of Hope: The Plight of Soviet Jewry Today* (London: Macmillan, 1984); Natan Sharansky, *Fear No Evil*, trans. Stefani Hoffman (New York: Random House, 1988).

30. The phrase 'provided by law' recurs in 'restrictive exception' provisions in other human rights treaties and has a specific meaning. In order to prevent unfair practices, such as penalizing individuals on the basis of previously non-existent laws, it stipulates that only prospective legislation (i.e. a law applicable only to cases arising after its enactment) may be used to curtail freedom of movement. The broad construction of the text of Article 12(3) means that any Soviet law that is not applied retroactively and is consistent with other ICPR rights may be used to restrict emigration.

31. See Article 12(3) of the International Covenant on Civil and Political Rights.

32. General Secretary Gorbachev stated on the eve of his October 1985 visit to France that the declassification period for state secrets ranged from 5 to 10 years. Nonetheless, people who have been removed from classified work for longer than a 5 to 10 year period have been routinely denied emigration permits. See 'M. S. Gorbachev Address on French Television', in *FBIS Daily Report: Soviet Union* 3 (2 October 1985), p. G10; Institute of Jewish Affairs, *Human Contacts, Reunion of Families and Soviet Jewry* (published on behalf of the International Council of the World Conference on Soviet Jewry in Cooperation with the Jewish Communities Concerned, 1986), p. 31. The state secrets classification and time limitations are to be addressed by a new law on entry into and exit from the USSR, which by September 1990 had yet to be passed by the Supreme Soviet.

33. See Jeffrey Barist, Owen C. Pell, Eugenia Oshman and Matthew E. Hamel, 'Who May Leave: A Review of Soviet Practice Restricting Emigration on Grounds of Knowledge of "State Secrets" in Comparison with Standards of International Law and the Policies of Other States', *Hofstra Law Review* 15 (3) (Spring 1987), pp. 434–7; Gerald F. O'Keefe, 'Soviet Legal Restrictions on Emigration', *Soviet Union/Union Soviétique* 14 (3) (1987), pp. 301–41.

34. See English translation, 'Types of Information Classified as State Secrets by a Decree of the USSR Council of Ministers, 28 April 1956', in Elizabeth C. Scheetz, 'State Secrets and the Right to Emigrate', *Radio Liberty Research*, RL 82/77 (13 April 1977), pp. 7–10. A 1947 decree on state secrets, which was superseded by the 1956 decree was issued in *Postanovlenie Soveta Ministrov SSSR* (8 June 1947). For an English translation see 'On the Establishment of a List of Information Comprising State Secrets, Disclosure of Which Shall be Punished by Law', in Scheetz, 'State Secrets and the Right to Emigrate'.

35. Individual cases are chronicled in 'Annex I', *Soviet Jewry and the Implementation of the Helsinki Final Act*, Report prepared on behalf of the Ongoing Presidium and Steering Committee of the World Conference on Soviet Jewry in Cooperation with the Jewish Communities Concerned (May 1977), unpublished report archived at the

Institute of Jewish Affairs, London.

36. See for example *The Position of Soviet Jewry 1977–1980: Report on the Implementation of the Helsinki Final Act Since the Belgrade Follow-Up Conference* (London: World Conference on Soviet Jewry in Cooperation with Jewish Communities Concerned, 1980). The best known case in the West of a Soviet-Jewish political prisoner during the latter half of the 1970s was that of Anatoly Sharansky, who was active in both the Soviet-Jewish emigration movement and the Moscow Helsinki Watch Group. Accused in 1977 of spying for the CIA, Sharansky was tried and convicted in 1978 of 'Treason' and 'Anti-Soviet Agitation and Propaganda' under Articles 64-a and 70 respectively of the RSFSR Criminal Code. He was sentenced to 3 years in prison and 10 years in a special regime camp. After serving 8 years of his sentence, Sharansky was included in what was termed an East–West spy exchange and freed on 11 February 1986.

37. For extensive coverage of individual cases see *Jews in the U.S.S.R.* (a news bulletin published by the Contemporary Jewish Library, London, under the auspices of the National Council for Soviet Jewry of the United Kingdom and Ireland), vols 1–2; Jewish Telegraphic Agency (JTA) reports throughout the period concerned.

38. 'Military Conscription: Why Some Prefer Jail', *Insight: Soviet Jews* 1 (November 1975), p. 5. Draft evasion was punishable under Article 80 of the RSFSR Criminal Code and under the equivalent articles in the criminal codes of the other union-republics.

39. The Final Act is often referred to as the 'Helsinki Accord(s)', the 'Helsinki Act', or simply 'Helsinki'.

40. For information on the history leading up to the CSCE, see Mojimir Povolny, 'The Soviet Union and the European Security Conference', *Orbis* 18 (Spring 1974), pp. 201–30; Harold S. Russell, 'The Helsinki Declaration: Brobdingnag or Lilliput?', *American Journal of International Law* 70 (April 1976), pp. 244–6.

41. The Final Act is not a treaty; it contains a provision that declares it ineligible for registration as a treaty under Article 102 of the United Nations Charter. For an interesting discussion of this point, see Suzanne Bastid, 'The Special Significance of the Helsinki Final Act', in Thomas Buergenthal (ed.), assisted by Judith R. Hall, *Human Rights, International Law and the Helsinki Accord* (Montclair, New Jersey: Allanheld, Osmun for the American Society of International Law, 1977), p. 13. Interestingly, the USSR wanted a legally binding instrument because it thought anything less would dilute the Final Act's impact. For its part, the US favored non-binding status which would enable it to conclude an international agreement without Congressional consent. See Russell, 'The Helsinki Declaration', pp. 246–9. Ironically, the USSR fell short of many of its Basket Three commitments while the US became extremely active in demanding compliance.

42. Oscar Schachter, 'Editorial Comment: The Twilight Existence of Nonbinding International Agreements', *American Journal of International Law* 71 (April 1977), p. 300. Louis Henkin wrote: 'That the

Helsinki Accord is not legally binding means there are no legal
remedies for their [sic] violation; adherence to the Accord is
nonetheless an international undertaking and violation of them [sic]
is a proper basis for international (non-legal) recourse and remedy
by other participants'. Louis Henkin, 'Human Rights and "Domestic
Jurisdiction"', in Buergenthal, *Human Rights*, p. 25.

43.   See, for example, 'Interview with Head of USSR Visa Department
[Col. Vladimir Obidin]', TASS in Russian for abroad, 20 January
1977, in BBC *Summary of World Broadcasts* (21 January 1977),
SU/5418/C/1 (A1, B).

44.   See 'Polozhenia o vezde v Soyuz Sovetskikh Sotsialisticheskikh Respublik i o vyezde iz Soyuz Sovetskikh Sotsialisticheskikh Respublik'
[Regulations on Entry into and Exit from the USSR], Decree no.
660, confirmed by the USSR Council of Ministers, 19 June 1959, in
Sobranie postanovlenii Pravitelstva SSSR, no. 13 (1959), item 80.
Decree no. 660 was updated and superseded by new regulations
(Decree no. 801, 22 September 1970) effective 1 January 1971,
which may be found in *Sobranie postanovlenii Pravitelstva SSSR*, no. 18
(1970), item 139. Amendments to the 1970 decree are embodied in
Decree no. 1064, dated 28 August 1986. The new decree became
effective 1 January 1987, and may be found in *Sobranie postanovlenii
Pravitelstva SSSR*, Section One, no. 31 (1986), item 163, pp. 563–6.

45.   See Principle VII of the Final Act's opening 'Declaration on Principles Guiding Relations between Participating States'. Soviet legal
theorists such as G. I. Tunkin raised no argument with the premise
that UN Charter Articles 55 and 56 establish a legal obligation to
respect human rights. See G. I. Tunkin, *Theory of International Law*,
trans., with an Introduction by William E. Butler (London: George
Allen & Unwin, 1974). However, problems arise because the UN
Charter does not *define* human rights. The UDHR does define a set
of human rights but: (a) the UDHR was originally not thought to
be legally binding and even now is controversial; (b) the rights
expressed in the UDHR do not always reappear in later treaties so
one cannot exclusively take the UDHR as the last word; and (c) the
UDHR rights themselves are unclear (e.g. the right to life contains
no mention of any exceptions for capital punishment). As a result,
certain rights included in the UDHR are subject to exceptions not
expressly stated. Consequently, the soundest legal basis for clearly
establishing particular human rights, together with their full definition, is a legally binding treaty, accepted by the respondent states.
The ICPR and its companion, the International Covenant on
Economic, Social, and Cultural Rights, are therefore the best examples of formal, binding documents guaranteeing human rights.

46.   See Opening Principle X: Fulfillment in Good Faith of Obligations
under International Law.

47.   The sixth Opening Principle of the Final Act addresses 'Non-
intervention in internal affairs' and states that '[t]he participating
States will refrain from any intervention, direct or indirect, individual or collective, in the internal or external affairs falling within

the domestic jurisdiction of another participating State.'
48. The USSR ratified the ICPR but it has accepted neither of the optional complaint provisions: the Optional Protocol to the International Covenant on Civil and Political Rights, which grants individuals the right to petition the UN Human Rights Committee in relation to alleged violations; and Article 41 of the ICPR, which provides an optional procedure for inter-state complaints. However, the Soviet Union announced in March 1989 that it would accept the binding arbitration of the International Court of Justice in disputes arising from the following five human rights documents sponsored by the United Nations: Convention on the Prevention and Punishment of the Crime of Genocide (1948), Convention on the Political Rights of Women (1953), International Convention on the Elimination of All Forms of Racial Discrimination (1966); International Agreement for the Suppression of the White Slave Traffic (1949); Convention Against Torture and Other Cruel, Inhuman or Degrading Treatment or Punishment (1984). See Paul Lewis, 'Soviet To Accept World Court Role in Human Rights', *New York Times* (9 March 1989), pp. A1, A15.
49. The first follow-up meeting was held in Belgrade from October 1977 to March 1978. The second follow-up meeting took place in Madrid, lasting from November 1980 through September 1983. The third follow-up conference was held in Vienna from November 1986 to January 1989.
50. The Concluding Document stated little more than that the signatories agreed to hold further meetings. See 'Appendix D – Text of the Concluding Document of the Belgrade Meeting 1977 of Representatives of the Participating States of the Conference on Security and Cooperation in Europe, Held on the Basis of the Provisions of the Final Act relating to the Followup to the Conference, March 8, 1978', pp. 74–6 in United States, Congress, House, Committee on International Relations, Commission on Security and Cooperation in Europe, *The Belgrade Followup Meeting to the Conference on Security and Cooperation in Europe: A Report and Appraisal*, (Washington, DC: US Government Printing Office, 17 May 1978).
51. For the Concluding Document of the Madrid CSCE Review Meeting held from 11 November 1980 to 9 September 1983, see Conference on Security and Co-operation in Europe, *Madrid CSCE Review Meeting*, in CIS Microfiche 1983: J892-4, pp. 64–103.
52. See US Commission on Security and Cooperation in Europe, *Concluding Document of the Vienna Follow-Up Meeting* (Washington, DC: US Government Printing Office, January 1989), pp. 25–9. The details of the Vienna Concluding Document are discussed later in this chapter.
53. Soviet-German emigration dropped from 6954 (1980), to 3773 (1981), 2071 (1982), 1447 (1983), 913 (1984), 460 (1985) and increased somewhat to 753 (1986). The source for German emigration statistics is the Deutsches Rotes Kreuz [German Red Cross], Hamburg. Armenian emigration fell from 6109 (1980) to 1905 (1981), 339 (1982), 194 (1983), 88 (1984) and increased slightly to

110 (1985) and to 246 (1986). The source for statistics on Armenian emigration is the US State Department.

54. See paragraph 24 in Decree no. 1064, 'O vnesenii dopolneniya v Polozhenia o vezde v Soyuz Sovetskikh Sotsialisticheskikh Respublik i o vyezde iz Soyuza Sovetskikh Sotsialisticheskikh Respublik' [On the Introduction of Additions to the Regulations on Entry Into the Union of Soviet Socialist Republics and on Exit From the Union of Soviet Socialist Republics], 28 August 1986 (effective 1 January 1987) in *Sobranie postanovlenii Pravitelstva SSSR*, Section One, no. 31 (1986), item 163, pp. 563–6. The application of the so-called first-degree relative rule was first noticed in Odessa, and by the end of 1979 was reported as being enforced in Kharkov, Kiev, Kishinev and Tashkent. See United States, Congress, House, Committee on International Relations, *Implementation of the Final Act of the Conference on Security and Cooperation in Europe: Findings and Recommendations Five Years After Helsinki*, Report by the Commission on Security and Cooperation in Europe, 96th Congress, 2nd session, 1 August 1980, p. 208.

55. United States, Congress, House, Committee on International Relations, *Implementation of the Final Act of the Conference on Security and Cooperation in Europe: Findings and Recommendations Seven Years After Helsinki*, report by the Commission on Security and Cooperation in Europe, 97th Congress, 2nd session, November 1982, p. 165.

56. United States, Commission on Security and Cooperation in Europe, *Implementation of the Final Act of the Conference on Security and Cooperation in Europe: Findings and Recommendations Seven Years After Helsinki*, p. 167; United States, Congress, House, Committee on International Relations, *Implementation of the Final Act of the Conference on Security and Cooperation in Europe: Findings Eleven Years After Helsinki*, Report by the Commission on Security and Cooperation in Europe, 100th Congress, 1st session, March 1987, pp. 35–6.

57. Z. Alexander, 'Jewish Emigration from the USSR in 1980', *Soviet Jewish Affairs* 11 (May 1981), p. 8; Elie Valk, 'Jewish Emigration from the USSR: Up in 1979 – Down in 1980', research report, rev. (New York: Soviet Jewry Research Bureau of the National Conference on Soviet Jewry, 15 June 1980), p. 1.

58. See Chapter 2, note 52.

59. See United States, Commission on Security and Cooperation in Europe, *Implementation of the Final Act of the Conference on Security and Cooperation in Europe: Findings and Recommendations Seven Years After Helsinki*, p. 166; Bernard Weinraub, 'The Kremlin is Said to Seize Mail From the U.S. for Jews', *New York Times* (9 June 1983), p. A10. During or shortly after the end of 1984, decreasing requests for invitations (prompted by limited permissions) reduced the number of invitations being sent to the USSR and postal problems became less frequent.

60. BBC jamming ceased in January 1987 and VOA jamming was stopped in March 1987. See *Twenty-second Semiannual Report by the President to the Commission on Security and Cooperation in Europe on the*

Implementation of the Helsinki Final Act, October 1, 1986–April 1, 1987,
Special Report no. 168 (August 1987), p. 33; *Twenty-third Semiannual
Report by the President to the Commission on Security and Cooperation in
Europe on the Implementation of the Helsinki Final Act, April 1, 1987–
October 1, 1987,* Special Report no. 172 (February 1988), p. 37.
Jamming of Radio Liberty's Russian-language broadcasts stopped in
December 1988. Jamming of Radio Israel also stopped in 1988.

61. See United States, Commission on Cooperation in Europe, *Implementation of the Final Act of the Conference on Security and Cooperation in
Europe: Findings and Recommendations Seven Years After Helsinki,* p.
173.

62. See 'O vnesenii izmenenii i dopolnenii v nekotorye zakonodatelnye
akti SSSR ob ugolovnoy otvetstvennosti i ugolovnom sudoproiz-
vodstve' [On the Introduction of Alterations and Additions to Some
of the USSR Legislative Acts on Criminal Responsibility and Criminal Legal Proceedings], Decree of the Presidium of the USSR
Supreme Soviet, 11 January 1984, in *Vedomosti Verkhovnogo Soveta
SSSR,* no. 3 (18 January 1984), item 58.

63. See, for example, 'The Increased Arrests of Soviet Jews in 1981',
Institute of Jewish Affairs, *Research Report,* no. 21 (December 1981).

64. The purpose of the Committee was stated in an appeal issued on 1
April 1983 calling for the Committee's creation. See *Pravda* (1 April
1983). For information about the Anti-Zionist Committee see *Anti-
Zionist Committee of Soviet Public Opinion: Aims and Tasks* (Moscow:
Novosti, 1983); Theodore H. Friedgut, 'Soviet Anti-Zionism and
Antisemitism – Another Cycle', *Soviet Jewish Affairs* 14 (February
1984), pp. 11–22; Julia Wishnevsky, '"Anti-Zionist Committee"
Formed in Soviet Union', *Radio Liberty Research,* RL 170/83 (26 April
1983); Lukasz Hirszowicz and Howard Spier, 'Eight Soviet Jews
Appeal for the Creation of an Anti-Zionist Committee', Institute of
Jewish Affairs, *Research Report,* no. 6 (April 1983); Howard Spier,
'The Soviet Anti-Zionist Committee – Further Developments', Insti-
tute of Jewish Affairs, *Research Report,* no. 13 (August 1983);
Howard Spier, 'Fulfilling a Restricted Role: The Soviet Anti-Zionist
Committee in 1984', Institute of Jewish Affairs, *Research Report,* no.
16 (December 1984).

65. See *Pochemu my vernulis na rodinu: svidetelstva reemigrantov* [Why We
Returned to the Motherland: Testimony of Re-emigrants] (Moscow:
Progress, 1983); David Abramovich Dragunsky, 'O chem govoryat
pisma' [What the Letters Say] (Moscow: Anti-Zionist Committee of
the Soviet Public, 1984). For further information see Spier, 'Fulfilling a Restricted Role'. In 1984 the prominence of the Anti-Zionist
Committee was downgraded, and reflecting changes in the USSR
under Gorbachev's leadership, it was reported in December 1987
that the Committee was to be dissolved. However, at the time this
book went to press in the autumn of 1990, the Committee had not
been disbanded.

66. *Literaturnaya gazeta* (22 June 1983). Zivs also declared: 'When parents
are, indeed, reunited with the children they lost during the war,

there is no question of treason. But if we are discussing a situation in which a person fell into the net of lying Zionist propaganda, I, as a lawyer, would say it is an unpatriotic act incompatible with our moral principles and disapproved of by Soviet society and by the absolute majority of the Jewish citizens of our country.' *Literaturnaya gazeta* (22 June 1983). The full text of the press conference, 'Press Conference of the Anti-Zionist Committee of Soviet Public Opinion', may be found in *Anti-Zionist Committee of Soviet Public Opinion: Aims and Tasks*, pp. 3–27.

67. For information on the Anti-Fascist Committee see Chapter 1.
68. The Committee was composed of 37 members, with a Presidium of 13 chosen from among them. Colonel-General David Dragunsky was appointed Chairman and Samuil Zivs was made First Deputy Chairman. Both Dragunsky and Zivs are Jewish, as are 6 other founding members of the Committee.
69. For appeals by refuseniks see *Jews in the U.S.S.R.*
70. For example, see United States, Commission on Security and Cooperation in Europe, *Implementation of the Final Act of the Conference on Security and Cooperation in Europe: Findings and Recommendations Five Years After Helsinki*, p. 211; United States, Commission on Security and Cooperation in Europe, *Implementation of the Final Act of the Conference on Security and Cooperation in Europe: Findings and Recommendations Seven Years After Helsinki*, pp. 170–1; 'Soviet Jews: Weather Permitting', *The Economist* (9 February 1985), pp. 49–50; Anthony Lewis, 'Crime and Punishment', *New York Times* (14 February 1985), p. A31; Elie Wiesel, 'Appeals for Refuseniks', *New York Times* (22 October 1985), p. A31.
71. 'Annual Survey – 1985', Wrap-Up ... Leadership Report of the National Conference on Soviet Jewry (New York), 31 December 1985.
72. Institute of Jewish Affairs, *The Position of Soviet Jewry, 1983–1986*, p. 11.
73. United States, Department of State, *Fourteenth Semiannual Report by the President to the Commission on Security and Cooperation in Europe on the Implementation of the Helsinki Final Act, December 1, 1982–May 31, 1983*, Special Report no. 109 (1983), p. 23.
74. United States, Department of State, *Ninth Semiannual Report by the President to the Commission on Security and Cooperation in Europe on the Implementation of the Helsinki Final Act, June 1, 1980–November 30, 1980*, Special Report no. 77 (1980), p. 15.
75. For historical analogies, see Chapter 1.
76. Donna L. Gold, 'Soviet Jewry: U.S. Policy Considerations', E 190 For. USSR, Report No. 85–88S, Congressional Research Service, Library of Congress (17 April 1985), p. 23.
77. The prisoner release was in connection with the freeing of individuals convicted of 'Anti-Soviet Agitation and Propaganda' under Article 70 of the RSFSR Criminal Code (and corresponding articles of the criminal codes of the other union-republics).
78. See Chapter 5 for a full analysis of post-1986 emigration trends.

79. Figures derived from data provided by the National Conference on Soviet Jewry (New York). For US policy changes that had the effect of curtailing emigration to the United States, see notes 5 and 23 above, and the discussion of this issue in Chapter 5.

80. Unless otherwise stated, this information and the data that follows in this section regarding numbers of refuseniks, numbers of invitations and numbers of emigrants are from unpublished materials compiled by Soviet Jewry monitoring bodies.

81. See 'The "Third Basket" for Deputies: How the USSR Fulfils [sic] its Vienna Commitments', interview conducted by Andrei Bezruchenko with Professor Yuri Kashlev in *Moscow News*, no. 45 (12–19 November 1989), p. 11. Kashlev also stated in the interview that 299 refusenik cases were upheld on review, i.e. in those cases the decision to deny permission to emigrate was confirmed. Kashlev was the head of the Soviet delegation at the Vienna CSCE meeting and at the time of this writing was assistant to the First Deputy Minister of Foreign Affairs of the USSR. See also *Jews in the U.S.S.R.*, 19 (2) (17 January 1990).

82. See Andrew Rosenthal, 'Soviet Anti-Zionist Agency May Go', *New York Times* (8 December 1987), p. A16; Ari L. Goldman, 'Soviet Jews to Join World Congress', *New York Times* (4 January 1989), p. A9.

83. Figures provided by the Deutsches Rotes Kreuz [German Red Cross] and the US State Department.

84. See above discussion in this chapter of the CSCE process.

85. The Vienna Concluding Document called for the simplification of administrative requirements and practices regarding visa applications and stipulated that documents submitted in connection with an emigration application would remain valid during the entire application procedure. It also provided for refusals to be made in writing (in the past they were made orally) and for an explanation and information regarding administrative or judicial remedies to accompany negative decisions. Laws and regulations regarding movement within one's country and between the 35 participant states in the CSCE process were to be published domestically and made easily accessible by January 1990. See US Commission on Security and Cooperation in Europe, *Concluding Document of the Vienna Follow-Up Meeting* (January 1989), pp. 26–7.

86. Individuals who cannot emigrate because they lack a financial waiver from their relatives are commonly known as 'poor relatives'.

87. See 'Cooperation in Humanitarian and Other Fields' in *Concluding Document of the Vienna Follow-Up Meeting*, p. 24. The text of the draft law may be found in Sidney Heitman, 'A Soviet Draft Law on Emigration', *Soviet Jewish Affairs*, 19 (3) (Winter 1989), pp. 41–5.

88. The number of demonstrations declined in the last 3 months of 1988, primarily due to the emigration of the majority of the participants. A decree on demonstrations, establishing among other things, civil and criminal penalties for participating in unauthorized demonstrations, was used to impede some public demonstrations of Soviet Jews but was not used to impede seminars and Hebrew classes

held in private homes. See 'Ukaz Prezidiuma Verkhovnogo Soveta SSSR o poryadke organizatsii i provedenia sobrany, mitingov, ulichnykh shestvy i demonstratsy v SSSR' [Decree of the Presidium of the USSR Supreme Soviet on the Procedures for Organizing and Conducting Meetings, Rallies, Street Processions and Demonstrations in the USSR], *Izvestia* (29 July 1988), p. 2.

89. See *Jews in the U.S.S.R.* 17 (1988).

90. See S. Rogov and V. Nosenko, 'Chto skazal "A" i chto skazal "B"', [What 'A' Said and What 'B' Said], *Sovetskaya kultura* (9 February 1989), p. 6.

91. By January 1989, approximately 100 individuals had registered to teach Hebrew and had formed the Union of Hebrew Teachers in the USSR, which planned to campaign for official recognition. See *Jews in the U.S.S.R.* 18 (5 January 1989), p. 1. Throughout 1989 and 1990 the publication *Jews in the U.S.S.R.* regularly reported on the formation of Hebrew study groups and officially endorsed classes. It also listed the towns in which Hebrew teaching was conducted on a regular basis. See *Jews in the U.S.S.R.* 18 (1989); *Jews in the U.S.S.R.* 19 (1990).

92. For information on religious developments see 'First Yeshiva in 60 Years Opens in the Soviet Union', *JTA Daily News Bulletin* 37 (24 February 1989) [JTA is the Jewish Telegraphic Agency]; Esther B. Fein, 'Lasting Faith of Soviet Jews Moves Wiesel', *New York Times* (13 February 1989), pp. A1, A14; Ari L. Goldman, 'Moscow to Get Academy of Jewish Learning', *New York Times* (19 February 1989), sec. 1, p. 25; Oxana Antic, 'The Situation of Religious Jews in the USSR: 1987–1989', Radio Liberty *Report on the USSR* 1 (47) (24 November 1989), pp. 7–9. For other developments see *Jews in the U.S.S.R.* 18 (1989); *Jews in the U.S.S.R.* 19 (1990).

93. For an example of a neo-Stalinist, anti-*perestroika* manifesto, using codewords to link Jews to responsibility for the problems of socialist society, see 'Letters to the Editor', letter by Nina Andreyeva, in *Sovetskaya Rossia* (13 March 1988), p. 3. (A condensed version of the letter is reprinted in translation in *Current Digest of the Soviet Press*, XL (13) (27 April 1988), pp. 1–6.

94. Pamyat, one of the best known of the Russian nationalist societies, was created in 1980, ostensibly for the preservation of Moscow's historical and cultural monuments. By late 1985 it emerged as an extreme Russian nationalist, anti-Semitic organization responsible for revitalizing the notion of a Zionist-Freemason conspiracy to take over the world (a theme first popularized in the 1905 *Protocols of the Elders of Zion*). Howard Spier states that belief in the Zionist-Freemason conspiracy against the Russian people has deep roots in Russia. 'It was the rallying-cry of the Black Hundreds organization, the Union of the Russian People, a reactionary monarchist and antisemitic body that fought against the planned reforms following the 1905 revolution.' Howard Spier, 'Soviet Antisemitism Unchained: The Rise of the "Historical and Patriotic Association Pamyat"', Institute of Jewish Affairs, *Research Report*, no. 3 (July 1987), p. 4.

95. See 'Letters to the Editor', *Moscow News* 32 (14–21 August 1988), p. 2; Esther B. Fein, 'For Moscow Jews, Fear of Prejudice is Stirring', *New York Times* (5 August 1988), p. A2; 'Ovations and Posters in Court', *Moscow News* 37 (17–24 September 1989), p. 15; Irina Ginzburg, 'We Russian Jews Fear for Our Lives', *New York Times* (5 May 1990), p. 25.

96. For example see Pavel Gutiontov, 'Podmena' [Substitution], *Izvestia* (27 February 1988), p. 3.

97. See L. Dymerskaya-Tsigelman, 'Anti-Semitism and Opposition to it at the Present Stage of the Ideological Struggle in the USSR', *Jews and Jewish Topics in Soviet and East-European Publications* 7 (Summer 1988), pp. 3–29; 'Letters to the Editor: Understanding Pamyat', *Moscow News*, 13 (2–9 April 1989), p. 4; Francis X. Clines, 'Anxiety Over Anti-Semitism Spurs Warning on Hate', *New York Times* (2 February 1990), p. A1; 'Do We Have to Wait for Bloodshed?', *Moscow News* 7 (25 February–4 March 1990), p. 14. For a sampling of Pamyat's documents see 'Documents of the Pamyat' Association', *Jews and Jewish Topics in Soviet and East-European Publications* 7 (Summer 1988), pp. 30–4.

98. It is also possible that individuals, such as the elderly, who might formerly have considered emigrating because they feared permanent separation from their families, were less inclined to emigrate once opportunities for tourism became viable.

4 Soviet Germans: A Brief History and an Introduction to Their Emigration

1. V. Auman and V. Chernyshev, 'Sovetskie nemtsi pered voinoi i segodnya' [Soviet Germans Before the War and Today], *Pravda* (4 November 1988), p. 8.

2. The first German settlers in Russia arrived in the mid-sixteenth century to help modernize the country and improve the army. Those Germans were urban dwellers – merchants, administrators, craftsmen, technical workers, professionals and military officers – invited by Ivan IV and his successors. The total number who remained permanently was not large and consequently not many of today's Soviet Germans are descended from the original German immigrants. For detailed histories of German immigration to Russia see Karl Stumpp, *The Emigration from Germany to Russia in the Years 1763 to 1862* (Lincoln, Nebraska: American Historical Society of Gemans from Russia, 1973); Fred C. Koch, *The Volga Germans* (University Park, Pennsylvania: Pennsylvania State University Press, 1977), pp. 4–89; Adam Giesinger, *From Catherine to Khrushchev: The Story of Russia's Germans* (Battleford, Saskatchewan, Canada: Marian, 1974), pp. 1–246.

3. For additional details on the various groups of Germans in Russia and the USSR, see Sidney Heitman, *The Soviet Germans in the USSR Today*, Berichte des Bundesinstituts für ostwissenschaftliche und internationale Studien no. 35 (Cologne: Bundesinstitut für ostwissenschaftliche und internationale Studien, 1980), pp. 32–5; CDU/

CSU Group in the German Bundestag, *White Paper on the Human Rights Situation in Germany and of the Germans in Eastern Europe* (Bonn: CDU/CSU Group in the Bundestag, 1977), pp. 55–8.

4.   Pinkus contends that the favorable policy towards the Soviet Germans in the first half of the 1920s related to both international and domestic factors. The former included the belief among Bolshevik leaders that a German revolution was imminent and that the Soviet Germans would be mobilized to help achieve the revolution. The latter related to the policy of co-opting the nationalities. Benjamin Pinkus, 'From the October Revolution to the Second World War', in Ingeborg Fleischhauer and Benjamin Pinkus (eds), *The Soviet Germans Past and Present*, with an Introduction by Edith Rogovin Frankel (London: C. Hurst in association with Marjorie Mayrock Center for Soviet and East European Research, Hebrew University of Jerusalem, Israel, 1986), p. 42.

5.   Six of the German National Districts were in the RSFSR (including one in the Altai Krai in Siberia and one in the Crimea), 8 in the Ukraine, and 1 each in Georgia and Azerbaijan.

6.   The deportation decree appears in translation in Robert Conquest, *The Nation Killers* (London: Macmillan, 1970, reprint edn, London: Sphere, 1972), pp. 62–3; and in Ingeborg Fleischhauer, '"Operation Barbarossa" and the Deportation', in Fleischhauer and Pinkus (eds), *The Soviet Germans Past and Present*, p. 81. Conquest and Fleischhauer cite *Vedomosti Verkhovnogo Soveta SSSR*, no. 38 (2 September 1941), item 153 as the source of the decree.

7.   The Volga German *raiony* (districts) were incorporated within the Saratov and Stalingrad provinces. See 'Ob administrativnom ustroistve territorii byvshei respubliki nemtsev povolzhia' [On the Administrative Arrangement of the Territory of the Former Volga German Republic], Decree of the Presidium of the USSR Supreme Soviet, 7 September 1941, in *Vedomosti Verkhovnogo Soveta SSSR*, no. 40 (1941). Reprinted in *Sbornik zakonov SSSR i ukazov Prezidiuma Verkhovnogo Soveta SSSR (1938–noyabr 1958)*, (Moscow: Gosudarstvennoe izdatelstvo yuridicheskoy literatury, 1959), p. 48.

8.   Karl Stumpp, 'Sterben die Russland-Deutschen aus?' [Are the Russian Germans Dying Out?], *Die Zeit* (23 April 1976), p. 40.

9.   In 1989 the Soviet newspaper *Argumenty i fakty* reported that as of 1 January 1953, a total of 1 224 931 Germans had been banished to 'special localities'. Included in this number were 855 674 Germans who had been deported as a result of the deportation decree, 208 388 who had been repatriated, 111 324 local Germans, 48 582 mobilized Germans and 963 others. See *Argumenty i fakty* (30 September–6 October 1989), p. 8.

10. The Warthegau, which had been annexed to the Reich, was the region surrounding the Warthe River on the Polish–German border.

11. Ann Sheehy and Bohdan Nahaylo, *The Crimean Tatars, Volga Germans, and Meskhetians: Soviet Treatment of Some National Minorities*, 3rd edn, Minority Rights Group Report no. 6 (London: Minority Rights Group, 1980), p. 19.

12. Sidney Heitman, 'Soviet German Population Change, 1970–79', *Soviet Geography: Review & Translation* 22 (November 1981), p. 553.
13. For details on the suppression of information regarding the Germans and other deported nationalities see Conquest, *The Nation Killers*, pp. 67–83.
14. Giesinger, *From Catherine to Khrushchev*, p. 316. Benjamin Pinkus cites a figure of 9678 in 'The Emigration of National Minorities from the USSR in the Post-Stalin Era', *Soviet Jewish Affairs* 13 (February 1983), p. 10. Angela Stent uses the figure of 9628 German POWs in *From Embargo to Ostpolitik: The Political Economy of West German–Soviet Relations, 1955–1980* (Cambridge: Cambridge University Press, 1981), p. 43.
15. For details of the Adenauer visit to Moscow, see Stent, *From Embargo to Ostpolitik*, pp. 20–47.
16. Sheehy and Nahaylo, *The Crimean Tatars*, p. 20; Heitman, *The Soviet Germans in the USSR Today*, p. 82. The terms of a repatriation agreement concluded in 1958 concerned only those individuals who possessed German citizenship before 21 June 1941. See Stent, *From Embargo to Ostpolitik*, p. 64.
17. See 'Ob amnistii sovetskikh grazhdan, sotrudnichavshikh s okkupantami v period Velikoy Otechestvennoy voyny 1941–1945' [On the Amnesty of Soviet Citizens Who Collaborated with the Occupiers in the Period of the Great Fatherland War, 1941–1945], Decree of the Presidium of the Supreme Soviet, 17 September 1955, in *Vedomosti Verkhovnogo Soveta SSSR*, no. 17 (4 October 1955), item 345; CDU/CSU Group in the German Bundestag, *White Paper*, p. 58. The 13 December Decree on the release from the special settlements and labor camps was not officially published in *Vedomosti Verkhovnogo Soveta SSSR*, but may be found in *German Samizdat*, A.S. no. 1776, according to Benjamin Pinkus, 'The Germans in the Soviet Union since 1945', in Fleischhauer and Pinkus (eds), *The Soviet Germans Past and Present*, p. 109, note 17.
18. Giesinger, *From Catherine to Khrushchev*, pp. 318–21.
19. Wolf Oschlies, 'The Status of Germans Living in the Soviet Union', in Karin Schmid (ed.), *The Soviet Union 1982–1983: Domestic Policy, The Economy, Foreign Policy* (London: Holmes & Meier, published with assistance of the Bundesinstitut für ostwissenschaftliche und internationale Studien, Cologne, 1985), vol. 7, pp. 109–10; Heitman, *The Soviet Germans in the USSR Today*, p. 39; Pinkus, 'The Germans in the Soviet Union since 1945', p. 132.
20. Sheehy and Nahaylo, *The Crimean Tatars*, p. 20.
21. 'The Germans and the Jews: A Study in Contrast', *Congress Bi-Weekly* 33 (5 December 1966), p. 30. See also Pinkus, 'The Germans in the Soviet Union Since 1945', p. 133.
22. Likewise the Germans would, in turn, be more vulnerable to a process of Sovietization than, for example, the Ukrainians. See the Introduction and Chapter 1 for details on this aspect of nationality policy.
23. See 'O vnesenii izmenenii v Ukaz Prezidiuma Verkhovnogo Soveta SSSR ot 28 avgusta 1941 "O pereselenii nemtsev, prozhivayushchikh

v raionakh Povolzhia"' [On the Introduction of Alterations to the Decree of the Presidium of the USSR Supreme Soviet of 28 August 1941, 'On Resettling the Germans Living in the Districts Along the Volga'], Decree of the Presidium of the USSR Supreme Soviet, 29 August 1964, in *Vedomosti Verkhovnogo Soveta SSSR*, no. 52 (28 December 1964), item 592.

24. By the end of the 1960s, a small number of Soviet Germans had returned to their former residences, apparently without encountering any obstacles, despite the express provisions in the December 1955 decree forbidding such resettlement. Koch, *The Volga Germans*, pp. 293–4. See also Giesinger, *From Catherine to Khrushchev*, p. 321. Today there are said to be approximately 40 000 Germans who have returned since the mid-1970s from Kazakhstan, Turkmenistan, Kirghizia and Siberia to live in the area formerly called the Volga German ASSR. See Victor Chistyakiv, 'German Autonomy – Projects and Realities', *Moscow News*, no. 35 (3–10 September 1989), p. 9.

25. Sheehy and Nahaylo, *The Crimean Tatars*, p. 20; Pinkus, 'The Germans in the Soviet Union since 1945', p. 110. Interestingly, although the rehabilitation decree was dated 29 August 1964, it was not published until 28 December 1964, and appeared only in *Vedomosti Verkhovnogo Soveta SSSR*. It was never printed in the principal central or local Russian-language press. According to Pinkus (p. 110) it was published only on 20 January 1965 in *Neues Leben*, a German-language paper published in Moscow by *Pravda*.

26. A delegation had gone to Moscow to meet with Mikoyan at the end of 1964 or early in 1965, but they were denied permission to see Mikoyan. Other than the fact that the Soviet Germans had submitted a petition bearing a sufficient number of signatures of Soviet Germans who supported the delegation's meeting with Mikoyan, Mikoyan's reasons for granting the meeting in June are not clear.

27. Mikoyan also agreed to work toward increasing Soviet-German representation in the Supreme Soviet. Sheehy and Nahaylo, *The Crimean Tatars*, p. 21. For an excerpt from the transcript of the meeting between Mikoyan and the German delegation on 7 June 1965, see 'The Question of the Restoration of the Volga German Republic', trans. by Ann Sheehy, in *American Historical Society of Germans From Russia*, Work Paper no. 11 (April 1973), pp. 13–15. For details of the visits of the German delegations to Mikoyan in 1965 and 1967 see E. Schwabenland-Haynes, 'The Restoration of the German Volga Republic', *American Historical Society of Germans From Russia*, Work Paper no. 11 (April 1973), p. 12; Ann Sheehy, *American Historical Society of Germans From Russia*, Work Paper no. 13 (1973), pp. 5–6; *American Historical Society of Germans From Russia*, Work Paper no. 22 (Winter 1976), p. 1; Boris Levytsky, 'Germans in the Soviet Union: New Facts and Figures', in *American Historical Society of Germans From Russia*, Work Paper no. 22 (Winter 1976), pp. 2–3.

28. The developments detailed below refer to those prior to the liberalization of the Gorbachev period. German sections in a number of

the writers' unions were established and German-language publications were increased over time (although the number remained
small compared to other nationalities). Press articles praising Soviet
Germans for their efforts during the Revolution as well as against
the Nazis in World War II began appearing in 1964 and continued
in following years. See Sheehy and Nahaylo, *The Crimean Tatars*, p.
21. A professional German variety ensemble was founded in 1968,
and the first (and possibly only) post-war German drama theater in
the USSR opened in 1980. See Yekaterina Kuznetsova, 'German
Theatre in Kazakhstan', *Moscow News* (13 September 1981), p. 11. In
1981, *Heimatliche Weiten*, a bi-annual German-language literary
almanac, was started. See 'Literary Almanac for Soviet Germans',
Radio Liberty Research, RL 205/81 (19 May 1981), annotations.

29. Census data revealed that the percentage of Soviet Germans declaring German as their native language declined from 75 per cent
(1959) to 66.8 per cent (1970), 57.0 per cent (1979) and 48.7 per cent
(1989). *Itogi Vsesoyuznoy perepisi naselenia 1970 goda*, 7 vols (Moscow:
Statistika, 1972–74), vol. 4 (1974), p. 9; the 1979 figure is based on
statistics in *Vestnik statistiki*, no. 7 (1980), p. 41; the 1989 figure is
from *Natsionalny sostav naselenia: Chast II* (Moscow: Finansy i statistika, 1989), p. 5.

30. In 1970, the urban and rural population percentages of Soviet
Germans were 45.4 and 54.6 respectively. (Figures based on population statistics in *Itogi Vsesoyuznoy perepisi naselenia 1970 goda*, vol. 4,
pp. 9, 27, 35.) The 1979 all-union census did not list the urban/rural
division by nationality, however Heitman estimated it to be 52 per
cent urban to 48 per cent rural. Heitman, *The Soviet Germans in the
USSR Today*, p. 20. The urban/rural statistics from the 1989 census
had not been published when this book went to press.

31. The USSR Supreme Soviet passed on 24 December 1958 a comprehensive law on educational reform and in 1959 the union- and
autonomous republics passed corresponding laws. The laws stated
that parents had the right to request instruction for their children in
their native language. *Pravda* (25 December 1958), pp. 1–2; see also
Yaroslav Bilinsky, 'The Soviet Education Laws of 1958–9 and Soviet
Nationality Policy', *Soviet Studies* 14 (October 1962), pp. 138–57;
Pinkus, 'The Germans in the Soviet Union Since 1945', pp. 125–6.

32. Giesinger, *From Catherine to Khrushchev*, pp. 325–8. German-
language study and cultural facilities were virtually inaccessible to
Soviet Germans living outside Kazakhstan, Kirghizia, western Si-
beria and Moscow. See 'Soviet German Asks for More Teaching of
German as Mother Tongue', *Radio Liberty Research*, RL 136/82 (23
March 1982), annotations. As late as January 1982, the Landsmann-
schaft der Deutschen aus Russland [Organization of Germans from
Russia] reported that there was still not a single German school in
the USSR. See Oschlies, 'The Status of Germans Living in the Soviet
Union', p. 108. In 1988 it was reported that the question of opening
German national schools was being raised, but when this book went
to press the issue had still not been resolved. See V. Auman and

V. Chernyshev, 'Sovetskie nemtsi pered voinoi i segodnya' [Soviet
Germans Before the War and Today], *Pravda* (4 November 1988),
p. 8.

33. See Gerd Stricker, 'A Visit to German Congregations in Central
Asia', *Religion in Communist Lands* 17 (1) (Spring 1989), pp. 19–33.
According to Oschlies ('The Status of Germans Living in the Soviet
Union', p. 111), in the mid-1980s there were 100 registered and 200
unregistered Lutheran congregations with 200–3000 members each;
10–12 Roman Catholic congregations with a total of 500 000 members; and German Baptist groups numbering 50 000–80 000, that
were part of Russian congregations. Heitman (*The Soviet Germans in
the USSR Today*, p. 46) estimated that there were 100 000 Mennon-
ites. Pinkus ('The Germans in the Soviet Union since 1945', p. 143)
noted that 25–30 per cent of Soviet Germans are religious believers.

34. There were 14 Soviet-German Supreme Soviet deputies before
World War II. However, following the war, Soviet Germans had no
representation in central government organs until 1970. At that time
two Germans became Supreme Soviet deputies, but this number had
not increased by 1979, the last date for which figures were available.
Verkhovny Sovet SSSR (Moscow, 1975), p. 402; Pinkus, 'The Germans
in the Soviet Union since 1945', p. 114, note 31; Oschlies, 'The Status
of Germans Living in the Soviet Union', p. 108. In the Congress of
People's Deputies elected in 1989, 10 out of a total of 2249 deputies
elected were Germans. See Valerii A. Tishkov, 'An Assembly of
Nations or an All-Union Parliament?', *Journal of Soviet Nationalities* 1
(1) (Spring 1990), p. 107. With respect to Party membership, Soviet
Germans have a low rate of representation. Out of a total German
population of 2 035 807 in 1989, only 89 550 (or 4.4 per cent) were
CPSU members. See 'Data on Population and Party Members by
Nationality', *Journal of Soviet Nationalities* 1 (1) (Spring 1990), p. 150.
While it is difficult to determine the degree to which political
participation is self-determined and the extent to which it reflects
discrimination in the selection process, it seems reasonable to assume
that both elements must be operating.

35. See the discussion in 'Our Aliens: The Destinies of Emigrants',
interview with Vyacheslav Kondratyev, interview conducted by
Yelena Vesyolaya, *Moscow News*, no. 44 (5–12 November 1989), p.
15.

36. For discussions of anti-German sentiment and discrimination, see
Oschlies, 'The Status of Germans Living in the Soviet Union', p. 114;
Juozas Kazlas, 'A Comparison of Ethnic Group Rights', unpublished
paper presented to the Conference on Problems of Soviet Ethnic
Policies: The Status of Jews in the USSR and the Impact of
Anti-Semitism, held at Columbia University, New York, 27 May
1980, pp. 75–8; John W. Kiser, 'Emigration from the Soviet Union:
The Case of the Soviet Germans', *Analysis*, no. 57 (June 1976), p. 6;
Andrei D. Sakharov, *My Country and the World*, trans. Guy V. Daniels
(London: Collins & Harvill, 1975), p. 58; Pinkus, 'The Germans in
the Soviet Union since 1945', pp. 144–9; Albert Plutnik, 'Ispoved
pered dalnei dorogoi' [Confession Before a Long Journey], *Izvestia*

(3 February 1989), p. 3.

37. See '"SSSR-nasha rodina", sozdano obshchestvo sovetskikh nemtsev' ['The USSR is Our Motherland', Society of Soviet Germans Created], *Pravda* (2 April 1989), p. 1; articles by Aleksandr Nikitin and Kurt Vidmaier under the general headline of 'Nemetskaya avtonomia: Gde? Kogda? Kak?' [German Autonomy: Where? When? How?], *Literaturnaya gazeta* (11 October 1989), p. 11.

38. Interview with Ms Wanda Wahnsiedler, Internationale Gesellschaft für Menschenrechte [International Society for Human Rights], Frankfurt, 27 March 1985.

39. Stent, *From Embargo to Ostpolitik*, p. 64. For information on Soviet-German emigration during 1918–41, see Benjamin Pinkus, 'The Emigration of National Minorities from the USSR in the Post-Stalin Era', *Soviet Jewish Affairs* 13 (February 1983), pp. 5–7.

40. Statistics regarding Soviet-German emigration were provided by the Deutsches Rotes Kreuz [German Red Cross], Hamburg.

41. Interview with Dr Enno Barker, Counsellor, Embassy of the Federal Republic of Germany, Washington, DC, 14 September 1984.

42. See Chapter 5 for a discussion of German emigration trends and policy analysis.

43. Sheehy and Nahaylo, *The Crimean Tatars*, p. 22.

44. One difference external to Soviet emigration procedure has been that the German Red Cross administers emigration of the Soviet Germans, whereas until the fall of 1989 when Jews wishing to immigrate to the United States began applying directly to the US (see the discussion in Chapters 3 and 5 on the policy change), the Israeli Foreign Ministry relayed all invitations.

45. See 'The Case of the Germans Resident in Estonia', *A Chronicle of Human Rights in the USSR*, no. 10 (July–August 1974), pp. 11–12; 'More Ethnic Germans Seek to Emigrate from the USSR', *Radio Liberty Research*, RL 26/77 (1 February 1977); 'Ethnic Germans Maintain Pressure to Emigrate', *Radio Liberty Research*, RL 121/77 (24 May 1977); 'Ethnic German Emigration from the USSR', *Radio Liberty Research*, RL 101/78 (5 May 1978); Anastasia Gelischanow, 'Penalties for Soviet Germans Applying to Emigrate', *Radio Liberty Research*, RL 309/82 (2 August 1982); Anastasia Gelischanow, 'Problems Still Face Soviet Ethnic Germans Wishing to Emigrate to the FRG', *Radio Liberty Research*, RL 40/83 (19 January 1983); Anastasia Gelischanow, 'No Concessions in Sight for Would-Be Ethnic German Emigrants from the USSR', *Radio Liberty Research*, RL 376/83 (7 October 1983).

46. For examples of Soviet anti-emigration propaganda, see 'Ethnic Germans Wanting to Settle in the FRG', *Sovetskaya Kirghizia* (30 October 1980), in BBC *Summary of World Broadcasts* (27 November 1980), SU/6586/C/1–2 (A1,B); 'Plight of Soviet Nationals who Emigrated to FRG', Moscow Radio in German, 16 August 1978 in BBC *Summary of World Broadcasts* (24 August 1978), SU/5899/A1/3–4; 'Disenchanted Emigrants to FRG Returning to USSR', TASS in English, 23 January 1976, in BBC *Summary of World Broadcasts* (26 January 1976), SU/5117/A1/6–7; Anastasia Gelischanow, 'Contrast-

ing Pictures of Ethnic German Emigration from the USSR', *Radio Liberty Research*, RL 172/79 (6 June 1979); Gelischanow, 'Penalties for Soviet Germans Applying to Emigrate'.

47. See Chapter 5 for further information on the surge in the number of German emigrants beginning in 1987.

48. Although several hundred thousand German descendants live in North America and are represented by organizations such as the American Historical Society of Germans from Russia and the Germans from Russia Heritage Society, no interest group has been formed to pressure the US government on behalf of the Soviet Germans. Until 1980, the strongest external support the Soviet Germans received was from the government of the Federal Republic of Germany. Beginning in 1980, when the FRG-based Soviet-German ethnic organization, the Landsmannschaft der Deutschen aus Russland, was internally restructured, non-governmental support in the FRG for the Soviet Germans increased. Sidney Heitman, 'Soviet German Emigration and Soviet Foreign Relations', paper prepared for the annual meeting of the American Association for the Advancement of Slavic Studies, Washington, DC, October 1982, p. 9.

49. In contrast, the US pursued a strategy of public diplomacy. See Chapter 5 for a discussion of the Jackson–Vanik amendment, an example of US public diplomacy regarding Soviet-Jewish emigration. The amendment linked US trade concessions to increased emigration.

50. One of the first instances since the start of large-scale Soviet-German emigration in which a West German Chancellor (Helmut Kohl) raised the issue publicly was at a Kremlin banquet on 4 July 1983.

51. See *Argumenty i fakty*, no. 12 (25–31 March 1989), p. 7; 'Natsionalny vopros: politika i praktika, vosstanovit spravedlivost' [The National Question: Politics and Practice, to Restore Justice], *Izvestia* (29 November 1989), p. 3.

5 The Domestic Context of Soviet Emigration Policy

1. Roy A. Medvedev, 'The Problem of Democratization and the Problem of Détente', October 1973, *samizdat* article published in translation in *Radio Liberty Special Report*, RL 359/73 (19 November 1973), p. 10.

2. See, for example, Robert O. Freedman, 'Soviet Jewry and Soviet–American Relations: A Historical Analysis', in Robert O. Freedman (ed.), *Soviet Jewry in the Decisive Decade, 1971–1980* (Durham, North Carolina: Duke University Press, 1984), pp. 38–67; Marshall Goldman, *Détente and Dollars* (New York: Basic, 1975), pp. 69–70; William Korey, 'The Future of Soviet Jewry: Emigration and Assimilation', *Foreign Affairs* 58 (1) (Fall 1979), pp. 74–7.

3. For details of the treaty see William E. Griffith, *The Ostpolitik of the Federal Republic of Germany* (Cambridge, Massachusetts: MIT Press, 1978), pp. 191–3. Walter Scheel was Chairman of the West German Free Democratic Party, a part of Willy Brandt's coalition government.

4. Z. Alexander, 'Immigration to Israel from the USSR', in *Israel Yearbook on Human Rights* (Tel Aviv: Tel Aviv University, 1977), vol. 7, special supplement, p. 324. (Z. Alexander is a pseudonym for Zvi Nezer.)
5. Indeed, the policy toward the emigration of Germans and Armenians was liberalized at the same time.
6. Invitations were sent to 79 711 Soviet Jews during 1968–71, to 67 895 in 1972, and to 58 216 in 1973. Alexander, *Israel Yearbook*, p. 326. These figures refer to first-request invitations and do not include those requested in order to replace expired invitations. Only a portion of *vyzov* (invitation) recipients eventually apply to emigrate.
7. See, for example, Marshall I. Goldman, 'Soviet–American Trade and Soviet Jewish Emigration: Should a Policy Change be Made by the American Jewish Community?', in Robert O. Freedman (ed.), *Soviet Jewry in the 1980s: The Politics of Anti-Semitism and Emigration and the Dynamics of Resettlement* (Durham, North Carolina: Duke University Press, 1989), pp. 148–59; Korey, 'The Future of Soviet Jewry: Emigration and Assimilation', p. 77. Korey also includes the passage of the Stevenson amendment (to the Export–Import Bank Act Amendment of 1974) as an additional reason for the decrease in emigration. For details of the Stevenson amendment, see note 13 below.
8. See Victor Zaslavsky and Robert J. Brym, *Soviet-Jewish Emigration and Soviet Nationality Policy* (London: Macmillan, 1983), pp. 120–2.
9. The amendment was sponsored by Henry Jackson in the Senate and Charles Vanik in the House of Representatives.
10. United States, Congress, *Trade Act of 1974*, Pub. L. 93–618, Title IV, sec. 402, in *United States Code Congressional and Administrative News* 2 (1974), pp. 2382–7.
11. The education tax imposed by the Soviet Union in August 1972 (see Chapter 2) is generally believed to be the catalyst that prompted the linkage of free emigration and US–Soviet trade. However, ideas had begun circulating regarding the relationship of trade and emigration before the tax was announced. Senator Henry Jackson had already been contemplating coupling trade and emigration, borrowing the concept of linkage from the Nixon administration, which had linked the trade concessions that were announced in the October 1972 US–Soviet Trade Agreement to a Soviet pledge to help the US withdraw from Vietnam. See Paula Stern, *Water's Edge: Domestic Politics and the Making of American Foreign Policy*, Contributions in Political Science, no. 15 (Westport, Connecticut and London: Greenwood, 1979), pp. 10–12, 21–2, 28–9; William Orbach, *The American Movement to Aid Soviet Jews* (Amherst, Massachusetts: University of Massachusetts Press, 1979), p. 131; Morris Brafman and David Schimel, *Trade and Freedom: Détente, Trade and Soviet Jews* (New York: Shengold, 1975), pp. 34–5.
12. Henry Kissinger, architect of détente in the Nixon and Ford administrations did not favor the linkage of trade to emigration,

viewing it as an inappropriate topic for public diplomacy and arguing instead that quiet (behind the scenes) diplomacy was the sole effective means of obtaining concessions on emigration. As a result of a compromise settlement, Secretary Kissinger and Senator Jackson agreed that Kissinger would assure that the USSR clarify its position on ending the harassment of individuals interested in emigrating, process visa applications in the order in which they were received, and increase the number of visas granted. See Joseph Albright, 'The Pact of Two Henrys', *New York Times Magazine* (5 January 1975), p. 29. Kissinger and Jackson publicly exchanged letters (Kissinger's conveying the Soviet assurances regarding emigration, and Jackson's detailing his understanding of the criteria discussed in Kissinger's letter and stipulating a minimum of 60 000 visas per year as a standard, or 'benchmark', of initial compliance) in a televised ceremony 2 months before the Senate vote on the Jackson–Vanik amendment. See Stern, *Water's Edge*, pp. 149–51, 154–62 for a discussion of the protracted negotiations concerning the exchange of letters. For the full text of the letters see United States, Congress, Senate, S. Rept. 1298 to accompany H.R. 10710, 93rd Congress, 2nd session, 1974, in *United States Code Congressional and Administrative News* 4 (1974), pp. 7335–8.

The Soviet Union, in a formal note from Foreign Minister Gromyko to Secretary Kissinger on 26 October 1974, flatly denied that figures concerning emigration were ever discussed and reiterated the Soviet position that emigration was an internal matter. (The Gromyko letter is reprinted in *A Chronicle of Human Rights in the USSR*, no. 11–12 (September–December 1974), pp. 10–11.) Despite the administration's objections, the Congress passed the Jackson–Vanik amendment, making it part of the Trade Act of 1974. On 10 January 1975, one week after the Trade Act of 1974 was signed into law, the Soviet government informed the United States that it did not accept the additions to the 1972 Trade Agreement (i.e. the Jackson–Vanik amendment) and therefore would not honor the Agreement. One immediate outcome of the Soviet rejection of the Trade Agreement was the halting of payments on the Lend-Lease debt.

13. The Stevenson amendment, one of the 1974 Export–Import Bank amendments, was also used restrictively. The amendment limited the dollar value of credits the Export–Import Bank could grant to the Soviet Union to $300 million over a 4-year period, and required the approval of Congress for any decision to grant credits above the $300 million ceiling. The decision on whether to allow additional credits would, according to the Stevenson amendment, be based on considerations of the 'national interest', such as Soviet emigration policy, the Middle East and arms talks. France, Great Britain, Japan and West Germany were willing to fill the gap between the $300 million ceiling the Stevenson amendment allowed the USSR and the USSR's needs. See United States, Congress, *Export–Import Bank Amendments of 1974*, Pub. L. 93–646, sec. 8, in *United States Code*

Congressional and Administrative News 2 (1974), p. 2715; William Korey, 'The Story of the Jackson Amendment, 1973–1975', *Midstream* 21 (3) (March 1975), p. 30.

14. Zaslavsky and Brym, *Soviet-Jewish Emigration*, pp. 120–2.

15. For statistics on emigration by republic of origin during 1968–77 see Alexander, *Israel Yearbook*, p. 324.

16. The number of new affidavits sent to Soviet Jews was 67 895 in 1972, 58 216 in 1973, 42 843 in 1974 and 34 145 in 1975. See Alexander, *Israel Yearbook*, p. 326. In general, trends in the number of invitations requested are reflected in the number of exit visas issued.

17. 36 104 new affidavits were sent in 1976 and 30 815 were issued in the first 9 months of 1977. Alexander, *Israel Yearbook*, p. 326.

18. The SALT II negotiations began in 1977, but the agreement was not signed until 1979.

19. President Gerald Ford stated in March 1976 that he had dropped the word 'détente' from his political vocabulary. James M. Naughton, 'Ford Says "In Time" He Expects To Talk With Nixon on China', *New York Times* (2 March 1976), p. 12.

20. Although President Carter had adopted a tough stance, his policy was prone to inconsistencies. In November 1980 Carter confirmed that approval had been granted for the export to the USSR of equipment for building the Siberian–Western European natural gas pipeline. See *Strategic Survey 1980–81* (London: International Institute for Strategic Studies, 1981), p. 121.

21. See note 13 above.

22. The amendment authorizes the President to waive the restrictions on most-favored-nation (i.e. non-discriminatory) tariff status if: (1) the waiver will substantially promote the objective of free emigration and (2) the country under consideration provides assurances that its emigration practices will more closely reflect the objectives of the amendment. A waiver is to remain in effect only for a specified period and may be extended annually if approved by a concurrent resolution of both Houses of Congress.

23. Although West German exports to the USSR began declining after 1974 (dropping from a peak level of 7.4 per cent in 1974 to 5.7 per cent by 1978), they still comprised 6.0 per cent of total USSR imports in 1979, and actually rose to 6.7 per cent in 1980. However, the percentage of imports from the FRG in total USSR imports dropped to 5.1 per cent in 1981 and to as low as 4.6 per cent in 1986. (This was still substantially higher than during the pre-détente era, e.g. imports in 1969 from the FRG comprised only 3.4 per cent of total Soviet imports.) *1979 Yearbook of International Trade Statistics*, 2 vols (New York: United Nations, 1980), vol. 1, p. 967; *1986 International Trade Statistics Yearbook*, 2 vols (New York: United Nations, 1988), vol. 1, p. 984.

24. Angela Stent, *From Embargo to Ostpolitik: The Political Economy of West German–Soviet Relations, 1955–1980* (Cambridge: Cambridge University Press, 1981), pp. 216–20. According to Stent (p. 217), in 1976, an estimated 300 000 people were employed in jobs resulting

from increased East–West trade (*Osthandel*).

25. Griffith, *The Ostpolitik of the Federal Republic of Germany*, p. 233. For instance, the US was not supported by the FRG on economic sanctions related to the Soviet invasion of Afghanistan. After the US announcement to embargo high-technology exports, the FRG began negotiations with the USSR over the Siberian gas pipeline.

26. German emigration reached 9704 in 1976. Annual levels dropped to 9274 (1977), 8455 (1978), 7226 (1979), 6954 (1980), 3773 (1981), 2071 (1982), 1447 (1983), 913 (1984) and 460 (1985). The number of German emigrants rose to 753 in 1986, and to astounding highs of 14 488 during 1987 and 47 572 in 1988. The source for these figures is the Deutsches Rotes Kreuz [German Red Cross], Hamburg.

27. *Itogi Vsesoyuznoy perepisi naselenia 1970 goda*, 7 vols (Moscow: Statistika, 1972–74), vol. 4 (1973), pp. 12–13; *Vestnik statistiki*, no. 2 (1980), pp. 27–8. Census figures for 1989 showed the Kazakh population in Kazakhstan to have grown to 39.7 per cent of the total, while the Russian population in the RSFSR held steady at 82.6 per cent. Figures are derived from *Natsionalny sostav naselenia: Chast II* (Moscow: Finansy i statistika, 1989), pp. 6, 68.

28. According to the 1979 census, Russians formed 40.80 per cent of the total population of the Kazakh SSR, Kazakhs comprised 36.02 per cent of the republic's population, Germans accounted for 6.13 per cent and Ukrainians represented 6.12 per cent. *Vestnik statistiki*, no. 9 (1980), p. 65. The figures from the 1989 census were: 39.7 per cent (Kazakhs), 37.8 per cent (Russians), 5.8 per cent (Germans) and 5.4 per cent (Ukrainians). Figures are derived from *Natsionalny sostav naselenia: Chast II*, pp. 68–70.

29. Percentages are based on statistics in *Vestnik statistiki*, no. 9 (1980), p. 65. According to data from the 1989 census, 54.4 per cent of Soviet Germans considered German to be their native tongue and 50.6 per cent considered Russian to be their second language. *Natsionalny sostav naselenia: Chast II*, p. 70.

30. Rasma Karklins, *Ethnic Relations in the USSR: The Perspective from Below* (Boston: Allen & Unwin, 1986), pp. 26–31. Karklins based many of her observations on interviews conducted in 1979 with a sample of 200 Soviet Germans who immigrated to the FRG in 1979.

31. Zaslavsky and Brym, *Soviet-Jewish Emigration*, pp. 71, 75.

32. For instance, the following, written by a well-known anti-Zionist propagandist was published in a major Moscow newspaper in 1978: 'The Zionists, fulfilling the role of shock troops of imperialism, strive to shake the foundations of the socialist multi-national state, to set the peoples of the USSR against one another, and to sow the seeds of nationalism, chauvinism and antisemitism.' L. Korneyev, *Moskovskaya pravda* (12 February 1978). A 1975 book entitled *Zionism and Apartheid* stated: 'the Jewish upper crust . . . nearly always found mutually profitable forms of symbiosis with the local exploitative elite.' V. I. Skurlatov, *Sionizm i aparteid* (Kiev: Politizdat Ukrainy, 1975), pp. 11–12.

33. Steven L. Burg, 'The Calculus of Soviet Antisemitism', in Jeremy R. Azrael (ed.), *Soviet Nationality Policies and Practices* (New York: Praeger, 1978), p. 206.

34. See S. Rogov and V. Nosenko, 'Chto skazal "A" i chto skazal "B"' [What 'A' Said and What 'B' Said], *Sovetskaya kultura* (9 February 1989), p. 6.

35. Zaslavsky and Brym, *Soviet-Jewish Emigration*, pp. 110–11. Zaslavsky and Brym term this an 'anti-Semitism of convenience'.

36. The US–PRC bilateral trade agreement, approved by the US Congress in January 1980, granted the People's Republic of China most-favored-nation status.

37. See Jonathan B. Stein, 'U.S. Controls and the Soviet Pipeline', *Washington Quarterly* 5 (Autumn 1982), pp. 52–9.

38. Although the grain negotiations were postponed, under a previous accord the USSR had until September 1982 to exercise an option to buy up to 25 million tons of US grain. See *Strategic Survey 1981–82* (London: International Institute for Strategic Studies, 1982), p. 33.

39. Whereas the natural population increase was 17.8 per thousand in 1960, the figure had fallen to 8.0 per thousand in 1980 and was projected to decline even further, to perhaps less than 2.5 per thousand in the year 2000. See Godfrey S. Baldwin, *Population Projections by Age and Sex: For the Republics and Major Economic Regions of the U.S.S.R. 1970 to 2000*, in *International Population Reports*, Series P-91, no. 26 (Washington, DC: US Department of Commerce, Bureau of the Census, Foreign Demographics Analysis Division, 1979), p. 14. Baldwin uses a projection series (high, medium, low) for natural increase rates in the year 2000. His projections are 8.4, 5.5 and 2.4 per thousand, respectively. According to *Narodnoe khozyaistvo SSSR v 1988 g.: Statisticheskii ezhegodnik* (Moscow: Finansy i statistika, 1989), p. 24, the natural population increase in 1988 rose slightly to 8.7 per thousand. It remains to be seen whether the long-term (Western) forecasts for continued decreases will prove accurate.

40. For detailed discussions see Ann Helgeson, 'Demographic Policy', in Archie Brown and Michael Kaser (eds), *Soviet Policy for the 1980s* (London: Macmillan for St Antony's College, Oxford, 1982), pp. 139–45; Gail Warshofsky Lapidus, 'Social Trends', in Robert F. Byrnes (ed.), *After Brezhnev: Sources of Soviet Conduct in the 1980s*, (Bloomington, Indiana: Indiana University Press in association with the Center for Strategic and International Studies, Georgetown University, Washington, DC, 1983), pp. 200–32.

41. For an interesting discussion see Alan Dowty, *Closed Borders: The Contemporary Assault on Freedom of Movement* (New Haven: Yale University Press, 1987), pp. 63–76.

42. See *New Times* (Moscow) (28 July 1987), pp. 24–6.

43. A comprehensive listing of refuseniks in mid-1986 included data on 11 137 Soviet Jews. The data is contained in *A Uniquely Jewish List – The Refuseniks of Russia* (New York: Anti-Defamation League of B'nai B'rith, 1986). An analysis of the data may be found in Mordechai

Altshuler, 'Who are the "Refuseniks"? A Statistical and Demographic Analysis', *Soviet Jewish Affairs* 18 (1), (Spring 1988), pp. 3–15.

44. This statistic is based on unpublished data compiled by the Israeli government.

45. See Resolution of the USSR Council of Ministers, 'O vnesenii dopolneniya v Polozhenia o verzde v Soyuz Sovetskikh Sotsialisticheskikh Respublik i o vyezde iz Soyuza Sovetskikh Sotsialisticheskikh Respublik' [On the Introduction of Additions to the Regulations on Entry into the Union of Soviet Socialist Republics and on Exit from the Union of Soviet Socialist Republics], *Sobranie postanovlenii Pravitelstva SSSR* (Section one), no. 31 (1986), item 163, pp. 563–6.

46. In an interview for American television conducted before the Reagan–Gorbachev summit meeting of 1987, Gorbachev stated: 'The United States wants . . . to be an active defender of the rights – of human rights, to resolve their own problems, *and what they're organizing is a brain drain.* And of course we're protecting ourselves. That's number one'. [Emphasis added.] 'Gorbachev Interview: The Arms Agreement, Nicaragua and Human Rights', *New York Times* (1 December 1987), p. A12. See also David K. Shipler, 'Gorbachev Mix on TV is Tough But Cooperative', *New York Times* (1 December 1987), pp. A1, A12. Two years later, Yuri Kashlev, assistant to the First Deputy Minister of Foreign Affairs of the USSR stated in an interview: 'Of course, such mass emigration cannot but cause anxiety and regret, the more so as this is a *brain drain.*' [Emphasis added.] 'The "Third Basket" for Deputies: How the USSR Fulfils [sic] its Vienna Commitments', interview conducted by Andrei Bezruchenko with Professor Yuri Kashlev in *Moscow News*, no. 45 (12–19 November 1989), p. 11.

47. See, for example, Viktor Perevedentsev, 'Domicile Registration Reappraised', *Moscow News*, no. 20 (22–29 May 1988), p. 3. See also Perevedentsev's subsequent article on this subject, 'Domicile Registration and *Perestroika*', *Moscow News*, no. 34 (28 August–4 September 1988), p. 2.

48. See, for example, Bill Keller, 'Soviet Poll Finds Deep Pessimism Over Gorbachev's Economic Plan', *New York Times* (5 November 1989), sec. 1, pp. 1, 13.

49. See G. Kanovich, 'Jewish Daisy', *Komsomolskaya pravda* [Vilnius] (5 October 1989), pp. 1, 3, trans. in *Current Digest of the Soviet Press*, 41 (46) (13 December 1989), pp. 19–20; Bulat Okudzhava, 'Russian Culture is a Source of Good, Not Evil', *Moscow News*, no. 41 (15–22 October 1989), p. 3. In a *Moscow News* interview, writer Vyacheslav Kondratyev stated: 'After all, today we are virtually forcing the Jewish population to leave, and it mustn't be thought that they don't understand that over there many will not be able to work in their specialty. There are few rich uncles waiting for them there, and they face a far from easy struggle for survival. But there nobody will tell them, either to their face, or from the pages of newspapers and magazines, that they are aliens. Incidentally, in exactly the same way

we are forcing the Germans out by not deciding the question of their autonomy quickly.' See 'Our Aliens: The Destinies of Emigrants', interview conducted by Yelena Vesyolaya, *Moscow News*, no. 44 (5–12 November 1989), p. 15.

50.   The emigration of Germans from Poland also increased enormously, growing from 27 188 in 1986 to 48 423 in 1987, 140 226 in 1988 and 250 340 in 1989. These figures are from the Deutsches Rotes Kreuz [German Red Cross].

51.   West Germany guarantees citizenship to ethnic Germans residing outside its borders. See Robert J. McCartney, 'Thousands from East Bloc Drawn by Westward Hopes', *Washington Post* (31 March 1989), pp. A1, A30.

52.   The figures on East German migration to the FRG in 1989 are from Ferdinand Protzman, 'As East German Emigrés Take Root in the West, Their Prosperity Unfurls', *New York Times* (26 September 1990), p. A6. The figures for other ethnic German migration to the FRG are from the Deutsches Rotes Kreuz [German Red Cross].

53.   See Craig R. Whitney, 'To West Germans, There is Less Joy in Latest Exodus', *New York Times* (7 November 1989), pp. 1, 7.

54.   With respect to Soviet Germans, the historian, Golo Mann, stated in an interview: 'The fact that families that went to Russia under Czar Alexander II, whose older members cannot speak German at all and whose younger members barely speak any, can all now come here, I really can't view as very sensible. We could have really helped better some other way.' See 'Golo Mann: Die SED wird Ja Sagen müssen zu freien Wahlen', *Die Welt* (6 November 1989), p. 7. (The excerpt is translated in Whitney, 'To West Germans, There is Less Joy in Latest Exodus', p. 7.)

55.   See Robert Pear, 'Emigrés' Stooped Ceiling', *New York Times* (14 September 1989), p. A8; 'Seekers of Visas Deluge U.S. Mission in Moscow', *New York Times* (3 October 1989), p. 4.

Select Bibliography

ARTICLES

Abramsky, Chimen. 'The Biro-Bidzhan Project, 1927–1959'. In *The Jews in Soviet Russia Since 1917*, pp. 64–77. 3rd edn. Edited by Lionel Kochan. Oxford: Oxford University Press for the Institute of Jewish Affairs, 1978.
———. 'The Rise and Fall of Soviet Yiddish Literature', *Soviet Jewish Affairs* 12 (November 1982), 35–44.
———. 'Russian Jews – A Bird's Eye View', *Midstream* 24 (December 1978), 34 –43.
Ainsztein, Reuben. 'Soviet Jewry in the Second World War'. In *The Jews in Soviet Russia Since 1917*, pp. 281–99. 3rd ed. Edited by Lionel Kochan. Oxford: Oxford University Press for the Institute of Jewish Affairs, 1978.
Albright, Joseph. 'The Pact of Two Henrys', *New York Times Magazine* (5 January 1975), 16–34.
Altman, Yochanan and Mars, Gerald. 'The Emigration of Soviet Georgian Jews to Israel', *Jewish Journal of Sociology* 26 (June 1984), 35–45.
Altshuler, Mordechai. 'Who are the "Refuseniks"? A Statistical and Demographic Analysis', *Soviet Jewish Affairs* 18 (1) (1988), 3–15.
Armstrong, John A. 'Mobilized and Proletarian Diasporas', *American Political Science Review* 70 (2) (June 1976), 393–408.
Aronsfeld, C. C. 'German Emigration from the Soviet Union', Institute of Jewish Affairs *Research Report*, no. 12 (September 1982).
Aronson, Gregor. 'The Jewish Question During the Stalin Era'. In *Russian Jewry 1917–1967*, pp. 171–208. Edited by Gregor Aronson, Jacob Frumkin, Alexis Goldenweiser, and Joseph Lewitan. Translated by Joel Carmichael. New York: Thomas Yoseloff, 1969.
Azrael, Jeremy. 'The "Nationality Problem" in the USSR: Domestic Pressures and Foreign Policy Constraints'. In *The Domestic Context of Soviet Foreign Policy*, pp. 139–53. Edited by Seweryn Bialer. Boulder, Colorado: Westview, 1981.
Barist, Jeffrey, Pell, Owen C., Oshman, Eugenia and Hamel, Matthew E. 'Who May Leave: A Review of Soviet Practice Restricting Emigration on Grounds of Knowledge of "State Secrets" in Comparison with Standards of International Law and the Policies of Other States', *Hofstra Law Review* 15 (3) (1987), 301–41.
Bastid, Suzanne. 'The Special Significance of the Helsinki Final Act'. In *Human Rights, International Law and the Helsinki Accord*, pp. 11–19. Edited by Thomas Buergenthal. Assisted by Judith R. Hall. Montclair, New Jersey: Allanheld, Osmun for the American Society of International Law, 1977.
Bilinsky, Yaroslav. 'The Soviet Education Laws of 1958–9 and Soviet Nationality Policy', *Soviet Studies* 14 (October 1962), 138–57.

Birman, Igor. 'Jewish Emigration from the USSR: Some Observations', *Soviet Jewish Affairs* 9 (Autumn 1979), 46–63.

Boim, Leon. 'The Passport System in the USSR and its Effect Upon the Status of Jews'. In *Israel Yearbook on Human Rights*, vol. 5, pp. 141–68. Tel Aviv: Tel Aviv University, 1975.

Breslauer, George W. 'Do Soviet Leaders Test New Presidents?', *International Security* 8 (Winter 1983–84), 83–107.

Bromlei, Y. V. 'Natsionalnye problemy v usloviakh perestroiki' [National Problems in the Conditions of Perestroika] *Voprosy istorii*, no. 1 (January 1989), 24–41.

Brunner, Georg. 'Recent Developments in the Soviet Concept of Human Rights'. In *Perspectives on Soviet Law for the 1980s*, pp. 37–51. Edited by F. J. M. Feldbrugge and W. B. Simmonds. The Hague: Martinus Nijhoff, 1982.

Brym, Robert J. 'The Changing Rate of Jewish Emigration from the USSR: Some Lessons from the 1970s', *Soviet Jewish Affairs* 15 (May 1985), 23–35.

——. 'Soviet Jewish Emigration: A Statistical Test of Two Theories', *Soviet Jewish Affairs* 18 (3) (1988), 15–23.

Burg, Steven L. 'The Calculus of Soviet Antisemitism'. In *Soviet Nationality Policies and Practices*, pp. 189–222. Edited by Jeremy R. Azrael. New York: Praeger, 1978.

Connor, Walker. 'A Nation is a Nation, is a State, is an Ethnic Group is a . . .', *Ethnic and Racial Studies* 1 (4) (October 1978), 377–400.

Daniels, Robert V. 'Soviet Politics Since Khrushchev'. In *The Soviet Union Under Brezhnev and Kosygin*. Edited by John W. Strong. New York: Van Nostrand Reinhold, 1971.

'The Decline of Soviet Jewish Emigration in 1980', Institute of Jewish Affairs *Research Report*, no. 17 (October 1980).

'Details of the Soviet "Diploma Tax"', Institute of Jewish Affairs *Research Report*, USSR/37 (23 February 1973).

Dinstein, Yoram. 'Soviet Jewry and International Human Rights'. In *Essays on Human Rights: Contemporary Issues and Jewish Perspectives*, pp. 126–43. Edited by David Sidorsky in collaboration with Sidney Liskofsky and Jerome J. Shestack. Philadelphia: Jewish Publication Society of America, 1979.

Domal'skii, I. 'New Developments in Anti-Semitism'. In *Anti-Semitism in the Soviet Union: Its Roots and Consequences*. 3 vols. Vol. 1 (1979): *Proceedings of the Seminar on Soviet Anti-Semitism held in Jerusalem on April 7–8, 1978*. Jerusalem: Hebrew University of Jerusalem, Centre for Research and Documentation of East-European Jewry, 1979–83, pp. 209–343.

'Dragunsky Proclaims Juridical Right of Jews to Emigrate', *Radio Free Europe Research*, USSR: Nationalities (24 February 1971).

Dymerskaya-Tsigelman, L. 'Anti-Semitism and Opposition to It at the Present Stage of the Ideological Struggle in the USSR', *Jews and Jewish Topics in Soviet and East-European Publications* 7 (Summer 1988), 3–29.

'Economic Trials: Death Sentences for Jews', *Jews in Eastern Europe* 2 (December 1962), 16–23.

Efron, Reuben. 'The Jackson Amendment and the Fight for Soviet Jewry's

Right to Emigrate', *International Problems* 15 (Spring 1976), 62–74.

'Ethnic German Emigration from the USSR', *Radio Liberty Research*, RL 101/78 (5 May 1978).

'Ethnic Germans Maintain Pressure to Emigrate', *Radio Liberty Research*, RL 121/77 (24 May 1977).

Ettinger, S. 'The Jews in Russia at the Outbreak of the Revolution'. In *The Jews in Soviet Russia Since 1917*, pp. 15–29. 3rd edn. Edited by Lionel Kochan. Oxford: Oxford University Press for the Institute of Jewish Affairs, 1978.

Felshtinsky, Yuri. 'The Legal Foundations of the Immigration and Emigration Policy of the USSR, 1917–27', *Soviet Studies* 34 (July 1982), 327–48.

Florsheim, Yoel. 'Demographic Significance of Jewish Emigration from the USSR', *Soviet Jewish Affairs* 10 (February 1980), 5–22.

Freedman, Robert O. 'Soviet Jewry and Soviet–American Relations: A Historical Analysis'. In *Soviet Jewry in the Decisive Decade, 1971–1980*, pp. 38–67. Edited by Robert O. Freedman. Durham, North Carolina: Duke University Press, 1984.

Freiman, Grigori. 'A Soviet Teacher's "J'accuse"', *New York Times Magazine* (25 November 1979), 122–7.

Friedgut, Theodore H. 'Interests and Groups in Soviet Policy-Making: The MTS Reforms', *Soviet Studies* 28 (October 1976), 524–47.

——. 'Soviet Anti-Zionism and Antisemitism – Another Cycle', *Soviet Jewish Affairs* 14 (February 1984), 3–22.

——. 'Soviet Jewry: The Silent Majority', *Soviet Jewish Affairs* 10 (May 1980), 3–19.

Gaddis, John Lewis. 'The Rise, Fall and Future of Détente', *Foreign Affairs* 62 (Winter 1983/84), 354–77.

Gelischanow, Anastasia. 'Contrasting Pictures of Ethnic German Emigration From the USSR', *Radio Liberty Research*, RL 172/79 (6 June 1979).

——. 'No Concessions in Sight for Would-Be Ethnic German Emigrants from the USSR', *Radio Liberty Research*, RL 376/83 (7 October 1983).

——. 'Penalties for Soviet Germans Applying to Emigrate', *Radio Liberty Research*, RL 309/82 (2 August 1982).

——. 'Problems Still Face Soviet Ethnic Germans Wishing to Emigrate to the FRG', *Radio Liberty Research*, RL 40/83 (19 January 1983).

'The Germans and the Jews: A Study in Contrast', *Congress Bi-Weekly* 33 (5 December 1966), 27–34.

Ginsburgs, George. 'Current Legal Problems of Jewish Emigration from the USSR', *Soviet Jewish Affairs* 6 (Autumn 1976), 3–13.

——. 'Soviet Law and the Emigration of Soviet Jews', *Soviet Jewish Affairs* 3 (Spring 1973), 3–19.

Gilboa, Yehoshua, A. 'The 1948 Zionist Wave in Moscow', *Soviet Jewish Affairs*, no. 2 (November 1971), 35–9.

Gitelman, Zvi. 'Are Nations Merging in the USSR?', *Problems of Communism* 32 (September–October 1983), 35–47.

——. 'Gorbachev's Reforms and the Future of Soviet Jewry', *Soviet Jewish Affairs* 18 (2) (1988), 3–15.

——. 'The Jewish Question in the USSR Since 1964'. In *Nationalism in the*

USSR and Eastern Europe in the Era of Brezhnev and Kosygin, pp. 324–34. Edited by George W. Simmonds. Detroit: University of Detroit Press, 1977.

——. 'Moscow and the Soviet Jews: A Parting of the Ways', *Problems of Communism* 29 (January–February 1980), 18–34.

——. 'Soviet Jewish Emigrants: Why are They Choosing America?', *Soviet Jewish Affairs* 7 (Spring 1977), 31–46.

——. 'Soviet Immigrant Resettlement in the United States', *Soviet Jewish Affairs* 12 (May 1982), 3–18.

Goble, Paul. 'Ethnic Problems in the USSR', *Problems of Communism* 38 (4) (July–August 1989), 1–14.

Goodman, Jerry. 'The Jews in the Soviet Union: Emigration and Its Difficulties'. In *Soviet Jewry in the Decisive Decade, 1971–80*, pp. 17–28. Edited by Robert O. Freedman. Durham, North Carolina: Duke University Press, 1984.

Hamilton, John A. 'To Link or Not to Link', *Foreign Policy*, no. 44 (Fall 1981), 127–44.

Hanson, Philip, 'Foreign Economic Relations'. In *Soviet Policy for the 1980s*, pp. 65–97. Edited by Archie Brown and Michael Kaser. London: Macmillan for St Antony's College, Oxford, 1982.

Harris, David. 'A Note on the Problem of "Noshrim"', *Soviet Jewish Affairs* 6 (Autumn 1976), 104–13.

Helgeson, Ann. 'Demographic Policy'. In *Soviet Policy for the 1980s*, pp. 118–45. Edited by Archie Brown and Michael Kaser. London: Macmillan for St Antony's College, Oxford, 1982.

Heitman, Sidney. 'Soviet German Emigration and Soviet Foreign Relations'. Paper prepared for the Annual Meeting of the American Association for the Advancement of Slavic Studies, Washington, DC, October 1982.

——. 'Soviet German Population Change, 1970–79', *Soviet Geography: Review & Translation* 22 (November 1981), 549–68.

——. 'Soviet Germans and the 1979 Census: A Note on the Reliability of Soviet Nationality Data', *Nationalities Papers* 9 (Fall 1981), 231–6.

Henkin, Louis, 'Human Rights and "Domestic Jurisdiction"'. In *Human Rights, International Law and the Helsinki Accord*, pp. 21–40. Edited by Thomas Buergenthal. Assisted by Judith R. Hall. Montclair, New Jersey: Allanheld, Osmun for the American Society of International Law, 1977.

Hirszowicz, Lukasz. 'Birobidzhan After Forty Years', *Soviet Jewish Affairs* 4 (Autumn 1974), 38–45.

——. 'Discrimination Against Jewish Students in the USSR', Institute of Jewish Affairs *Research Report*, USSR/56 (August 1976).

——. 'Further Statistical Data on Soviet Jewry: The Use of Languages', Institute of Jewish Affairs *Research Report*, no. 13 (September 1980).

——. 'Less Noted Sides of Soviet Jewish Policies: Elections at the Recent Party Congress', Institute of Jewish Affairs *Research Report*, USSR/53 (April 1976).

——. 'Ominous Changes in the Soviet Criminal Code', Institute of Jewish Affairs *Research Report*, no. 5 (May 1984).

——. 'The Soviet Census: New Data on the Jewish Minority', Institute of

Jewish Affairs *Research Report*, no. 5 (April 1980).
——. 'The Soviet-Jewish Problem: Internal and International Developments, 1972–1976'. In *The Jews in Soviet Russia Since 1917*, pp. 366–409. 3rd edn. Edited by Lionel Kochan. Oxford: Oxford University Press for the Institute of Jewish Affairs, 1978.
——. 'The Twenty-Seventh Congress of the CPSU', *Soviet Jewish Affairs* 16 (May 1986), 3–27.
——. 'Uni-National and Mixed Marriages in the USSR', Institute of Jewish Affairs *Research Report*, no. 19 (December 1983).
—— and Spier, Howard. 'Eight Soviet Jews Appeal for the Creation of an Anti-Zionist Committee', Institute of Jewish Affairs *Research Report*, no. 6 (April 1983).
'A Historical Aside on the New "Education Tax"', *Radio Liberty Research*, CRD 232/72 (4 September 1972).
Huntington, Samuel P. 'Renewed Hostility'. In *The Making of America's Soviet Policy*, pp. 265–89. Edited by Joseph S. Nye, Jr. New Haven, Connecticut and London: Yale University Press for the Council on Foreign Relations, 1984.
——. 'Trade, Technology, and Leverage: Economic Diplomacy', *Foreign Policy*, no. 32 (Fall 1978), 63–80.
'The Increased Arrests of Soviet Jews in 1981', Institute of Jewish Affairs *Research Report*, no. 21 (December 1981).
'Jewish Culture in the USSR Today', Institute of Jewish Affairs *Research Report*, no. 10 (December 1985).
'Jewish Influence in the US Presidential Election as Seen in Moscow', Institute of Jewish Affairs *Research Report*, USSR/54 (June 1976).
Jones, Ellen. 'Committee Decision-making in the Soviet Union', *World Politics* 36 (January 1984), 165–88.
Kashlev, Yuri. *Helsinki–Belgrade: The Soviet Viewpoint*. Moscow: Novosti, 1978.
Katz, Zev. 'The Jews in the Soviet Union'. In *Handbook of Major Soviet Nationalities*, pp. 355–69. Edited by Zev Katz. London: Collier Macmillan for the Massachusetts Institute of Technology, 1975.
Kazlas, Juozas. 'A Comparison of Ethnic Group Rights'. Unpublished paper presented to the Conference on Problems of Soviet Ethnic Policies: The Status of Jews in the USSR and the Impact of Anti-Semitism, held at Columbia University, New York, 27 May 1980.
Kelley, Donald R. 'Environmental Policy-Making in the USSR: The Role of Industrial and Environmental Interest Groups', *Soviet Studies* 28 (October 1976), 570–89.
——. 'Group and Specialist Influence in Soviet Politics: In Search of a Theory'. In *Social Scientists and Policy Making in the USSR*. Edited by Richard B. Remnek. London: Praeger, 1977.
Kiser, John W. 'Emigration from the Soviet Union: The Case of the Soviet Germans', *Analysis*, no. 57 (June 1976).
Knisbacher, Mitchell. 'Aliyah of Soviet Jews: Protection of the Right of Emigration under International Law', *Harvard International Law Journal* 14 (Winter 1973), 89–110.
Kohl, Helmut. 'Germans in the Soviet Union', *Journal of Social and Political Studies* 3 (Spring 1978), 17–25.

Korey, William. 'International Law and the Right to Study Hebrew in the USSR', *Soviet Jewish Affairs* 11 (February 1981), 3–18.

——. 'Jackson–Vanik and Soviet Jewry', *Washington Quarterly* 7 (Winter 1984), 116–128.

——. 'The Legal Position of Soviet Jewry: A Historical Enquiry'. In *The Jews in Soviet Russia Since 1917*, pp. 78–105. 3rd edn. Edited by Lionel Kochan. Oxford: Oxford University Press for the Institute of Jewish Affairs, 1978.

——. ' The "Right to Leave" for Soviet Jews: Legal and Moral Aspects', *Soviet Jewish Affairs*, no. 1 (June 1971), 5–12.

——. 'The Story of the Jackson Amendment, 1973–1975', *Midstream* 21 (March 1975), 7–36.

Kudinov, V., and Pletnikov, V. 'Ideological Confrontation of the Two Systems', *International Affairs* (Moscow), no. 12 (1972), 57–64.

Lapidus, Gail Warshofsky. 'Ethnonationalism and Political Stability', *World Politics* 36 (July 1984), 555–80.

——. 'Gorbachev's Nationalities Problem', *Foreign Affairs* 68 (4) (Fall 1989), 92–108.

——. 'The Nationality Question in the Soviet System'. In *The Soviet Union in the 1980s*, pp. 98–112. Edited by Erik P. Hoffmann. Proceedings of the Academy of Political Science, vol. 35, no. 3. New York: The Academy of Political Science, 1984.

——. 'Social Trends'. In *After Brezhnev: Sources of Soviet Conduct in the 1980s*, pp. 186–249. Edited by Robert F. Byrnes. Bloomington, Indiana: Indiana University Press in association with the Center for Strategic and International Studies, Georgetown University, Washington, DC, 1983.

Larrabee, F. Stephen. 'Soviet Attitudes and Policy Towards "Basket Three" Since Helsinki', *Radio Liberty Research*, RL 135/76 (15 March 1976).

Lederhendler, Eli M. 'Resources of Ethnically Disenfranchised'. In *Nationality Group Survival in Multi-Ethnic States: Shifting Support Patterns in the Soviet Baltic Region*, pp. 194–227. Edited by Edward Allworth. New York: Praeger, 1977.

Lendvai, Paul. 'Jews Under Communism', *Commentary* 52 (December 1971), 67–74.

Lenin, V. I. 'O prave natsii na samoopredelenie' [On the Right of Nations to Self-Determination]. In *Sochinenia* [Works], vol. 20 (1913–14), pp. 365–424. Moscow: Gosudarstvennoe izdatelstvo politicheskoi literatury, 1948.

Levine, Norman. 'Lenin on Jewish Nationalism', *Wiener Library Bulletin* 33 (1980), 42–55.

Lewis, Philippa. 'The "Jewish Question" in the Open: 1968–1971'. In *The Jews in Soviet Russia Since 1917*, pp. 349–65. 3rd edn. Edited by Lionel Kochan. Oxford: Oxford University Press for the Institute of Jewish Affairs, 1978.

Lowenthal, Richard. 'East–West Détente and the Future of Soviet Jewry', *Soviet Jewish Affairs* 3 (Spring 1973), 20–5.

Mark, Judel. 'Jewish Schools in Soviet Russia'. In *Russian Jewry 1917– 1967*, pp. 250–8. Edited by Gregor Aronson, Jacob Frumkin, Alexis Goldenweiser, and Joseph Lewitan. Translated by Joel Carmichael. New

York: Thomas Yoseloff, 1969.

Medvedev, Roy A. 'The Problem of Democratization and the Problem of Détente', October 1973. *Samizdat* article published in translation in *Radio Liberty Special Report*, RL 359/73 (19 November 1973).

Meeter, Stephen H. 'The Relation of the Helsinki Final Act to the Emigration of Soviet Jews', *Boston College International and Comparative Law Journal* 1 (1977), 111–47.

Mehl, Fred, and Rappoport, Sandra E. 'Soviet Policy of Separating Families and the Right to Emigrate', *International and Comparative Law Quarterly* 27 (October 1978), 876–89.

Miller, Jacob. 'Soviet Theory on the Jews'. In *The Jews in Soviet Russia Since 1917*, pp. 46–63. 3rd edn. Edited by Lionel Kochan. Oxford: Oxford University Press for the Institute of Jewish Affairs, 1978.

Mills, Richard M. 'The Formation of the Virgin Lands Policy', *Slavic Review* 29 (March 1970), 58–69.

'More Ethnic Germans Seek to Emigrate from the USSR', *Radio Liberty Research*, RL 26/77 (1 February 1977).

Morgenthau, Hans J. 'The Question of Détente', *Worldview* 19 (March 1976), 7–13.

Nezer, Zvi. 'The Emigration of Soviet Jews', *Soviet Jewish Affairs* 15 (February 1985), 17–24.

Nezer, Zvi, [Z. Alexander]. 'Immigration to Israel from the USSR'. In *Israel Yearbook on Human Rights*, vol. 7, pp. 268–335. Special supplement. Tel Aviv: Tel Aviv University, 1977.

——. 'Jewish Emigration from the USSR in 1980', *Soviet Jewish Affairs* 11 (May 1981), 3–21.

O'Keefe, Gerald. 'Soviet Legal Restrictions on Emigration', *Soviet Union/Union Soviétique* 14 (3) (1987), 301–41.

Okuneva, Ruth. 'The Position of the Jews in the Soviet School Syllabus of World and Russian History: What Soviet Schoolchildren Read about the History of the Jewish People'. In *Anti-Semitism in the Soviet Union: Its Roots and Consequences*. 3 vols. Vol. 3 (1983), Jerusalem: Hebrew University of Jerusalem, Centre for Research and Documentation of East-European Jewry, 1979–83, pp. 51–92. Edited by Shmuel Ettinger.

Orbach, William. 'A Periodization of Soviet Policy Towards the Jews', *Soviet Jewish Affairs* 12 (November 1982), 45–62.

Oschlies, Wolf. 'The Status of Germans Living in the Soviet Union'. In *The Soviet Union 1982–1983: Domestic Policy, The Economy, Foreign Policy*, vol. 7, pp. 105–15. Edited by Karin Schmid. London: Holmes & Meier with the assistance of the Bundesinstitut für ostwissenschaftliche und internationale Studien, Cologne, 1985.

'The Paris Pledge: Kosygin on Reunification of Families', *Jews in Eastern Europe* 3 (May 1967), 14–16.

Pettiti, Louis E. 'The Right to Leave and to Return in the USSR'. In *Israel Yearbook on Human Rights*, vol. 5, pp. 264–75. Tel Aviv: Tel Aviv University, 1975.

Pinkus, Benjamin. 'The Emigration of National Minorities from the USSR in the Post-Stalin Era', *Soviet Jewish Affairs* 13 (February 1983), 3–36.

——. 'National Identity and Emigration Patterns Among Soviet Jewry',

Soviet Jewish Affairs 15 (November 1985), 3–28.

——. 'Soviet Campaigns Against "Jewish Nationalism" and "Cosmopolitanism", 1946–1953', *Soviet Jewish Affairs* 4 (Autumn 1974), 53–72.

——. 'Yiddish-Language Courts and Nationalities Policy in the Soviet Union', *Soviet Jewish Affairs*, no. 2 (November 1971), 40–60.

Povolny, Mojimir. 'The Soviet Union and the European Security Conference', *Orbis* 18 (Spring 1974), 201–30.

'*Pravda* Equates Zionism with Fascism'. Institute of Jewish Affairs *Research Report*, no. 2 (March 1984).

Reddaway, Peter. 'Dissent in the Soviet Union', *Problems of Communism* 33 (November–December 1983), 2–15.

——. 'Policy Towards Dissent Since Khrushchev'. In *Authority, Power and Policy in the USSR: Essays Dedicated to Leonard Schapiro*, pp. 158–92. Edited by T. H. Rigby, Archie Brown, and Peter Reddaway. New York: St. Martin's, 1980.

——. 'Theory and Practice of Human Rights in the Soviet Union'. In *Human Rights and American Foreign Policy*, pp. 115–29. Edited by Donald P. Kommers and Gilbert D. Loescher. Notre Dame, Indiana: University of Notre Dame Press, 1979.

Redlich, Shimon. 'Ha'atzumot shel yehudei brit ha'moatsot k'bitui l'hitorrut leumit (1968–1970)' [Petitions of Soviet Jews as an Expression of National Revival (1968–1970)], *Behinot* 5 (1974), 7–24.

——. 'Jews in General Anders' Army in the Soviet Union 1941–42', *Soviet Jewish Affairs*, no. 2 (November 1971), 90–8.

Rigby, T. H. 'Addendum to Dr. Rigby's Article on CPSU Membership', *Soviet Studies* 28 (October 1976), 615.

——. 'Soviet Communist Party Membership Under Brezhnev', *Soviet Studies* 28 (July 1976), 317–37.

Ro'i, Yaacov. 'The Soviet Jewish Anomaly', *Jerusalem Quarterly*, no. 10 (Winter 1979), 106–16.

Roth, Stephen J. 'Madrid Ends and Helsinki Continues: The Agreement at the CSCE Follow-Up Conference', Institute of Jewish Affairs *Research Report*, no. 14 (September 1983).

——. 'New Chapter in the Helsinki Process: The Vienna Conference and Its Aftermath', Institute of Jewish Affairs *Research Report*, no. 4 (1989).

Rothenberg, Joshua. 'Jewish Religion in the Soviet Union'. In *The Jews in Soviet Russia Since 1917*, pp. 168–96. 3rd edn. Edited by Lionel Kochan. Oxford: Oxford University Press for the Institute of Jewish Affairs, 1978.

Russell, Harold S. 'The Helsinki Declaration: Brobdingnag or Lilliput?', *American Journal of International Law* 70 (April 1976), 242–72.

Salitan, Laurie P. 'Domestic Pressures and the Politics of Exit: Trends in Soviet Emigration Policy', *Political Science Quarterly* 104 (4) (Winter 1989–90), 671–87.

——. 'The Dynamics of Emigration and Nationality in the Soviet Union', *The Harriman Institute Forum* 2 (2) (February 1989).

——. 'Politics and Nationality: The Soviet Jews'. In *Politics, Society, and Nationality Inside Gorbachev's Russia*, pp. 175–91. Edited by Seweryn Bialer. Boulder, Colorado: Westview, 1989.

Sawczuk, Konstantyn. 'Soviet Juridical Interpretation of International Documents on Human Rights', *Survey* 24 (Spring 1979), 86–91.

Schachter, Oscar. 'Editorial Comment: The Twilight Existence of Non-binding International Agreements', *American Journal of International Law* 71 (April 1977), 296–304.

Schachner, Gerhard. 'The Soviet-German Newspaper "Freundschaft" and the Cultural Transformation of the Soviet-Germans in Kazakhstan', *Nationalities Papers* 9 (Spring 1981), 81–98.

Schapiro, Leonard B. 'Antisemitism in the Communist World', *Soviet Jewish Affairs* 9 (1) (1979), 42–52.

Scheetz, Elizabeth C. 'Emigration from the USSR in the Post-Helsinki Period', *Radio Liberty Research*, RL 2/77 (1 January 1977).

———. 'State Secrets and the Right to Emigrate', *Radio Liberty Research*, RL 82/77 (13 April 1977).

Scherer, John L. 'A Note on Soviet Jewish Emigration, 1971–84', *Soviet Jewish Affairs* 15 (May 1985), 37–44.

Schroeter, Leonard. 'How They Left: Varieties of Soviet Jewish Exit Experience', *Soviet Jewish Affairs* 2 (Autumn 1972), 3–30.

Schwarz, Solomon. 'Birobidzhan: An Experiment in Jewish Colonization'. In *Russian Jewry 1917–1967*, pp. 342–95. Edited by Gregor Aronson, Jacob Frumkin, Alexis Goldenweiser, and Joseph Lewitan. Translated by Joel Carmichael. New York: Thomas Yoseloff, 1969.

Shapiro, Leon. 'An Outline of the History of Russian and Soviet Jewry 1912–1974'. In *History of the Jews in Russia and Poland: From the Earliest Times Until the Present Day*, edited by S. M. Dubnow. Translated by I. Friedlaender. 3 vols. Vol. 3: *From the Accession of Nicholas II Until the Present Day*. Philadelphia: Jewish Publication Society of America, 1916–20; reprint edn, New York: Ktav, 1975.

Sheehy, Ann. 'Andropov and Nationalities Policy', *Radio Liberty Research*, RL 412/83 (28 October 1983).

———. 'The National Composition of the Population of the USSR According to the Census of 1979', *Radio Liberty Research*, RL 123/80 (27 March 1980).

Shukman, Harold. 'Lenin's Nationalities Policy and the Jewish Question', *Bulletin on Soviet and East European Jewish Affairs*, no. 5 (May 1970), 43–50.

Simes, Dimitri K. 'The Death of Détente?', *International Security* 5 (Summer 1980), 3–25.

———. 'Soviet Policy toward the United States'. In *The Making of America's Soviet Policy*, pp. 291–322. Edited by Joseph S. Nye, Jr. New Haven, Connecticut and London: Yale University Press for the Council on Foreign Relations, 1984.

'Sionizm – Udarny otryad imperializma: Press-konferentsia antisionistsko-go komiteta sovetskoy obshchestvennosti' [Zionism – Shock Troops of Imperialism: A Press Conference of the Anti-Zionist Committee of the Soviet Public], *Literaturnaya gazeta*, 22 June 1983. Full English translation in 'Documents: The Soviet Anti-Zionist Committee', *Soviet Jewish Affairs* 13 (November 1983), 55–68.

Skilling, H. Gordon. 'Interest Groups and Communist Politics', *World*

Politics 18 (April 1966), 435–51.

——. 'Interest Groups and Communist Politics Revisited', *World Politics* 36 (October 1983), 1–27.

Slider, Darrell. 'A Note on the Class Structure of Soviet Nationalities', *Soviet Studies* 37 (October 1985), 535–40.

Sonntag, Jacob. 'Yiddish Writers and Jewish Culture in the USSR: Twenty Years After', *Soviet Jewish Affairs*, no. 2 (1972), 31–8.

Sorensen, Theodore C. 'Most-Favored-Nation and Less Favorite Nations', *Foreign Affairs* 52 (January 1974), 273–86.

'The Soviet "Diploma Tax"', Institute of Jewish Affairs *Background Paper*, no. 24 (November 1972).

'Soviet "Education" Decree', *Jews In Eastern Europe* 5 (November 1972), 45–56.

Spier, Howard. 'Fulfilling a Restricted Role: The Soviet Anti-Zionist Committee in 1984', Institute of Jewish Affairs *Research Report*, no. 16 (December 1984).

——. 'Soviet Antisemitism Unchained: The Rise of the "Historical and Patriotic Association Pamyat"', Institute of Jewish Affairs *Research Report*, no. 3 (July 1987).

——. 'The Soviet Anti-Zionist Committee – Further Developments', Institute of Jewish Affairs *Research Report*, no. 13 (August 1983).

Stalin, I. V. 'Marksizm i natsionalny vopros' [Marxism and the National Question]. In *Sochinenia* [Works], vol. 2 (1907–13), pp. 290–367. Moscow: Gosudarstvennoe izdatelstvo politicheskoi literatury, 1946.

Stein, Jonathan B. 'U.S. Controls and the Soviet Pipeline', *Washington Quarterly* 5 (Autumn 1982), 52–9.

Stewart, Philip D. 'Soviet Interest Groups and the Policy Process: The Repeal of Production Education', *World Politics* 22 (October 1969), 29–50.

Stricker, Gerd. 'A Visit to German Congregations in Central Asia', *Religion in Communist Lands* 17 (1) (Spring 1989), 19–33.

Suny, Ronald Grigor. 'Nationalist and Ethnic Unrest in the Soviet Union', *World Policy Journal* (Summer 1989), 503–28.

Talbott, Strobe. 'Social Issues'. In *The Making of America's Soviet Policy*, pp. 183–205. Edited by Joseph S. Nye, Jr. New Haven, Connecticut and London: Yale University Press for the Council on Foreign Relations, 1984.

——. 'U.S.–Soviet Relations: From Bad to Worse', *Foreign Affairs* 58 (1980), 515–39.

Tishkov, V. 'Narody i gosudarstvo' [Peoples and State], *Kommunist*, no. 1 (January 1989), 49–59.

Valenta, Jiri. 'The Bureaucratic Politics Paradigm and the Soviet Invasion of Czechoslovakia', *Political Science Quarterly* 94 (1979), 55–76.

Voronel, Aleksandr, 'The Aliyah of Russian Intellectuals', *Midstream* 22 (April 1976), 28–35.

Weinryb, Bernard D. 'Antisemitism in Soviet Russia'. In *The Jews in Soviet Russia Since 1917*, pp. 300–32. 3rd edn. Edited by Lionel Kochan. Oxford: Oxford University Press for the Institute of Jewish Affairs, 1978.

Wishnevsky, Julia. '"Anti-Zionist Committee" Formed in the Soviet Union', *Radio Liberty Research*, RL 170/83 (26 April 1983).
Zand, Mikhail. 'Fate, Civilization, Aliya'. In *In Search of Self: The Soviet Jewish Intelligentsia and the Exodus*, pp. 23–34. Edited by David Prital. Jerusalem: Mount Scopus Publications, for the Scientists Committee of the Israel Public Council for Soviet Jewry, 1982.
Zaslavsky, Victor and Luryi, Yuri. 'The Passport System in the USSR and Changes in Soviet Society', *Soviet Union/Union Soviétique* 6 (1979), 137–53.
Ziegler, Charles E. 'Issue Creation and Interest Groups in Soviet Environmental Policy: The Applicability of the State Corporatist Model', *Comparative Politics* 18 (January 1986), 171–92.

BOOKS, MONOGRAPHS and PAMPHLETS

Alexeyeva, Ludmilla. *Soviet Dissent*. Middletown, Connecticut: Wesleyan University Press, 1985.
Allworth, Edward, ed. *Ethnic Russia in the USSR: The Dilemma of Dominance*. New York: Pergamon, 1980.
——. *Nationality Group Survival in Multi-Ethnic States: Shifting Support Patterns in the Soviet Baltic Region*. New York: Praeger, 1977.
Altshuler, Mordechai. *Soviet Jewry Since the Second World War – Population and Social Structure*. Studies in Population and Urban Demography, no. 5. New York: Greenwood, 1987.
Anti-Semitism in the Soviet Union: Its Roots and Consequences. 3 vols. Jerusalem: Hebrew University of Jerusalem, Centre for Research and Documentation of East-European Jewry, 1979–83.
Anti-Zionist Committee of Soviet Public Opinion: Aims and Tasks. Moscow: Novosti, 1983.
Azbel, Mark Ya. *Refusenik: Trapped in the Soviet Union*. Boston: Houghton Mifflin, 1981.
Azrael, Jeremy. *Emergent Nationality Problems in the USSR*. Santa Monica, California: Rand, 1977.
——, ed. *Soviet Nationalities Policies and Practices*. New York: Praeger, 1978.
Bahry, Donna. *Outside Moscow: Power, Politics, and Budgetary Policy in the Soviet Republics*. New York: Columbia University Press, 1987.
Baldwin, Godfrey S. *Population Projections by Age and Sex: For the Republics and Major Economic Regions of the U.S.S.R. 1970 to 2000*. International Population Reports, Series P-91, no. 26. Washington, DC: U.S. Department of Commerce, Bureau of the Census, Foreign Demographics Analysis Division, 1979.
Baron, Salo W. *The Russian Jew under Tsars and Soviets*. New York: Macmillan, 1964.
Begun, V. Ya. *Vtorzhenie bez oruzhia* [Invasion without Arms]. Moscow: Molodaya gvardia, 1977.
Bialer, Seweryn, ed. *The Domestic Context of Soviet Foreign Policy*. Boulder, Colorado: Westview, 1981.
Bourdeaux, Michael, Hebly, Hans and Voss, Eugen, eds. *Religious Liberty in the Soviet Union. WCC and USSR: A Post-Nairobi Documentation*. Keston

Book no. 7. Kent: Centre for the Study of Religion and Communism, Keston College, 1976.

Brafman, Morris and Schimel, David. *Trade and Freedom: Détente, Trade and Soviet Jews*. New York: Shengold, 1975.

Brandt, Willy. *People and Politics: The Years 1960–1973*. Translated by J. Maxwell Brownjohn. Boston: Little, Brown, 1978.

Brown, Archie. *Soviet Politics and Political Science*. London: Macmillan, 1974.

—— and Kaser, Michael, eds. *Soviet Policy for the 1980s*. London: Macmillan for St Antony's College, Oxford, 1982.

Brownlie, Ian, ed. *Basic Documents on Human Rights*. 2nd edn. Oxford: Clarendon Press, 1981.

Brzezinski, Zbigniew K. and Huntington, Samuel P. *Political Power: USA/USSR*. New York: Viking, 1965.

Buergenthal, Thomas, ed., assisted by Hall, Judith R. *Human Rights, International Law and the Helsinki Accord*. Montclair, New Jersey: Allanheld, Osmun for the American Society of International Law, 1977.

Butler, W. E., comp., trans. and ed. *Basic Documents on the Soviet Legal System*. New York: Oceana, 1983.

Byrnes, Robert F., ed. *After Brezhnev: Sources of Soviet Conduct in the 1980s*. Bloomington, Indiana: Indiana University Press in association with the Center for Strategic and International Studies, Georgetown University, Washington, DC, 1983.

Commission on Security and Cooperation in Europe. *The Belgrade Followup Meeting to the Conference on Security and Cooperation in Europe: A Report and Appraisal*. Washington, DC: U.S. Government Printing Office, 1978.

——. *Concluding Document of the Vienna Follow-Up Meeting*. Washington, DC: US Government Printing Office, 1989.

Carrère d'Encausse, Hélène. *Decline of an Empire: The Soviet Socialist Republics in Revolt*. Translated by Martin Sokolinsky and Henry A. La Farge. New York: Newsweek Books, 1979.

CDU/CSU Group in the German Bundestag. *White Paper on the Human Rights Situation in Germany and of the Germans in Eastern Europe*. Bonn: CDU/CSU Group in the German Bundestag, 1977.

Chalidze, Valery. *To Defend These Rights: Human Rights and the Soviet Union*. Translated by Guy Daniels. London: Collins & Harvill, 1975.

Concluding Document of the Madrid Meeting of the Conference on Security and Cooperation in Europe, September 6, 1983. In Edmund Jan Osmanczyk, ed., *The Encyclopedia of the United Nations and International Agreements*. Philadelphia and London: Taylor & Francis, 1985, pp. 487–91.

Connor, Walker. *The National Question in Marxist–Leninist Theory and Strategy*. Princeton: Princeton University Press, 1984.

Conquest, Robert. *The Nation Killers*. London: Macmillan, 1970; reprint edn, London: Sphere, 1972.

Dowty, Alan. *Closed Borders: The Contemporary Assault on Freedom of Movement*. New Haven: Yale University Press, 1987.

Dragunsky, David Abramovich. *O chem govoryat pisma* [What the Letters Say]. Moscow: Anti-Zionist Committee of the Soviet Public, 1984.

Edmonds, Robin. *Soviet Foreign Policy: The Brezhnev Years*. Oxford: Oxford University Press, 1983.

Fainsod, Merle. *How Russia is Ruled*. Cambridge, Massachusetts: Harvard University Press, 1953.

Feldbrugge, F. J. M., ed. *The Constitutions of the USSR and the Union Republics: Analysis, Texts, Reports*. Alphen aan den Rijn, The Netherlands: Sijthoff & Noordhoff, 1979.

Final Act of the Helsinki Conference on Security and Cooperation in Europe, August 2, 1975. In Edmund Jan Osmanczyk, ed., *The Encyclopedia of the United Nations and International Agreements*. Philadelphia and London: Taylor & Francis, 1985, pp. 333–44.

Fleischhauer, Ingeborg and Pinkus, Benjamin. *The Soviet Germans Past and Present*. Edited with an Introduction by Edith Rogovin Frankel. London: C. Hurst in association with Marjorie Mayrock Center for Soviet and East European Research, Hebrew University of Jerusalem, 1986.

Ford, Gerald R. *A Time to Heal*. New York: Harper & Row and Reader's Digest, 1979.

Freedman, Robert O., ed. *Soviet Jewry in the Decisive Decade, 1971–1980*. Durham, North Carolina: Duke University Press, 1984.

——. ed. *Soviet Jewry in the 1980s: The Politics of Anti-Semitism and Emigration and the Dynamics of Resettlement*. Durham, North Carolina and London: Duke University Press, 1989.

Friedrich, Carl J. and Brzezinski, Zbigniew, K. *Totalitarian Dictatorship and Autocracy*. 2nd edn, rev. Cambridge, Massachusetts: Harvard University Press, 1965.

Ganji, Manouchehr. *International Protection of Human Rights*. Geneva: E. Droz, 1962; Paris: Minard, 1962.

Gelman, Harry. *The Brezhnev Politburo and the Decline of Détente*. Ithaca, New York and London: Cornell University Press, 1984.

Giesinger, Adam. *From Catherine to Khrushchev: The Story of Russia's Germans*. Battleford, Saskatchewan, Canada: Marian, 1974.

Gilbert, Martin. *The Jews of Hope: The Plight of Soviet Jewry Today*. London: Macmillan, 1984.

Gilboa, Yehoshua A. *The Black Years of Soviet Jewry 1939–1953*. Translated by Yosef Shachter and Dov Ben-Abba. Boston: Little, Brown, 1971.

Gitelman, Zvi Y. *Jewish Nationality and Soviet Politics: The Jewish Sections of the CPSU 1917–1930*. Princeton: Princeton University Press, 1972.

Gold, Donna L. *Soviet Jewry: U.S. Policy Considerations*. Congressional Research Service Report 85–88S, 17 April 1985.

Goldhagen, Erich, ed. *Ethnic Minorities in the Soviet Union*. New York: Praeger, 1968.

Goldberg, B. Z. *The Jewish Problem in the Soviet Union: Analysis and Solution*. New York: Crown, 1961.

Goldman, Marshall I. *Détente and Dollars: Doing Business with the Soviets*. New York: Basic, 1975.

Govrin, Yosef. *Israel–Soviet Relations: 1964–1966*. Research Paper no. 29. Jerusalem: The Soviet and East European Research Centre of the Hebrew University of Jerusalem, January 1978.

Griffith, William E. *The Ostpolitik of the Federal Republic of Germany*. Cambridge, Massachusetts: MIT Press, 1978.

Gustafson, Thane. *Reform in Soviet Politics, Lessons of Recent Policies on Land and Water.* Cambridge: Cambridge University Press, 1981.

Heitman, Sidney. *The Soviet Germans in the USSR Today.* Berichte des Bundesinstituts für ostwissenschaftliche und internationale Studien no. 35. Cologne: Bundesinstitut für ostwissenschaftliche und internationale Studien, 1980.

Hoffman, Stefani. *Shades of Gray: The Current Soviet Press on Israel and Zionism.* Research Paper no. 70. Jerusalem: Marjorie Mayrock Center for Soviet and East European Research, Hebrew University of Jerusalem, June 1989.

Hoffmann, Stanley. *Duties Beyond Borders.* Syracuse, New York: Syracuse University Press, 1981.

Hough, Jerry F. *The Soviet Union and Social Science Theory.* Cambridge, Massachusetts: Harvard University Press, 1977.

Institute of Jewish Affairs. *Human Contacts, Reunion of Families and Soviet Jewry.* London: International Council of the World Conference on Soviet Jewry in Co-operation with the Jewish Communities Concerned, 1986.

——. *The Position of Soviet Jewry: Human Rights and the Helsinki Accords 1985.* London: International Council of the World Conference on Soviet Jewry in Co-operation with the Jewish Communities Concerned, 1985.

Ivanov, Yuri. *Ostorozhno: Sionizm!* [Beware Zionism!]. Moscow: Politizdat, 1969.

Itogi Vsesoyuznoy perepisi naselenia 1959 goda SSSR (Svodny tom) [The Results of the USSR All-Union Population Census of 1959, Summary Volume]. Moscow: Gosstatizdat, 1962.

Itogi Vsesoyuznoy perepisi naselenia 1970 goda [The Results of the All-Union Population Census of 1970]. 7 vols. Moscow: Statistika, 1972–74.

Karklins, Rasma. *Ethnic Relations in the USSR: The Perspective from Below.* Boston: Allen & Unwin, 1986.

Katz, Zev. ed. *Handbook of Major Soviet Nationalities.* London: Collier Macmillan for the Massachusetts Institute of Technology, 1975.

Khronika tekushchikh sobytiy [Chronicle of Current Events]. (*Samizdat* journal that circulated in the early 1970s.)

Kichko, Trofim. *Iudaizm bez prikras* [Judaism without Embellishments]. Kiev: Akademia nauk URSR, 1963.

Kissinger, Henry. *Years of Upheaval.* Boston: Little, Brown, 1982.

Klinghoffer, Arthur Jay, with Apter, Judith. *Israel and the Soviet Union: Alienation or Reconciliation?* Boulder, Colorado: Westview, 1985.

Koch, Fred C. *The Volga Germans.* University Park, Pennsylvania: Pennsylvania State University Press, 1977.

Kochan, Lionel, ed. *The Jews in Soviet Russia Since 1917.* 3rd edn. Oxford: Oxford University Press for the Institute of Jewish Affairs, 1978.

Kolarz, Walter. *Religion in the Soviet Union.* New York: St. Martin's, 1961.

Korey, William. *The Soviet Cage: Anti-Semitism in Russia.* New York: Viking, 1973.

Korneev, Lev. *Klassovaya sushchnost sionizma* [The Class Essence of Zionism]. Kiev: Politizdat Ukrainy, 1982.

Kulturnoe stroitelstvo SSSR: Statisticheskii sbornik [The Cultural Development of the USSR: A Statistical Collection]. Moscow: Gosudarstvennoe statist-icheskoe izdatelstvo, 1956.

Kuznetsov, Edward. *Prison Diaries.* Translated by Howard Spier. New York: Stein & Day, 1975.

Lauterpacht, Hirsch. *International Law and Human Rights.* London: Stevens, 1950.

Lenin, V. I. *Collected Works.* 45 vols, 4th edn 1963–70. Moscow: Foreign Languages (vols 1–17). Moscow: Progress (vols 18–45).

——. *Natsionalnii vopros* [The National Question]. Moscow: Gosudarstvennoe izdatelstvo, 1936.

——. *The Right of Nations to Self-Determination.* Moscow: Foreign Languages, 1947.

——. *Polnoe sobranie sochinenii* [Complete Collected Works]. 55 vols, 5th edn, 1958–65. Moscow: Gosudarstvennoe Izdatelstvo politicheskoi literatury (vols 1–42). Moscow: Izdatelstvo politicheskoi literatury (vols 43–55).

Liebman, Charles S. *Pressure Without Sanctions: The Influence of World Jewry on Israeli Policy.* London: Associated University Presses, 1977.

Löwenhardt, John. *Decision-Making in Soviet Politics.* New York: St. Martin's, 1981.

Marx, Karl, and Engels, Friedrich. *Collected Works.* 43 vols. New York: International, 1975.

Millar, James R., ed. *Politics, Work, and Daily Life in the USSR: A Survey of Former Soviet Citizens.* New York: Cambridge University Press, 1987.

Miller, Jack, ed. *Jews in Soviet Culture.* New Brunswick, New Jersey and London: Transaction Books for the Institute of Jewish Affairs, 1984.

Modzhoryan, Lidia Artemevna. *Mezhdunarodny sionizm na sluzhbe imperialis-ticheskoy reaktsii: Pravovoy aspekt* [International Zionism in the Service of Imperialist Reaction: The Legal Aspect]. Moscow: Mezhdunarodnye otnoshenia, 1984.

Moskva v tsifrakh (1966–1970 gg.): Kratkii statisticheskii sbornik [Moscow in Figures 1966–1970: A Short Statistical Collection]. Moscow: Statistika, 1972.

Moskva v tsifrakh: Statisticheskii ezhegodnik [Moscow in Figures: A Statistical Yearbook]. Moscow: Statistika, 1980–1981.

Narodnoe khozyaistvo SSSR: Statisticheskii ezhegodnik [The National Economy of the USSR: A Statistical Yearbook]. Moscow: Finansy i statistika. See annual volumes 1958–88. [Published 1958–80 by Statistika].

Narodnoe obrazovanie, nauka i kultura v SSSR: Statisticheskii sbornik [National Education. Science and Culture in the USSR: A Statistical Collection]. Moscow: Statistika, 1977.

Natsionalny sostav naselenia: Chast II [The National Composition of the Population: Part II]. Moscow: Finansy i statistika, 1989.

Nove, Alec. *The Soviet Economic System.* 3rd edn. Boston: Allen & Unwin, 1986.

Nye, Joseph S., Jr, ed. *The Making of America's Soviet Policy.* New Haven, Connecticut and London: Yale University Press for the Council on Foreign Relations, 1984.

Oglesby, Samuel C. 'Soviet Emigration Policy: Exit Visas and Fees'.

Congressional Research Service, 11 April 1973.

Orbach, William. *The American Movement to Aid Soviet Jews*. Amherst, Massachusetts: University of Massachusetts Press, 1979.

Pinkus, Benjamin. *The Jews of the Soviet Union: The History of a National Minority*. Cambridge: Cambridge University Press, 1988.

——. *The Soviet Government and the Jews 1948–1967: A Documented Study*. Cambridge: Cambridge University Press in association with Hebrew University of Jersualem-Institute of Contemporary Jewry and Israel Academy of Sciences and Humanities, 1984.

Pipes, Richard. *The Formation of the Soviet Union: Communism and Nationalism 1917–1923*. Rev. edn. Cambridge, Massachusetts: Harvard University Press, 1980.

Ploss, Sidney. *Conflict and Decision-Making in Soviet Russia: A Case Study of Agricultural Policy, 1953–1963*. Princeton: Princeton University Press, 1965.

Pochemu my vernulis na rodinu: svidetelstva reemigrantov [Why We Returned to the Motherland: Testimony of Re-emigrants]. Moscow: Progress, 1983.

The Position of Soviet Jewry 1977–1980: Report on the Implementation of the Helsinki Final Act since the Belgrade Follow-Up Conference. London: Presidium and Steering Committee of the World Conference on Soviet Jewry in Co-operation with the Jewish Communities Concerned, 1980. [Available at the Institute of Jewish Affairs, London.]

Prital, David, ed. *In Search of Self: The Soviet Jewish Intelligentsia and the Exodus*. Jerusalem: Mt. Scopus Publications for the Scientists' Committee of the Israel Public Council for Soviet Jewry, 1982.

Prudnik, Ivan Vasilevich. *Sionistskoe lobbi v SShA* [The Zionist Lobby in the USA]. Minsk: Belarus, 1984.

Rothenberg, Joshua. *The Jewish Religion in the Soviet Union*. New York: Ktav, 1971.

Rubenstein, Joshua. *Soviet Dissidents: Their Struggle for Human Rights*. Boston: Beacon, 1980.

Rukhadze, Avtandil. *Jews in the USSR: Figures, Facts, Comment*. Moscow: Novosti, 1982.

Sakharov, Andrei D. *My Country and the World*. Translated by Guy V. Daniels. London: Collins & Harvill, 1975.

——. *Sakharov Speaks*. Edited by Harrison E. Salisbury. New York: Alfred A. Knopf, 1974; reprint edn, New York: Vintage, 1974.

Samuel, Maurice. *Blood Accusation: The Strange History of the Beilis Case*. New York: Alfred A. Knopf, 1966.

Sawyer, Thomas E. *The Jewish Minority in the Soviet Union*. Boulder, Colorado: Westview, 1979.

Schroeter, Leonard. *The Last Exodus*. Jerusalem: Weidenfeld & Nicolson, 1974.

Schwarz, Solomon M. *The Jews in the Soviet Union*. Syracuse, New York: Syracuse University Press, 1951.

Semenyuk, V. A. *Natsionalisticheskoe bezumie: Ideologia, politika i praktika mezhdunarodnogo sionizma* [Nationalist Madness: The Ideology, Politics and Practice of International Zionism]. Minsk: Belarus, 1976.

Shaffer, Harry G. *The Soviet Treatment of Jews.* New York: Praeger, 1974.

Sharansky, Natan. *Fear No Evil.* Translated by Stefani Hoffman. New York, Random House, 1988.

Sheehy, Ann and Nahaylo, Bohdan. *The Crimean Tatars, Volga Germans, and Meskhetians: Soviet Treatment of Some National Minorities.* 3rd edn. Minority Rights Group Report no. 6. London: Minority Rights Group, 1980.

Shindler, Colin. *Exit Visa: Détente, Human Rights and the Jewish Emigration Movement in the USSR.* London: Bachman & Turner, 1978.

Sieghart, Paul. *The International Law of Human Rights.* Oxford: Clarendon, 1983.

Skilling, H. Gordon and Griffiths, Franklyn, eds. *Interest Groups in Soviet Politics.* Princeton: Princeton University Press, 1971.

Skurlatov, V. I. *Sionizm i aparteid* [Zionism and Apartheid]. Kiev: Politizdat Ukrainy, 1975.

Solodar, Tzezar Samoilovich. *Dikaya polyn* [Wild Wormwood]. Moscow: Progress, 1980.

Solomon, Peter H., Jr. *Soviet Criminologists and Criminal Policy: Specialists in Policy-Making.* New York: Columbia University Press, 1978.

Solomon, Susan Gross, ed. *Pluralism in the Soviet Union: Essays in Honour of H. Gordon Skilling.* London: Macmillan, 1983.

Soviet Antisemitic Propaganda: Evidence from Press and Radio. London: Institute of Jewish Affairs, 1978.

Soviet Jewry and the Implementation of the Helsinki Final Act. Presidium and Steering Committee of the World Conference on Soviet Jewry in Co-operation with the Jewish Communities Concerned, May 1977. [Available from the Institute of Jewish Affairs, London].

Stalin, I. V. *Sochinenia* [Works]. 13 vols. Moscow: Gosudarstvennoe izdatelstvo politicheskoi literatury, 1946–51.

Stalin, Joseph. *Marxism and the National and Colonial Question: A Collection of Articles and Speeches.* New York: International, 1935?

Stent, Angela. *From Embargo to Ostpolitik: The Political Economy of West German–Soviet Relations, 1955–1980.* Cambridge: Cambridge University Press, 1981.

Stern, Paula. *Water's Edge: Domestic Politics and the Making of American Foreign Policy.* Contributions in Political Science, no. 15. Westport, Connecticut and London: Greenwood, 1979.

Stumpp, Karl. *The Emigration from Germany to Russia in the Years 1763 to 1862.* Lincoln, Nebraska: American Historical Society of Germans from Russia, 1973.

Taylor, Telford. *Courts of Terror: Soviet Criminal Justice and Jewish Emigration.* New York: Vintage, 1976.

Tunkin, G. I. *Theory of International Law.* Translated with an Introduction by William E. Butler. London: George Allen & Unwin, 1974.

Ulam, Adam. *Dangerous Relations.* New York: Oxford University Press, 1983.

Valenta, Jiri and Potter, William, eds. *Soviet Decisionmaking for National Security.* London: George Allen & Unwin, 1984.

Voronel, Aleksander and Yakhot, Viktor, eds. *Jews in the USSR: Collection of Materials on the History, Culture and Problems of Jews in the USSR,* no. 1

(October 1972), Moscow. In *I am a Jew: Essays on Jewish Identity in the Soviet Union*. Edited, with a Foreword by Moshe Decter. Introduction by Lewis A. Coser. N.p.: Academic Committee on Soviet Jewry and the Anti-Defamation League of B'nai B'rith, 1973.

Wixman, Ronald. *The Peoples of the USSR: An Ethnographic Handbook*. Armonk, New York: M. E. Sharpe, 1984.

Zaslavsky, Victor and Brym, Robert J. *Soviet-Jewish Emigration and Soviet Nationality Policy*. London: Macmillan, 1983.

Index